More Brickwall Solutions

To Genealogy Problems

Published by Family Chronicle Magazine
www.familychronicle.com

Thank you to: Ed Zapletal and all Brickwall Solutions submitters

First published in December 2004

Portions of this book have previously appeared in *Family Chronicle* Magazine © 2004

Published by Family Chronicle Magazine
500-505 Consumers Road
Toronto ON M2J 4V8
416-491-3699, 1-800-326-2476
www.familychronicle.com

ISBN 0-9731303-7-7

Library and Archives Canada Cataloguing in Publication

More brickwall solutions to genealogy problems / Victoria L. Moorshead, Marc Skulnick, editors.

Includes index.
ISBN 0-9731303-7-7

1. Genealogy. I. Moorshead, Victoria L., 1970- II. Skulnick, Marc, 1972- III. Title:

CS16.M76 2004   929'.1'072   C2004-906837-7

Printed and bound in Canada by Transcontinental Printing Inc.

$2

More Brickwall Solutions

To Genealogy Problems

Table of Contents

Introduction

Since beginning work on this second collection of brickwall solutions, we have noticed how important networking with fellow genealogists, family historians, family, friends and neighbors has become. Somebody, somewhere can help you, be it with advice, ideas, experience or support.

In addition, the Internet has become an increasingly important resource in genealogy and family history research. Many of the maxims that were demonstrated in the first book, *500 Brickwall Solutions to Genealogy Problems*, are still true today; examine original documents, review your information for new clues, on-site and local research is crucial, make educated guesses, keep an open mind and never, ever give up. These solutions, whether found across the ocean or across the street, are applicable for most countries and most research periods.

The key to success in genealogy is to always "think outside the box". After all, each brickwall is as unique as the individuals you are researching and therefore no solution is the same. The diversity of ideas and research techniques presented in this collection will hopefully inform and inspire.

All submissions were edited for length, style and consistency; however, we tried to retain the original wording and personality of each submitter. The illustrations came from numerous sources and as such, their quality is not consistent. Illustrations were selected for relevance to the story, not quality.

To save on unnecessary repetition, several abbreviations have been used throughout the text, but a glossary can be found at the end of the book. Great-great-grandparents are identified as second-great-grandparents, great-great-great-grandparents are identified as third-great-grandparents and other generations in the same manner to avoid any misunderstandings in the text.

Please note that each submitter was given the choice of credit and contact information. *Family Chronicle* cannot provide any more information than is published here and unfortunately we are unable to forward any reader requests for information onto brickwall submitters. *Family Chronicle* would also like to make it clear that the brickwall submitters are under no obligation to respond to any inquiries from readers.

Marc Skulnick and Victoria Moorshead, Editors

It's Not A Brickwall Until...

Introduction by Emily A. Croom

"My great-great-grandmother is my biggest brickwall, and I haven't started on her yet!"

Have you ever felt this bewildered? Indeed, a brickwall declaration is often a cry for help instead of a real dead end. It is frequently a state of mind, perhaps impatience, rather than a failure of past record keepers or intentional deception by the ancestor. So don't despair; maybe you don't have a brickwall after all.

As you consider your tough genealogy questions, try breaking the process into the manageable steps outlined below. They can help you tackle the challenge with appropriate preparation, research, documentation and evaluation. You don't really have a brickwall until you've taken these steps.

Preliminary Step
Before confronting your problem ancestor, assess the state of your family tree, beginning with yourself. Check the facts you've learned from relatives and research, and collect the documents that confirm each generation's link to the previous one — your link to your parents (perhaps with your birth certificate), their link to their parents, etc. Don't skip a generation. This way, you know you're working on the correct ancestors. Then, instead of researching all great — or second-great-grandparents at once, focus on one or two so you can concentrate on details, using the following steps as a guide.

Step 1. Gather and organize your facts about the focus ancestor. Regardless of your preferred system for organizing documents and notes, here's a great tool for summarizing your information and centering your

attention — a four-column chronological profile that is easy to create as a table in a word processing document or as a spreadsheet. Column 1 shows the date of every known event in the ancestor's life; column 2, the ancestor's age at the time of the events; column 3, a description of events and where they took place; and column 4, documentation (the source) of your facts. If a computer isn't convenient, try an index card for each event. Continually update the profile as you learn new details about the ancestor's life — birth,

Clarence B. Sweeney, undated.

marriage, children, death, census entries, migrations, etc. (See the example of Clarence B. Sweeney's profile on the next page).

Step 2. Evaluate the facts and sources listed on the profile. Watch for inconsistencies. Does your information make sense for the ancestor's circumstances, location and time period? Do dates suggest a daughter was born before her mother? Do

For Steps 1 and 3 — Gather and organize your facts. Highlight holes and questions in color.
Chronological profile example:

Chronological Profile of Clarence B. Sweeney

Date	Age	Event	Documentation
1871	born	*Reportedly in September, possibly in Texas or Mississippi, parents unknown, no siblings yet identified. No 1880 census entry yet found. What was his middle name?*	U.S. Census of 1900, roll 1642, Harris County, TX, Houston, e.d. 82, sheet 2A, family 53, household of Clarence B. Sweeney, 28, b in Sept 1871 in Texas; U.S. Census of 1910, roll 1574, Llano County, TX, e.d. 176, sheet 2A, household of Clarence B. Sweeney, 38, b in Miss.
1887-1888	c16	First entry in Houston, Texas, city directory; worked as a clerk, residing at home of Mrs. F.F. Stephans. *Why was a 16-year-old in town, working and residing with someone of a different surname? Study Mrs. Stephans.*	1887-1888 Houston (Texas) City Directory, p. 297. *Add Clarence's other entries; last entry 1903-1904.*
1894	23	Dec. 19, married Miss Mary Ella Super in Houston.	Harris County, TX, Marriage Book M:373, #2348, FHL microfilm #25226.
1904	32	March 13, wife Mary Ella died. Dau of M/M John G. Super, burial at Glenwood Cemetery. Three children survive her. *Add children to profile.*	Mary Ella Sweeney obituary, *Houston (Texas) Chronicle*, 14 Mar 1904, sec. 1, p. 1; Glenwood Cemetery, Sec. C4, lot 197, no tombstone, visited 12 July 2004.
c1905-1906	c34	Married Kate Tompkins of Llano County, TX. No marriage record found in Llano or Harris County; no Llano newspaper available from the period.	Llano County, TX, Clerk's Office, marriage index, no record; Harris County, TX, marriage records, 1903-1908, FHL film #25229, 25230, no record found. *Try San Saba County.*
1911	40	Oct. 1, died in Llano, TX. Funeral held at home of father-in-law John G. Super, Houston, TX. Burial at Glenwood Cemetery, Houston. Four children survive him. No death certificate filed (county and state indexes do not name him).	Probate file 495, Llano County, TX, County Clerk's Office, Llano, TX; obituary of Clarence B. Sweeney, Houston (Texas) Chronicle, 3 Oct 1911; Glenwood Cemetery, Washington Ave., Houston, records show burial in Oct. 1911 (no tombstone).

sources disagree on how many wives a man had? As part of Step 5 below, you can try to reconcile such discrepancies.

How reliable are the informants and sources that provided your facts? Were the informants in a position to know correct information? Were the sources contemporary with the ancestor? Documents from the ancestor's lifetime are often more dependable than materials compiled decades later.

If you have undocumented information from websites, books or relatives, you have clues, not facts. You shouldn't accept the data until you confirm it with reliable sources. For example, if the ancestor's profile shows an unsubstantiated death date, try to get a death certificate, obituary, burial or probate record and/or other verification of the date and place.

When I created my mother's chronological profile, I realized I didn't have a copy of my parents' marriage record to confirm the date and place of their wedding, and no copy was among their papers after their deaths. When I mailed a request to the county clerk in the county where they married, I was told "No record found." Then it dawned on me that my dad worked elsewhere at the time and probably got the marriage license in the county where he lived. Indeed, that county's clerk provided a copy of the license, which confirmed what my parents had told me. The effort of checking my facts and sources had let me focus on the details and complete the documentation.

Step 3. Identify specific holes and questions in your data to address as you research. I like to highlight these in color on the ancestor's profile as I enter and study information. I also indicate uncertainties with words like *probably*, *possibly* and *check*.

Genealogists eagerly seek the names of ancestors' parents in order to move back in time. However, with a problem ancestor, you often have many other unknowns to resolve first. Thus, focusing solely on identifying the parents could be a frustrating initial goal. Instead, tagging other gaps to fill in — such as a marriage date and place, census entries and names of siblings — can help you build a foundation of facts with which to work as you try to identify the previous generation.

Clarence B. Sweeney, first wife Mary Ella (Super) Sweeney, son Johnnie, daughter Hazel and baby daughter Grace, taken in 1902.

Step 4. Plan your research by identifying sources that (1) could help you answer your questions and (2) are available from the ancestor's era and known locations. When applicable, these sources include records relating to birth, marriage and death and all accessible censuses taken during the ancestor's life.

Books and articles about research

in your ancestral jurisdictions (town, parish, county, state, province or nation) can give you ideas, even if you don't live near enough to go there in person. To learn about US records, consult *The Genealogist's Companion and Sourcebook* (2nd ed., Betterway Books, 2003), *Ancestry's Red Book: American State, County and Town Sources* (3rd edition, Ancestry, 2004) and *The Family Tree Resource Book for Genealogists* (Family Tree Books, 2004). For Canadian sources, see the *Genealogist's Handbook for Atlantic Canada Research* (2nd ed., New England Historic Genealogical Society, 1997), *Genealogy in Ontario* (Rev. 3rd ed., Ontario Genealogical Society, 2002) and *In Search of Your Canadian Roots* (3rd ed., Genealogical Publishing Co., 2000).

The Family History Library in Salt Lake City holds numerous records. To identify microfilmed

Steps 4 and 7 — Plan your research... Write down your plan...
Step 7 — Research log

Research Log: William J. and Ella Jane (Hill) Everett
Goal: Identify their parents

Date	Activity/Subject	Results/Notes/Questions	Profile Entry
27 Apr 04	Focus on Wm. J. and Ella Jane (Hill) Everett	Created profile. No luck with 1880 census. Found them in 1900 census. *Who is Betsy Price in 1900 census with Everetts? No relationship stated.*	✔ ✔ ✔
1-4 May 04	Search online censuses, SSDI on their kids, death record index, etc. *Need WJ's death date so I can get obit and/or death certificate.*	Got Everett family and Jack Hill's 1910, 1920, 1930 censuses. Got Ella Jane's and Jack Hill's death dates + 3 for the Everett kids. *Try to get all 5 obituaries.*	✔ ✔ ✔
7 May 04	University library — newspaper research: Look for Ella Jane's obit and others.		
7 May 04	Order Jack Hill's obit from Hillsboro library.		
11 May 04	FHC — order film for marriage records, 1880-1910.		
May 04	Library — look for cemetery indexes and church records.	*Betsy Price in these records?*	
May 04	Library — check for county records and county history		

---

records from your ancestor's location, consult this library's online catalog at FamilySearch.org, using the "place" search. You can rent microfilm from the library through thousands of Family History Centers worldwide; consult the FamilySearch site to locate a center near you. Microfilmed records are also available on inter-library loan from some state and provincial archives and the National Archives of Canada.

Don't forget online indexes, digitized records and reference sites. Try to find other genealogists working on the same family so you can share information and research efforts.

Write down your goal and plan, perhaps on a research log that will show sources you've tried or want to consult, the dates you sent requests and received answers, microfilm you've ordered, etc. (See the example from the Everett search on the previous page.)

Step 5. Research according to your plan, but remain alert to new sources and strategies to try. Keeping an open mind is important to progress, whereas concentrating only on preconceived ideas can hinder your success. Be sure to note each source you consult, whether it provides new information or not.

When you find abstracts and transcriptions of records that name your ancestor, try to get copies of the actual documents. Seek records created closest in time to the events in the ancestor's life. You can obtain copies of many original documents and first-generation copies on microfilm, by mail, or by hiring a researcher in the ancestor's location, if you cannot go there yourself. (Many libraries maintain lists of local researchers; their fees vary.)

Your ancestors knew relatives, neighbors, friends and others in their community. When you work on genealogical problems, branch out to study some of these individuals. I call the process "cluster genealogy." For example, some ancestors asked relatives to witness their legal documents and religious events. Thus, studying witnesses to ancestors' records may help you discover new details about the ancestors and their family.

Investigate any problem ancestor's spouse(s) and children as thoroughly as available records allow. Likewise, for an ancestor with a common surname, you frequently need to research in the context of a specific nuclear family — for example, identifying and studying your ancestor's siblings in order to locate records that name the parents.

You'll almost always find inconsistencies in the spelling of your ancestors' names. However, such variations are not necessarily discrepancies to resolve. The question is not to determine one correct spelling but to learn more about the correct ancestors, regardless of how their names appear in documents.

Kate Kegans, c.1895.
See attached chronological profile for more information.

Step 6. Record and evaluate new data. Carefully examine each new record, including the small details, for all it can tell you. Update the ancestor's chronological profile. Do the new facts change, confirm or clarify anything? What new questions do they raise? Could a lack of new information suggest that the ancestor was in a different location?

Genealogists often ask, "How many sources does it take to prove a fact?" My reply is "as many as it takes." One record may furnish enough indisputable details to confirm a fact, but a different question may require half a dozen documents for a logical, likely, convincing answer.

Step 7. Log and evaluate your progress. Review your plan, and revise it as necessary. Re-examine your notes and documents periodically for clues you may have missed.

Another tool, that I call a progress report, may help you evaluate your findings. For example, in trying to identify an ancestor's parents, you think you've discovered her brother's name. Write down your reasons for this tentative conclusion; note

Step 7 — Progress Report example:

Progress Report on Kate (Kegans) Ollre
Goal: to identify and confirm Kate's parents

Photograph is labeled Kate Kegans Ollre; her marriage record, Sept. 1899, also gave her maiden name as Kegans. After studying city directories, marriage record, and censuses of 1900-1930, I think Kate's parents were William H. and Savanah Kegans:

1. Katie and her husband, Clarence J. Ollre, lived as nearest neighbors to William H. Kegans, from at least 1910 to 1932, at 106 and 120 Drennan St., respectively, as shown in censuses and city directories. (It's a short street; both houses standing in 2004, with 2 newer houses now between them.) (Kate married in Sept. 1899. For the 1900 census, she and Clarence were not neighbors of the Kegans family.)

2. Kate's birth date of Dec. 1880 (from 1900 census) would place her in birth order between William H. Kegans' children Hamilton (born Jan. 1879) and Adele (born Feb. 1883).

3. Kate's parents were reportedly born in Texas and South Carolina, according to the 1900 census; this is consistent with reports of Wm. H. Kegans' children in the 1900-1930 censuses. No census entry for Kate and her husband or for William H. Kegans family has been found for 1910. Inconsistencies: the 1920 and 1930 censuses reported Kate's parents' birthplaces both as Texas.

4. William H. Kegans married Savanah A. King in 1867. Kate's only child was Savanah Jewel Ollre.

5. Notes: If Kate's reported birth date of Dec. 1880 was correct, she would not have been reported in the 1880 census. William Kegans and family have not been located in the 1880 census; thus, can't determine whether any infant was listed younger than Hamilton and therefore provides contradictory evidence for Kate being part of this family. No other Kate Kegans has been found in the area.

Next: Try to find death dates to look for obits for Kate and Kegans family members. Check Social Security Death Index, state death index.

---

other sources that might verify the sibling relationship. After all, establishing her brother's identity may provide her maiden name and bring you closer to learning the names of her parents. (See the example progress report on Kate Kegans Ollre on the previous page.)

Step 8. Continue learning as you pursue your genealogy. What approaches and sources have you not yet tried? Read case studies to discover how other genealogists have answered tricky questions. An excellent journal with case studies is the *National Genealogical Society Quarterly.* Case studies also appear in books such as *A Genealogist's Guide to Discovering Your African-American Ancestors* (Betterway Books, 2003), *Ancestry's Guide to Research* (Ancestry, 1985), *Applied Genealogy* (Ancestry, 1988) and *500 Brickwall Solutions to Genealogy Problems* (*Family Chronicle* Magazine, 2003).

Then What?
Repeat these steps as needed. Because each ancestor was unique, each search is unique. No one can tell you in advance which sources will answer your hard questions, but the strategy described here helps with many genealogical problems.

If you've diligently followed these steps and still have unanswered questions, you have several more options. (1) Lay the search aside temporarily while you study a different ancestor. Sometimes a change of scenery helps, figuratively or literally. Reopen your quest after you've gained more experience or confidence. (2) Hire someone to investigate your ancestor or to guide you. (3) As a last resort, recognize that every lineage comes to a research halt due to the lack or destruction of records that might have confirmed the genealogical links we seek. Or at some point in the

Kate Kegans Ollre, c.1900.

past, our ancestors lived and died without being named in records created in their community. Or they lived in a time or place before written records of lineage were kept. These situations are real brickwalls.

Fortunately, many of our brickwalls are perceptions that we can often conquer with good planning, research, documentation and evaluation.

About the Author...

Emily Croom is an active genealogy researcher, lecturer, teacher and author. Her books include The Sleuth Book for Genealogists *(2000), about problem-solving strategies, with a detailed guide to documentation, and* Unpuzzling Your Past *(4th edition, 2001), a well known basic guide to genealogy. For more information visit her website at www.unpuzzling.com.*

Take Time For Spelling

In solving brickwalls, one problem I have run into over and over again is taking name spelling and where people lived for granted. Last names can be spelled several different ways. When people came to North America from overseas, many immigration authorities spelled the immigrants' last names the way it sounded to them.

Many North Americans' ancestors had problems speaking English or perhaps their English was a little different than North American English, so this made it hard to communicate with the immigration officers. Also, some people did not like the way their names were spelled so they changed it or they changed the spelling to fit in (for example, the MacGreys may have changed their last name to Grey so that people would not know they came from Scotland).

If you check some ancestors' records, you will find they did not actually live in areas they listed or talked about. This was because certain names did not fit into that area and some people did not want their descendants to know they came from, for example, Germany. — Mary Rosevear, NB

The Case Of The Missing Mary Jane

Mary Jane was missing! She appeared with her parents, David and Elizabeth Marshall Dell, her younger brothers and an older child Tabithy (who may or may not have been her sister, but probably was her mother's youngest sister) in the 1861 census for Charlotteville Township, Norfolk County, ON. By the 1871 Canadian census, 15-year-old Mary Jane was living with Mary and Joseph Cullimore, her maternal aunt and uncle in Woodhouse Township.

Her brothers, Jonathon and Solomon, were living with other relatives and mother Elizabeth and the two youngest boys were living with Elizabeth's parents, John and Tabitha Marshall, (father David was nowhere to be seen nor was the sister/aunt Tabithy). That was the last we saw of Mary Jane. Searches of marriage and death registrations under any type of spelling proved fruitless.

Gravestone for Mary Jane Trinder.

I had started searching for Mary Jane Dell in 2000 and came to the conclusion that many members of the Vittoria Baptist Church in Norfolk County had disregarded the laws about birth, marriage and death registrations, unless they had married outside their faith. It looked like Mary Jane was one of these exceptions. In frustration, I left her and concentrated on other family members that had obligingly obeyed the registration laws.

In July 2003, while camping near Simcoe, ON, we came across the Eva Brook Donly Museum that houses the Norfolk Genealogical Society archives. On a whim, we decided to see if they held any records of the

Vittoria Baptist Church. Disappointment again, but the volunteer there convinced us to stay to check the data that they did have on the Dell families in Norfolk County. While we browsed, the volunteer was busy going through various shelves of material. Then, "Were you looking for someone with the initials M J? I have the listing here for Vittoria Baptist Cemetery done in the 1960s and there is an interesting note here."

Assuring him I had checked the Ontario Cemetery Finding Aid online and had even been to the cemetery, I asked what he had found. Believe or not, there was our Mary Jane! In the 1960s, while recording gravestones for the local society, some wonderful person had noted that the gravestone of a "Mary Jane Trinder" was very similar to the gravestone right beside it. That nearby gravestone was Elizabeth Marshall Dell!

It only took a few minutes on our next trip to our local library to check the death, birth and marriage records to find that Mary Jane Dell had married John Trinder, had a daughter Susan, then died two days later and was buried beside her mother Elizabeth. If it had not been for that observant person who added extra notes to her work (something not noted in the 1980s recording of that cemetery that I had worked from) and the sharp eyes of the volunteer in 2003, we would not have seen what was right before our eyes. From now on, I will double check at local societies to see if any earlier transcriptions or lists are available.

Now, if only we could find her father David Dell and Aunt Tabitha A.W. Marshall! — Maureen Beecroft, ON, tmbee_2@hotmail.com

The Search For Aunt Florence

My grandfather spent many years trying to find his sister who went missing sometime around 1940 when she was close to 40 years old. The only real clue that grandpa ever had to go on was that Florence went to Hartford, CT. He made many trips to Hartford to try to track her down; but to no avail. My mother remembers the heavy disappointment on her father's face each time he came home with nothing. Sadly, he never found her before he died in 1965 — but then he didn't have the luxury of the Internet.

In 1999, I decided to plug Florence's maiden name into the online SSDI for Connecticut. I came up with six different women with the same name. From the list, my mother picked out the one that had our Florence's birth year (which Mom knew) and which also showed a Hartford, CT address. I warned her that we still might not have our Florence, but we mailed the request anyway.

Soon we received our reply in the mail. Bingo! It was our Florence. The card listed both her parents' names, which confirmed it was her. I then plugged her name into the online Connecticut Death Index by matching the birthdates, and again, we were able to find our Florence — this time with the date and place of her death. All of the information pointed to the fact that she had lived in Hartford, CT and seemingly had never married. It showed that she had died in Manchester, CT — a suburb of Hartford, in March 1984. We excitedly mailed away to Manchester for her death certificate.

When the death certificate arrived we found more clues. The "informant" listed on her certificate was the Department of Income Maintenance. It also listed the name of the nursing home where she was living when she died. (We checked with the nursing home for records but they had discarded them). The death certificate told us that she was cremated at Cedar Hill Cemetery in Hartford. My mother and I were so excited that we had finally found so much information about Florence, we located the cemetery on a map, jumped in the car and drove there thinking we would certainly find a grave for her. Needless to say, we were extremely disappointed when we got there after a two-hour drive and found the office closed; in our excitement we had jumped the gun.

The next day my mother called the cemetery. They didn't have a burial record for Florence but they suggested we call the funeral home listed on the death certificate which was still in business. My mother called and told the owner of the funeral home her story and that all she wanted to know was

The day of the funeral, in March 2000, Florence's urn was laid next to the spot where she was to be buried in the family plot.

where Florence was buried. He then asked her to hold for a couple of minutes. When he returned to the phone my mom got the shock of her life. He told her that he actually had Florence right there at the funeral home! "What?" My mother cried out, "What are you talking about?" The funeral director chuckled a little and told her that when Florence died no family members could be located, so the State of Connecticut required that she be cremated. Her cremated remains were returned to the funeral home where they were placed on a shelf with others. (Yes, there are many others in many funeral homes, left

unclaimed for different reasons, so we found out.) He was also able to provide my mother with the information from his file that the nursing home had given him at the time of her death, such as previous jobs held and other personal information.

Apparently, Florence had told the nursing home she had two brothers and one sister, which was correct. The only sibling she actually named was my grandfather, but no location where to find him. We have reason to believe she knew that her sister and other brother had already died at that time, but we don't think she knew for sure that my grandfather had also passed away.

Well, we certainly were not going to leave her at the funeral home after we had come this far. As luck would have it, my mother happened to recall that her father received a copy of a will from the last living member of his family, an unmarried aunt, who had died in 1956. She quickly located it. The will only mentioned Florence in one spot, it stated if Florence was to ever return to her home in New Haven and needed a place to be buried, her remains could be put in the family plot in the cemetery; otherwise the family plot was to be closed forever. The only stipulation was that Florence could only be put there if she had never married. (Strange request, I know, but not to me, the more research I do on this side of the family!)

We called the cemetery and sure enough they confirmed that the last family member had listed a "conveyance in trust" for Florence and they agreed that she would be able to be buried in the family plot. Thanks initially to the Internet, not only were we able to find Florence, but we brought her home too! — Mary Byrne, NY

The More We Visit, The Luckier We Get

My parents told me I was related to Thomas Alva Edison but not directly descended from the famous inventor.

Early on in our genealogy research, we determined my second-great-grandmother was Elizabeth Jane Edison Putnam who, we later learned, was the daughter of Captain Samuel Edison and his second wife Elizabeth (Yokum) Cook. Thomas Alva was the son of Samuel Edison Jr., a son of the Captain and his first wife, Nancy Simpson. This means we share Captain Samuel Edison as a common ancestor; he is Thomas' grandfather, my third-great-grandfather, and we are distant cousins.

The Edison family Bible lists "Capt. Samuel Edison married to Elizabeth Cook on Sep 5th 1825..." It was during a visit to relatives that the Edison family Bible surfaced as a primary source of confirmation that Peter Bradish was related to Thomas Alva Edison.

All we had for evidence of these relationships in the Edison family were the *Haggan Papers Genealogies* and a few other secondary sources. We had no primary, or even close to, primary documents.

Not long after learning the basics of the Edison relationship, we decided to visit a cousin of mine in northwest Minnesota whom I hadn't seen since I was a very young boy. We renewed our friendship during a very enjoyable day and continued on our travels. During this first visit we discussed our genealogy research and what we had learned so far. The widow of another cousin in the same family was there and expressed the thought she might have a family Bible but she wasn't certain where it was.

A few years later, we stopped by again and the widow asked if we were interested in the Edison Bible. You can bet we were! She left and returned with the Bible of Captain Samuel Edison. We now had a primary source for some of the Edison lineage. While it wasn't complete with all the births, marriages and deaths in the Edison family, it certainly contained many details and information we hadn't encountered yet.

Two more family Bibles of related lines have shown up during our visits with this cousin's family. Of course, all the relevant Bible pages have been scanned into our computer. A copy of the first page of the Samuel Edison Bible, the title page with publishing data, two birth pages, a marriage page and a death page were given to the Edison Museum of Vienna, ON along with an excellent copy of Elizabeth Jane Edison Putnam's photograph. Incidentally, our copy of Elizabeth Jane's photograph wasn't identified until we visited the museum where they had a newspaper article which portrayed the same photograph with her name below it.

Research can take many forms. Finding and visiting relatives and old friends has been one of our most enjoyable and rewarding efforts.

None of these Bibles or many other family documents would likely have surfaced during our lifetimes had we not continued to search for, and visit, our still living relatives. Additionally, all of them have been wonderful to spend time with! — Peter Bradish, FL, bradish@attglobal.net

'Til Death Do Us Part

My second-great-grandfather Eli Barber Spray just showed up in Madison County, MT. We know he was there prior to 1866 when he married Martha E. Hinch. According to the census and his death certificate, he was born in Illinois in 1839. A slightly older William H. Spray can be found in Madison County, but, in correspondence with his descendants, William was born in Ohio in 1829 and came to Montana five or more years after Eli via Texas, Missouri and Nebraska.

A search in the 1850 federal census for Illinois didn't turn up any good candidates for Eli's parents. He couldn't be found on the rosters of the Union Soldiers of the Civil War. So, I put the search aside... until I stumbled upon him listed in the 1890 Civil War Veterans and Widows census for Washington state.

I then sent for his Civil War pension application. His application had been rejected, but in it he told the story of how he had been orphaned at age nine in Texas! I was then able to find his parents and a sister listed in the 1850 Texas mortality census. I was eventually able to find a record of him selling his father Elias Spray's headright in the Peter's Colony (Cooke County, Texas) to a Samuel Spray. I was also able to track this family back to Ohio where they were documented in the Quaker records. The William H. Spray I had found earlier turned out to be Eli's older brother who had left Texas after their parents' deaths. He

had headed back to Ohio but stopped and got married in Missouri instead. — Vicki Hutchison, CA

A Second Request

When I first began researching my Waters ancestors, I knew my great-grandfather William Weard Waters was born in Clarion, PA in 1854, had moved to Lock Haven, PA by 1881 where he married, and finally on to Ohio where he died. My goal was to trace William's line.

I began by sending for his death record from Ohio, hoping to learn his parents' names. When it arrived, it showed the parents' names as John and Mary Waters. Marriage records for William didn't give any additional information.

Being such common names — John, Mary, William — I began searching, but without any success for several years.

I found a John and Mary Waters in census records for 1850, but since this was before William was born I wasn't sure this was my family. By 1860, there was no record for them at all. I contacted various Pennsylvania libraries requesting information on the surname Waters, but without success. I also posted messages on numerous message boards.

One day I received a reply to one of my posts from a man named Nick who said that the facts for my great-grandfather looked a lot like his facts for his great-grandmother Frances E. (Waters) in that she was born near Clarion and moved to Lock Haven area; plus her parents' names were John and Mary Waters. He also said his great-grandmother was referred to as Fanny. Coincidentally, one of William's daughters was named Frances Elizabeth and nicknamed Fanny. This was looking promising, but we needed proof of a relationship!

Nick had a marriage application for Fanny's marriage, stating her parents' names and mentioning her mother's maiden name, however, it wasn't entirely legible, so we had several different possibilities. The record also had the name of Clement which led us to believe Mary had remarried a Clement.

With the new clue of Clement, I went back to message boards and census records and found a John Clement living in Venango County, PA in 1870 with wife Mary Ann and son William Waters, but no Fanny. I again went to the Internet to try to determine Mary's death date and location, learning she had died in 1906. I sent for her death record and was told they had no such person's record of death. A dead end.

NAME	JOINED: BY/FROM	DISMISSED/DIED
Berringer, George, Sr. *	1838 transfer	died 11/__/1895
Berringer, Margaret	between 1838 -1879 transfer	died 6/28/1889
Boundy, Sarah A.	10/__/1884 letter	to Clarion Co
Bowman, Ann S.	between 1838 -1879 letter	died 1905
Bowman, Jennie A.	between 1838 -1879 prof.	moved away
Bowman, Robert	between 1838 -1879 prof.	to Butler Co.
Bowman, Sarah Ellen	between 1838 -1879 prof.	to Sandy Lake, Pa.
Brye, Rachel, Miss	6/9/1918 prof.	10/3/1926 Clintonville P. Ch.
Buchanan, Bertha	11/4/1894 prof.	
Buchanan, David K.	3/25/1887 prof.	10/1/1904 to Franklin
Buchanan, Edna	11/4/1894 prof.	
Buchanan, Luther	4/21/1901 prof.	
Buchanan, Marietta	3/25/1887 prof.	
Buchanan, May	4/__/1891 prof.	to Franklin
Buchanan, William	11/4/1894 prof.	
Buchannan, Ethel	4/21/1901 prof.	
Buck, Hettie	11/4/1894 prof.	to Oil City
Buck, James	11/4/1894 prof.	to Oil City
Buck, Margaret J.	2/4/1888 prof.	to Oil City
Buck, Reuben	2/4/1888 prof.	died 4/19/1901
Buck, William	11/4/1894 prof.	to Oil City
Bumgardner, Absalom	3/25/1887 prof.	dead
Bumgardner, Elizabeth	between 1838 -1879 prof.	gone
Bumgardner, Maggie	1872	died 11/__/1877
Carnahan, Winifred L., Miss	4/18/1915 prof.	gone
Carr, D. A.	as of 1915	
Carson, Cora	4/__/1891 prof.	moved away
Cassidy, __w/C. J.	9/8/1901 cert.	joined M.E. Ch.
Cassidy, Kate M., Mrs.	10/18/1903 letter	moved away
Cassidy, Maud, w/C. J.	9/8/1901 letter	moved away
Cassidy, Milton	10/18/1903 prof.	moved away
Clements, John H.	1/__/1879 prof.	died 10/__/1900
Clements, Mary A.	between 1872 -1879 prof	died 3/11/1906

Finding the member roster of the Cumberland-Kennerdell Presbyterian Church allowed Linda Wright to learn an exact date of death and ultimately to obtain Mary's death certificate.

Back to online searching, I found a website which mentioned a church near where John and Mary Clement lived and a person's name who had written a booklet about this church. I wrote her to see if perhaps Mary had been a member of this church. Yes, she had! Graciously, the author sent me copies of some records she had in her possession. I doubt Marilyn realized how important one little bit of information was that she included. One page stated Mary's exact date of death! I sent a second request for a death certificate and this time Pennsylvania was able to find it! The informant's name on the certificate was Fanny (Nick's great-grand-mother) proving Fanny and William were siblings and proof Nick and I shared a common ancestor.

On the death certificate there was an additional bonus of the names of Mary's parents. With these names, I've been in contact with other researchers who have these two branches well documented back to the 1700s, so I've added several additional generations.

In time, I sent for widows' pension papers knowing John Clement was in the Civil War. I really didn't have high expectations of finding any new information, but I was totally wrong. It was a banner day when the records arrived as they documented Mary's marriage to John Waters and listed his death date of 1856, two years after William was born — explaining why there were no 1860 census records for John Waters. Mary had also been married to a Jacob Weaver (first husband) who had died 1843.

If I had accepted the fact that a death record for Mary didn't exist, I would still be in the dark about her life. Digging a little deeper and sending a second request opened up a window in my brickwall.

I'm still trying to locate further information on John Waters, but now I have no doubt that I'll eventually learn more about him. In the meantime, I've found a third-cousin in Nick and corresponded with so many wonderful people, many of them volunteers. I've found that no one person is responsible for breaking down that brickwall; it takes wonderful volunteers willing to help, new-found cousins and those people who contribute to genealogy websites and share their knowledge. — Linda Wright, OH, lwright@greenapple.com

The Mystery Of Mary Farris Tyner Tyler

The moral of this story is don't give up, be persistent. I learned the name of my second-great-grandmother, Mary Farris, when I started doing genealogy about 12 years ago. I also learned from my great-grandfather's death certificate that she was born in Tennessee.

The name Farris is very common in early Tennessee. She was a widow with eight children when she married my second-great-grandfather, John Alexander Tyler. She came to California from Arkansas with her first husband, Thomas Tyner, during the gold rush and shortly thereafter she was

Mary Farris Tyner Tyler.

widowed. Looking for the common name of Mary in the 40 Farris families in Tennessee at that time is like looking for a needle in a haystack. To complicate matters, Mary seemed to be unsure where she was born. In the earlier census she put Tennessee, while later she put Alabama. This told me that the family probably moved from one state to another.

Over the years I wrote letters to just about everyone who was researching the Farris name asking "Might you have a Mary Farris born about 1816?" Finally I heard from a researcher who said that one of Isaac Farris' sons name was Thomas Tyner Farris, which was Mary's first mar-

ried name. That indicated that Isaac and Mary probably were related and Isaac had named a child after his brother-in-law. Finally after years of research I found a land record showing that Mary Tyner sold land and the witness was Isaac Farris. This record definitely indicated that they knew each other.

Shortly thereafter one of Isaac's descendants found a photo with the name Mary Tyler. It was one of those photographs that people have that fortunately was marked with the name but everyone had forgotten who it was. We now have two siblings to fit into the family. I am working on Isaac and lateral lines to fit both Isaac and Mary into the family. It helps to have siblings to fit into the picture. I have birthdates, birthplaces, children's birthdates and places, migration patterns and naming patterns all to help me. — Carolyn Peterson, CA, corksterr@sbcglobal.net

Not All Brickwalls Are Created Equal

Some brickwalls come crumbling down when a key piece of information is found. Typically these walls have missing information, incorrect assumptions or some unexpected location as the foundation.

My brickwall has as its foundation a shortage of information, lack of state record keeping and changing county boundaries. I have worked very hard to breach this wall and have succeeded in breaking down portions of it but every time I gain ground on the main part of the challenge there is another wall waiting.

Very little was known about my maternal grandfather. My mother never knew him and my grandmother still has a very sharp mind but she has 75-year-old memories of a 16-year-old girl involved in a short marriage. Not a good starting point for research. The man's name was Oscar Eugene Gregg and grandma knew he was from Georgia.

Diligent and slow genealogical research has been the way I have tackled this problem. First was a marriage record which told Oscar's age, birth state and parents' names. A request for a birth record from the state of Georgia came back negative. It seems only the counties kept records prior to 1909. The SSDI yielded a death date but no benefits address or death place. The SS-5 yielded a birth date and place (Sycamore, GA, March 1902) and place of employment in Rome, GA in 1934 when he applied for his social security card. A trip to Rome yielded nothing from the city directories around that time and the mill where he worked was long since closed with no known records surviving. However, a very helpful genealogy department librarian did assist, by finding a death date and place on a subscription service genealogy website, thus the trip was not wasted. A request to the vital records department of two Georgia counties yielded the run-around about who should have the Sycamore, GA birth records from 1902.

A search of the 1910 US census showed Oscar's mother as a widow with four children. The last sibling was born in 1906 so it is assumed that Oscar's father (David Clarence Gregg) died between 1906 and 1910. Repeated searches of the 1900 census Soundex yielded no sign of the David

Gregg family. Finally a name-by-name search of the Soundex revealed D.C. Gregg and family living in the Sycamore area. I now have an approximate date of birth for David Gregg. His birth place is listed as Texas and his birth year can be estimated. There looms a new brickwall with almost no information.

The second layer of the wall in the Gregg line continues to challenge me and I will continue to try to chip away at it with the slow thorough research methods and constant review of what I know what I don't know and what can be read between the lines.

With such a sturdy foundation this wall may stand for a while. — Greg Wight, TN, eggwight@msn.com

West Not, Want Not

I had been trying to find the birth and death records for Amelia Porter, the sister of my second-great-grandfather Eli Sisler for more than five years. Other family members had been searching for many years.

According to family tradition, Amelia and her husband Johnson had moved out west but we did not know where. I placed a query on the Halton County, Ontario, Ancestry.com page. This was the last place we knew where she had lived. In a few days, someone answered my query and referred me to the excellent website of the Halton/Peel Branch of the Ontario Genealogical Society. There was a death notice listed for an Amelia Porter in the *Acton Free Press* newspaper.

I visited the Archives of Ontario in Toronto where they have a massive microfilmed collection of Ontario newspapers. I found the death notice. Amelia's full name was Emily Amelia Porter, she had been named after her mother Emily. Amelia died on 10 November 1916 in Toronto. Her husband was still alive at the time of her death. Also at the Archives of Ontario,

I was able to find Amelia's death record. By her age at death, I figured out she was born on 1 September 1854. Amelia was born in Whitchurch Township, York County, ON.

Amelia had moved out west, but only as far as Acton. This was about 50 miles from where she was born. So the family tradition was correct. We thought she had moved out to western Canada or the western United States. — Ken Sisler, ON

Death And Taxes

There is an old joke circulating among musicians that says there are three sure things in life — death, taxes and faulty intonation. Being an amateur violist, I was well aware of faulty intonation, but it wasn't until I started family history research that I became aware of the importance of death and taxes in genealogy.

For several years now, I have been researching my mother's family, the Fishers, who came to Canada from Devon. The family history told me that Richard Fisher, my second-great-grand-father lived in Yarnscombe, North Devon. I then visited the FHC and ordered several films from their catalogue.

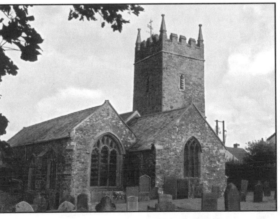

St. Andrew's Church, Yarnscombe, Devon, showing the gravestones of the Fisher family.

Sure enough, I found Richard Fisher in the 1881 British census living at Gibbing's Down Farm, Yarnscombe, and born in George Nympton, about 13 miles east of Yarnscombe, Devon.

Next, I ordered the parish register film for George Nympton, and found my second-grandfather baptized in 1797 along with his three brothers. His parents were listed as Henry and Rachel Fisher.

Meanwhile, I had studied the parish registers for Yarnscombe and found many entries for the Fisher family including a Henry Fisher, baptized in 1748 and married in 1785 to Rachel Pow. Was this Henry Fisher mine? Was this Henry Fisher Richard's father? I had come to a standstill.

I must admit that when I ordered the land tax assessment film for Yarnscombe from the FHC, I was not too sure what I would find. It turned out to be a gold-mine of information showing the owner, the occupier, the name of the farm and the taxes owing for all of the properties in this village.

Then I compared this report with the land tax assessment for George Nympton of 1780-1832. Bingo! Henry and Rachel Fisher lived at Yarnscombe from 1785 to at least 1793, paying taxes each year.

According to the land tax assessment for George Nympton, Henry Fisher lived there from 1796 to 1805 when his name disappeared from the listings.

However, in 1805 his name turned up again in Yarnscombe where he farmed until 1815. In this way, I was able to show that Henry Fisher, the relocator, was present in Yarnscombe, moved to George Nympton, and finally returned to Yarnscombe. This discovery allowed me to go back one more generation.

Rachel Fisher was buried in Yarnscombe on 18 April 1822 at the age of 60 while her husband, Henry, was buried one year later on 26 March 1823, also at Yarnscombe. He was 75 years old.

Were Henry and Rachel musical like me? If so, their tunes have long since eroded like their names on the gravestones in Yarnscombe parish churchyard — Ruth Miller Downs, BC, jrdowns@smartt.com

The Little Drummer Boy

James Neville, the son of Henry and Aramintha Neville, was born in Greene County, PA in 1803. The family lived in Pickaway, OH for about 30 years, then settled in Edgar, IL from about 1834 through 1856. At that time the family migrated to Osage, IA where they were in the 1860 census. The entire family "disappeared" by 1870.

After searching for them for a few years, they re-surfaced near Pawnee,

James Neville was the oldest person in his regiment when he enlisted as a drummer at age 59.

NB in the 1870 census. Solomon Neville, the son of James, was living near his wife's parents. Living in the same household was Mary Ann Neville, the mother of Solomon. The logical conclusion was that James had died, but when and where?

After looking in every possible place for several years, I decided to try a Google.com search for James Neville. I found James in a list of Iowa volunteers in the Civil War. It turns out that he was the oldest person in his regiment when he enlisted as a drummer at age 59. He was in the war for one year and six months and was discharged for disability and died shortly thereafter. The moral of this story is to not leave any stone unturned. — Carolyn Peterson, CA, corksterr@sbcglobal.net

Try And Try Again

I was trying to find the death record for my grandmother who had been born in 1852 and died in the late 1920s. I am one of the youngest in a large family and my grandmother had died when I was just a toddler. My older siblings all told me that she had died in Bowling Green, OH where she was living at the time.

However, in checking the county records I could find no death record for her. I then wrote to the state to obtain her death certificate but was again told they had no record of her death. I decided that somehow, her record must have been lost or just not recorded or there was some other explainable reason for its absence. My siblings were all old enough to have known her and knew where she had lived. I then contacted the church she had attended. Again they had no record but said that records from that time period would have been sent to a depository. They sent me the address and I wrote to the depository in question. I received an answer stating they did not have the record and gave me an address for another depository at which I would find the record.

I wrote to this depository and the answer I received told me they did not have the record and recommended that I should write directly to the church she had attended.

Frustratingly, I was right back where I had started. I decided to let it rest for awhile. I then went to work on my grandfather's records. He had died many years before my grandmother and I knew they were living in Michigan when he had died. I sent away for his death record and received a letter back saying that although they did not have his record, they did have one for his wife! More by accident than design, I had stumbled across my grandmother's record.

I, of course, sent for the record and discovered that my grandmother had been visiting her daughter, who was living across the state line into Michigan, when she had died.

The lesson here is to check the neighboring state records when one lives close to the border. It's good to know that death records are in fact, kept where the person died and not where they resided. (Through a newspaper item I did learn that my grandfather had also died while on a trip in another state.) — Marjorie C. Alderks, PA

Portrait Of My Great (Or Not So Great) Uncle

One person my great-grandmother hardly mentioned was her brother, Willie Watkins. (Not his real name, mind you.) While at the NARA, looking through the census records, I decided to see if I could find out what happened to Great-Uncle Willie. Since I had no idea of his locality, I began to search through a few different states in the Soundex index. At last, I did find his name, and the age matched, too — but I couldn't believe that he was listed as an inmate at the state prison!

After getting over the initial shock that my relatives weren't all perfect, I thought I would try to investigate further. Through the local library, I was able to find newspaper articles about his arrest. I also found there is quite a paper trail, when researching someone who has been through the legal system. I wrote a letter to the prison where he was incarcerated, asking for information. They referred me to the prison archives. Here is where the real treasure was found! I was able to get his prison file (more than 40 years' worth), court records and also two 8x10 photos of him. Nice and clear too! I had never seen a picture of him before that time.

Not everyone has a front view *and* a side view of their relative — and fully identified too — along with a serial number! — Marianne Hale, CA, hhmachshop@aol.com

Back To The Present

Brickwalls have been a repeated challenge during the 34 years I've been searching for family. My search has mainly concentrated on living cousins rather than long-dead ancestors, so I assumed it would be relatively simple.

However, I soon learned that in order to find people in the present, one has to begin with the past. So I started more or less with the fathers of my four grandparents, seeking all their descendants.

My latest brickwall collapsed as a direct result of my computer and a website, so that's the story I want to tell. But before telling the story, it will be easier for you to follow if I give you a cast of characters: Kate, my maternal grandmother; Doll and Roe, two of Kate's sisters; Frances, one of Doll's daughters; Nancy, one of Doll's granddaughters (and Frances' niece); and Helen, Roe's daughter-in-law (and widow of her son Ralph, who was Doll's nephew).

My most recent search was for the descendants of Kate's siblings who married and raised families. Aunt Doll, who lived in a distant city, had visited us twice when I was a child. I knew her name and where she lived, so I started with her. However, there were more than 200 people with the same surname listed in the city's phone directory — a formidable challenge to say the least.

So I turned to Aunt Roe, with whom my grandmother had corresponded when I was a child. Through the miracle of computers, within 30 minutes of searching I was talking on the phone to Helen — widow of Aunt Roe's son Ralph — who put me in touch with additional family members.

In the process, I learned about Kate's other siblings, with whom I was completely unfamiliar. My computer helped me identify the descendants of all of those siblings and put me in touch with quite a few of them. Although I eventually got Aunt Doll's obituary with the names of all of her children — including the married

(L-R) Bob Hartsell's Great-Aunt Doll, grandmother Kate and first-cousin, once-removed Frances in 1941. He had wondered for months who the young lady in the photo was. In a twist of fate, he was reunited with his cousin Frances after 60 years.

names of her daughters — I still couldn't locate any of her descendants. None of the cousins I found knew anything about her family; not even Helen, who had put me in touch with many other family members.

So I posted messages on appropriate genealogical surname message boards. A few months later, I received an e-mail from Nancy, one of Aunt Doll's granddaughters who had just enrolled in a genealogy class and was only beginning her research. Just like that, the wall collapsed. Nancy gave me the name and address of her Aunt Frances — Aunt Doll's sole surviving child and my mother's sole surviving first-cousin. Frances was in her mid-eighties. If my mother had been living, she would have been 108; but she had been dead 49 years. Almost half-a-century after her death, I made contact with her cousin and made plans to visit her the following summer, which I did. We had a wonderful reunion, just a couple of months before she died.

But other than my actual visit with Frances, one of the most rewarding parts of the story is this: In Kate's trunk I found a snapshot taken when Aunt Doll visited us in 1941. It showed Kate and Aunt Doll and a young lady I couldn't identify. I had only a vague, but very fond, memory of someone who had accompanied Aunt Doll on her visit — the "unidentified young lady" in the snapshot, I assumed. When I asked cousin Frances if she could identify the unknown person for me, it turned out to be Frances herself! After 60 years I was in direct contact with someone who was only a vague, but pleasant, memory from my childhood; one whose photograph had puzzled me for months since I had discovered it in my grandmother's trunk!

It was sad to say good-bye so soon to Frances after being reunited with her after so many years, but every letter, phone conversation and our few hours of personal reunion were celebrations of the joy of family rediscovered and reunited; thanks to the marvel of computers and the generosity of those who maintain websites! — Bob Hartsell, AR, u4eah@hsnp.com

James A. Saxman: A Forgotten Ancestor

Sometimes, while working on our own genealogy mysteries, we inadvertently solve someone else's.

The Saxman vault in Unity Cemetery in Latrobe, PA, has seven occupants. By the time I visited the vault, I already knew the identities of those within, but this was not true for another, older member of my extended family, someone I had never even met.

My maternal grandfather, Shields Albert Saxman, was born in 1884 in Westmoreland County, PA, not far from Latrobe. I never knew much about his ancestry, so when I began my family digging several years ago, I turned to my sister and our cousins. I discovered an aunt had once given my cousin some names and dates and that seemed a likely starting place.

We all knew our great-grandfather's name was Albert Saxman and that his father had made a name for himself in the coal industry. Unfortunately, my aunt had only guessed at the lineage and gave the wrong first name for Albert's father, thereby sending me in the wrong direction.

I contacted a man with the same "wrong" name, assuming we were closely related, but he had never heard of Shields Albert Saxman and said I must be mistaken. Embarrassed, I apologized and kept looking.

Seven members of the Saxman family are interred in the Saxman family vault in Unity Cemetery, Latrobe, PA.

Researching the name Saxman in county histories provided the big breakthrough:

Mr. (Mathias) Saxman married first (1858) Susan Armel, who died after the birth of her only son, James Albert Saxman" (*Old And New Westmoreland* by John N. Boucher).

This revelation jogged some memories and several members of my family then remembered Albert's first name was James. One cousin, whose given names are James Albert, realized he had been named for our great-grandfather.

We also knew Albert had died in his twenties. A tip from another researcher directed me to the Unity Cemetery records where I found the Saxman vault. The earliest occupant had died on 21 May 1886. His name was James A. Saxman. Near his place was his father Mathias, who died in 1913.

I felt the need to go back to the man who had never heard of my branch and explain how our families were connected. He was very happy to hear from me, especially when I mentioned the Saxman vault. The other occupants were all from his branch. He thanked me for solving the mystery of who James A. Saxman was, since no one in his generation or his father's had any idea of James' true identity. Since then we have both learned a great deal about our common ancestors.

Sadly, though, he regretted his father had not lived to this "new age of genealogy" via the Internet, where connections are made swiftly and mysteries are solved quickly. — Kathy Borne, OH, Kathyborne@aol.com

Bureau of Land Management Website

I started researching my Norwegian ancestry about four years ago. I found my paternal great-grandmother's family and her parents. Then I found my paternal great-grandfather's family and his parents, except for one brother in a family of seven. I could not find his place or date of death anywhere after nearly a year of searching. I found Palmer Clemetson in the 1870 and 1880 censuses for Minnesota as a young man still at home. I found him later in North Dakota as a married man with six young children in the 1900 census.

After that I lost him. I scanned hundreds of pages for the 1910 census for both counties where I suspected he lived. Two brothers lived close to him in North Dakota. I made requests to Minnesota and North Dakota for death certificates, to both Roseau and Walsh counties and to different historical societies requesting help. All were unsuccessful. One day, I was searching the Bureau of Land Management website looking for homestead/land records for my great-grandfather Ole. I found it, but I also found a record for Jane Thompson, widow of Palmer Clemetson, which she filed to complete in 1904.

Finally, after all this time, a morsel; a hint of an approximate date of death for my great-uncle. I ordered the land papers for Jane Thompson and there it was. She stated that her husband Palmer had died on 1 March 1902. She remarried an Ole Thompson and filed to complete the patent on that homestead in Roseau County, MN.

I still don't have Palmer's death certificate, but at least I know when and where he died leaving behind a pregnant wife and seven young children. I just don't know how, yet! — Terri (Clemetson) Schmitke, BC, wayter@telus.net

Search For The Sister Solution

One of my most interesting brickwalls was my ancestor Elizabeth Ann Holt (born in 1869). I was fortunate to meet with her daughter Lillian, who told me a bit about Elizabeth's life.

Elizabeth was placed in foster care, along with a sister Ida. After an abusive life in foster care, Elizabeth entered into a marriage of the same nature. She worked hard to ensure her children never went into foster care. The sisters found each other as young women. Neither Elizabeth nor Ida ever spoke of their parents. Lillian had many wonderful memories of her mother but could tell me little in the way of names and dates. However, she did tell me that Elizabeth was buried in Lakefield Cemetery, just outside Peterborough, ON.

I decided I would start with the

cemetery. I could not find her gravestone in the local cemetery, however, I found her husband's father, William Graham. I decided to leave Elizabeth alone for the time being, afraid of the dead end I might be facing.

After attending a seminar where experienced researchers shared their tips, I got the idea to look more closely at the grave. It seemed to be a large plot for just William and Sarah (Manning) Graham. I used a stick with a steel tip on the end to feel around for buried stones. As luck would have it, I discovered two tiny name stones, buried just under the grass. It had only first names: "Elizabeth" and "Frederick". I was hesitant about going to the cemetery office, which was someone's home. However they were very friendly and helpful. My first real information on Elizabeth came from the burial records.

Elizabeth Ann Holt.

With a death date, I sent away for Elizabeth's death certificate. It listed her parents as Simon Holt and Mary Jane Killbride. The informant was Charles Genge, Elizabeth's brother-in-law and Ida's husband. Elizabeth's death certificate stated she was born in Kingston, ON. I began an exhaustive search of the 1871 Canadian census for Kingston, ON, and other resources. I found nothing of her or her parents. I searched the Peterborough area again, and still nothing.

I figured I should locate every piece of paperwork on the family. I was unable to find Elizabeth's daughter's birth certificate but I did locate

the next oldest. I also found them in the 1891 Smith Township Census. I thought I could find Elizabeth, in the 1881 census, most likely in an orphanage. She wasn't listed as a residence in any. I contacted local archives, and family historians to find out if there are records for foster care in the 1880s. No one knew of any. I read up on the subject and found most children were put out to work. Elizabeth most likely would have been put out to work at age 12. I tried three more times to find her in Peterborough County in 1881.

I had run out of ideas for her. I thought searching for her sister's information might shine a new light on the research. So I turned my attention to Ida.

I searched the Ontario marriage index for Ida's marriage to Charles Genge. Her marriage certificate had an extra notation regarding Hill being an adoptive name. I went on to find her birth record which listed Simon Holt and Mary Killbride as her parents. Ida was born in Peterborough in 1874. I also found her on the 1881 census living with the Hills, as their daughter. Through the local genealogy society's project of transcribing old newspapers, I found that Elizabeth and Ida had a brother, George Henry, who died in 1877.

A timeline started to form; I began listing the years, location and events for this family. I found a city directory for 1876, which listed Simon as living in Peterborough, but not in 1881 and this didn't tell me whether the children were with him. I found Bridget

Holt, widow of Simon, buried in Young's Point Cemetery. I then use the Ontario marriage index to locate the marriage of a Simon and Bridget in 1878. Simon was listed as a widower. I figured I was on the right track. I also found a Simon and Bridget Holt living in Harvey Township in 1881. That gave me a location to find his death registry in 1888. I figured Mary Killbride Holt must have died in the period 1877-78. I searched all Holts on the Ontario death index for that time period. There was nothing. Even though there are many blanks left, I managed to find Simon, a second marriage and more about Ida and her adoptive family.

By starting with only my second-great-grandmother's name, I have managed to pull together quite a bit on her family.

Even when it looks hopeless, don't give up! — Tina Hansen, YK, idigupfamily@hotmail.com

Digging Deeper

When I started my research on my paternal grandmother's Boatfield family, I only had a few loose pieces of paper showing her with her siblings, parents, paternal grandparents and cousins. The information listed only names, with some marriages in various hand writing. The family had lived in Pavilion, Genesee County, NY since 1880. A trip to the county historical society in Le Roy, NY proved very successful. A deceased cousin had previously worked on this Boatfield family and her records were housed there. These records added more names, some dates, but few places. They added nothing on my great-grandmother, Maria Ann (Wellington) Boatfield except that she had died in 1926.

I learned that the Boatfield family had immigrated from Atherton, UK in 1880. Taking these records, along with the other information I had gathered,

I started my search. I gathered information from census records. I wrote for vital records from the county and visited cemeteries, recording information on everyone I could locate. The courthouse provided more information. A search of Atherton records at the FHC revealed nothing.

When I finally got my great-grandfather Samuel Boatfield's death record, I realized why. It indicated that they were not from Atherton at all, but were actually from

Maria Ann Wellington Boatfield.

Atherington, Devon, UK. These two towns are in different counties entirely. A later search in Atherington has taken this Boatfield family back to 1699 in the church records.

Each new record added more meat to the bones of this family, but one record was missing that I really wanted. That was my great-grandmother Maria Boatfield's death certificate. I knew that she had died in 1926 in Pavilion, NY but I could not locate her death record.

On a trip to Pavilion some time later, I decided to stop by the First Baptist Church. This was the church the family had attended for generations. I found the minister and asked to see any records they might have that would show this family. It was a Saturday and the church secretary was not there. The minister knew that the older records were not in the church, but were kept at the home of the secretary. He called her at home to see if she would let me view those records. She agreed, but said she would have to get them out. The old church records were stored in a cardboard box in her garage. Fortunately, she was planning to be home and I was welcome to go to her house to look through the box.

After obtaining directions from the minister, I went to the secretary's home. When I arrived, she had the box sitting out on her front steps. We sat on the steps and she brought out the records that she thought might help me. She handed me the journal of the First Baptist Church for the years 1870-1930. I obviously was not prepared for this trip, as the only paper I had was a very small note pad and a pencil.

Using my little note pad and this journal, I recorded all entries I could find on my Boatfield family and related cousins. The main data recorded were baptismal dates, dates of admission by letter, dates of dismissals and dates of deaths. The members were listed in order of first entry, not alphabetical. There it was, Maria Boatfield was baptized on 19 April 1908 and she died 1 March 1926, but her last name of Boatfield was crossed out and the name Weber was written in the margin. She had remarried (I did not know this), and none of the other records indicated a second marriage for Maria. I now had a new last name to help me continue my search.

I wrote for her death certificate under Maria Boatfield Weber. When her death certificate arrived I found out that her father was George Wellington and her mother's name was not known. She had been born on 12 June 1858 in Barnstable, Devon, UK. This information opened up a whole new search in England.

If you can't find a death record for your female ancestor that you know should be there, check for additional marriages. You might have to dig a little deeper, but the information is there. — Carolyn H. Brown, OR, sidcarol@escapees.com

Don't Reinvent The Wheel

After beginning my genealogical research about six or seven years ago, I did the usual things beginning researchers usually do, like contacting relatives for information, checking the house for old photographs, family Bibles, etc. I contacted relatives that I knew, asking if they had old family Bibles, especially any which belonged to the Poston family as I had decided to research my father's Poston family. One cousin thought that a Poston Bible existed, but wasn't sure who had it.

I had several old family Bibles, including one that had a 3" x 5" old yellowed paper, handwritten on both sides, listing what appeared to be the Minert family. This information had been transferred to an old typewritten page listing the Minert family. Since I didn't know where they fit onto the family tree, I put the information on hold and pursued the elusive Poston family. I did know that my grandmother's maiden name was Starr and she married grandfather Poston. Now I had two names to pursue.

I spent a good deal of time at the Yuma FHC (before FamilySearch.org came online) researching the FHL catalog on cd-rom. I found the name Starr listed in many books and films in the catalog. Since each listing shows prominent surnames in the book or film, I skipped through the surnames listed with Starr. On one film it listed the surname Meinert. Since it was a similar name to my almost-forgotten name Minert, I ordered the film. My idea was to compare my old typed list of Minerts to the filmed book.

I was so excited when the film arrived that I forgot my Minert list. However, I soon found I didn't need my list because my branch of the Starrs and Postons were listed. My sister and I were even listed. The filmed book listed the name and address of the authors and even though the book was published in 1989, I decided to write to the authors at the address given in the book. I was really lucky because the authors still lived at that address. After much correspondence and some phone calls, the authors, Roy and Jean Minert, along with their son, Roger P. Minert, Ph.D., A.G., decided to republish and update their book. Dr. Roger Minert researched in Germany for the roots of the Minerts and others updated their lines of the family.

The book, *Gerhard Henrich Meinert: His Ancestors And His Descendants* was published in 2000. Dr. Minert wrote about his research in Germany giving a vivid picture of the Minert ancestors and pictures of the old home. His research in church records of vital events shows the family back to the 1600s and some of the family are mentioned in documents as old as 1300.

3" x 5" sheets of paper, like the one shown above, were found in an old family Bible listing the various Minerts.

The book also tells of memories told by descendants and along with Dr. Minert's wonderful, thorough research, brings the Minert family to life. The book far exceeded my fondest hope.

How do the Starrs and Postons fit into the Minert family? My great-grandmother, Maria Minert, married my great-grandfather, Adam Starr. Their daughter (my grandmother), Ada Louise, married my grandfather, Adam Poston.

The brickwall solved (who were the Minerts) and the lesson learned: Check and see if someone has researched and published a "limb" from your family tree. I found new relatives and played a very small part in helping with the updated Minert book. I will forever be grateful to the Minert family. — Patricia Ann Poston Weaver, AZ

The Sister And The Journal

Aaron Nelson, a great-grandfather of mine, born in 1823 in England, was one of 12 children and the only one of them to immigrate to America. I made it my goal to locate his siblings in England, in as many censuses as I could, starting with 1841 and running to 1881. Aaron had an older sister named Elizabeth. Family records mistakenly had her married to a man who turned out to be her niece Elizabeth's husband. I could understand the confusion on the name:

there were so many Elizabeth Nelsons in the family and in the area. But the dates hadn't made sense. However, with some diligence in investigating marriage records, I did eventually find the right Elizabeth, married to a William Taylor in 1834. In 1841, William and Elizabeth were still in the family hometown of Lambley, but were not there in 1851 or 1861.

I needed to find the right William Taylor in those censuses, married to an Elizabeth, so I could find more of their children. Even a good index would have been no help as there were many William and Elizabeth Taylors. How to find them?

Aaron Nelson.

Fortunately, my ancestor Aaron kept a journal of his travels during his last few years in England (1858-61). He wrote about going to see his parents, and occasionally mentioned the given name of a sister or brother. I had a few pages of this journal which mentioned a visit to his "sister Charlotte at Lenton." Heartened by this, I located the rest of the journal in a university library, obtained a copy and carefully read the entries. I soon found one that talked about a visit to his "sister Mary at Carrington." The entries led me to find the families in the census, as well as giving me interesting details of Aaron's lifestyle, occupation and journeys.

This is what his journal said to lead me to Elizabeth and William Taylor's family in the census:

1860, Oct. 1: "Monday" morning. Went to Carlton with my son William to see my sister. Afternoon returned to Nottingham. At night attended a Social Party...

Though he did not say "my sister Elizabeth," I knew it must be her, because I had already located the others. Once I had the name of the town where William and Elizabeth lived, I then easily found them in the 1861 census, and also in the 1851 census. — Marcia Green, CA, mwverde.mwg@verizon.net

The Old Christmas Card

My father left Stockholm, Sweden to come to the US in 1927 at the age of 17. He kept his plan to leave Sweden a secret from all family members and friends, forging his mother's name on all needed documents.

On my father's last day in Stockholm, he invited his step-brother to spend the day with him and told him of his plans. They visited their grandparents, ate dinner and together they rode the train to the port of Goteburg, where my father departed on the ship *Stockholm (1)* for the US. He asked his step-brother not to tell anyone until the ship was on its way.

Father made his home in the greater Seattle area, became a US citizen and changed his name. He married and had two daughters, of which I am the oldest. Father returned to Sweden only once, which was in 1946.

He visited his many relatives. When he returned to the US he never talked about his Swedish relatives; maybe we didn't ask.

Many years later, an old Christmas card came into my possession, which was sent to my father from his step-brother in 1973 (my father died in January 1974). A few years later, I became interested in genealogy. The only names I had other than the step-brother were my father's parents' names on his birth certificate. I sent a few letters to Sweden for information but never received any response. I sent two letters to the step-brother but they were returned to me as "unable to deliver".

In my frustration, I started sending letters to all the people I could find with the step-brother's last name in Stockholm. Then I started sending letters outside of Stockholm. Still no response.

In July of 2003, my husband's Danish cousin visited. I asked her if she could read the handwritten message in the Christmas card. She was able to give me the name of the step-brother's son. I immediately found his name and address in the Swedish phone book and mailed him a letter. In two weeks' time, I heard from him and his father and mother.

These wonderful people have given me so much information and sent pictures. Father's step-brother is blind but he records messages to me about my father's childhood and his sister-in-law writes them out for me in English. His wife writes often and keeps me posted on the events in their family.

She also introduced me to a family friend that has been doing genealogy for many years. He has provided me with names and information about my father's family; on about 200 people dating back to 1712. He has also found some living cousins, with whom I am in communication with at this time.

This brickwall turned into a gold-mine for me. All of this information because of one old Christmas card. A treasure for sure.

My husband and I plan to visit Sweden in 2005 to meet all these people. I just want to hug them all for the kind and generous help they have given me. — Pat L., WA, GGBeach372@aol.com

The Name Game

While researching my husband's family, I discovered a son of the family named Charles. In the next census, Charles, who should have been 10 at the time, was only six. I first put it down as a human error made by the census taker but later discovered that the first Charles had, in fact, died and they had another child which they also named Charles.

In fact, this was a very common practice; our ancestors, depending on their background, had a naming pattern for their kids (for example, naming the first-born son after the father's father and the second son after the mother's father). — Mary Rosevear, NB

World Family Trees

Order the World Family Trees for one month on Genealogy.com. This is not an advertisement for them. I bought it for a month and I found six different lines that I had been looking for.

Search for an unusual name that is in the line you are looking for and when it comes up, you will not believe the information you get; it will keep you busy for months! I had a step-great-grandmother by the name of Hollenbeck and I had to prove I had the correct surname for her because someone questioned me, saying that it was wrong. There it was in the Austin family tree and it only cost me $9.95 (at the time).

It was so simple that I would never have thought of it. — Mary Jo Sibel

Pieces Of A Puzzle

My great-grandfather Walter James was born in Cornwall, England. He didn't know his birth date or his mother's name. His mother died when he was two, I found out later, from consumption. She was only 32.

He did know his father's name, also Walter James and his grandfather's name, Nicholas James. He had two siblings — one older and one younger that had also died young that he didn't know about. When I started trying to find out about his ancestors, I didn't have a lot to go on.

I found Walter James (age nine months), with his father, Walter James (a miner, age 26) and his mother, Elizabeth James (age 28) on the 1861 British census in Gwinear parish, Hayle, Cornwall. Knowing the location, I was able to locate an 1860 birth registration from the Reduth registration district for a Walter James. I ordered a birth certificate. Walter James was born on 10 June 1860 and his mother's maiden name was listed. His mother's maiden name was Elizabeth Carter. I was able to find the marriage certificate for Walter's parents. This listed their marriage date and the names of the bridal couple's fathers. I also found the christening and burial records of Walter's two siblings. I found his mother's burial record and ordered a death certificate for her.

Walter James.

I made several wrong turns along the way. Walter's father married again to another Elizabeth. I researched this Elizabeth and her family thinking it was Walter's mother. I did this before I found out his mother's death date.

There was a Nicholas James living in Gwinear near Walter's father in the 1861 census. He was also a miner and the right age. I traced this Nicholas, thinking it was my ancestor. After a lot of searching, I found a Nicholas James, a farmer in the 1861 census, living in Cold Harbor, Cornwall. This was my ancestor, I later found out. I found Walter living with his parents, Nichalls and Susanna James in the 1851 census. It was hard to find them as they had moved. I also found the family in the 1841 census — this time it was Nicholas listed.

I didn't give up though I hit several brickwalls and went down several wrong trees. The one thing that kept me searching for the right Nicholas was that if the miner was the right Nicholas, Walter was born before they were married. Now that FamilySearch.org is available, I have added seven more generations. I haven't had time to research this myself but will get to it.

I have found out quite a lot about my great-grandfather's ancestors. I wish he could have known more about his family before he died on 23 May 1949 in Le Grand, Merced County, CA. I always thought it was very sad not to know when you were born. — Sharon White, UT, slmwhite@aol.com

Go To The Source

Sometimes it pays to go directly to the source when you hit a brickwall, even if you think you have correct documentation. This happened when my sister, who has been searching the English side of our family for many years, obtained a copy of a birth registration for my great-grandmother.

According to the microfilm of births in Bromyard, Herefordshire, for the 1860s, Lilian Jessie Weltch was listed. But her name appeared in pencil between the lines and above the name of Pauline Emily Weltch, born on 23 February 1861. Since there was no registration number for Lilian, the aid at the FHC suggested she send to the FHL for the certificate with Pauline's number, thinking that there might be twins or a mistake had been made in the records.

When the certificate arrived, it was for Pauline Emily. Where was Lilian Jessie? Were they twins? Had Pauline died? One possibility was a name change after registration; however the column that would indicate this had a line drawn through it, indicating that this had not taken place. British records are usually very thorough; however there seemed to be no sign of Lillian's birth.

When I became interested in the research, my sister gave me copies of her records and told me the mystery. I checked the various censuses, and there was Pauline Emily in the 1861 census, aged one month. Lilian Jessie appeared in the 1871 census aged 10 years. A name change seemed the most likely, but when did it happen?

It wasn't until a cousin, who worked for the British government, came to visit us here in Canada and we told him of our mystery that there seemed to be any hope. He offered to get any certificates we needed from the Public Records Office in London. A couple of months later, the certificates arrived and the mystery was solved. On the new certificate was the answer. The column "Name changed after registration" was clearly filled in — Lilian Jessie. It seems that her father, an Anglican minister, had not only changed little Pauline's name at baptism, but a few years later did the same for his youngest son, registered as Edward Herbert and baptized as Herbert Lea.

The Church of Latter-day Saints do a great job preserving and transcribing records, but it does pay to check the records from the source, especially if those records come from overseas or Canada. I have found many errors in transcriptions done by Americans who do not understand the hand writing or language of an area or even the geography. It might cost more, but you just might find great-grandmother as we did. — Maureen Beecroft, ON, tmbee_2@hotmail.com

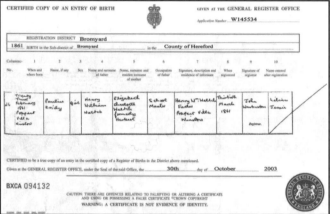

The birth registration for Pauline Emily Weltch, who had had her name changed after registration by her father to Lilian Jessie (see column 10 on the right).

Think Outside The Box

Once I decided to pursue it, my wife's surname, McHatton, seemed an easy research project. For several reasons. Unlike my Murphy line with its mix of many surname backgrounds which I'd traced to England, France and Germany (among other places), my wife, from the start of our marriage, had always claimed to be more Irish than me. I really wanted to disprove her claim, if I could.

A first-cousin of my wife had already supplied several years of her family research for this McHatton surname. This frustrated me slightly for I'd been earnestly researching my Murphy line for several years without a great deal of success. This cousin, who sadly died just recently, had even worked in our Washington State Vital Records Office. Thus, I knew she had acquired most of the available McHatton local family details from their records and it would be quite reliable.

This material, loaned to my wife for copying, included a local history and cemetery excerpts from the Mt. Sterling area of Brown County, IL. It was published in 1975 by the Schuyler-Brown County Genealogical Society. These counties, including Morgan County, IL, were areas where the McHattons had lived for several generations. I discovered some of this data had been developed by an ancestor of the McHatton family, supplying many details of my wife's original McHatton line from Northern Ireland, County Antrim, in 1859. It mentioned a neighboring family from nearby Belfast; the Robert Kerrs, who had even traveled to America with the first McHattons. This Illinois local history excerpt also declared that one member of the original McHatton family in Ireland had become an architect and remained in that country.

One day, I decided to perform some modest research on my wife's family. So I placed several queries on the Internet relating to the County Antrim, Ireland McHattons. I'd reached this point after failing to locate any McHattons in County Antrim materials that seemed to match my wife's family. My research had included trips to the FHL and other major genealogy libraries around the country, all without locating any helpful details about my wife's Irish McHatton line. After some months passed without any helpful responses I turned to other, more productive, lines to research.

It was nearly a year later, long after I'd forgotten about my McHatton queries I'd placed on the Internet, when an unusual e-mail arrived from a stranger in Belfast, Ireland. This person stated she'd received an inquiry from Australia tracing a McIlhatton line. The Belfast person was researching her husband's family, also a McIlhatton, from north of Belfast. It seems he traced back to a McIlhatton from north of Belfast who had been a master carpenter. They both had come across one of my queries about my wife's McHatton folks and wished to further explore details. My first impression was there's no connection, of course. However, I was willing to examine matters a bit further.

As e-mail exchanges followed, including information from the Public Records Office of Northern Ireland visited by this wonderful Belfast lady, I slowly realized the data coming from the Belfast woman about her husband's McIlhatton family eerily matched much of the data I'd seen about my wife's Ireland McHatton original family.

At this point I shared this news with my wife who was also skeptical at first, to say the least. Shortly after these early exchanges, as more and more information about the origination and location in County Antrim of the McIlhatton family was received, I came to the realization that indeed these were the one and same family.

I was then even able to persuade my wife, once she saw the matching details, that these were connected families. No mention of any hints of that surname alteration had been passed down through the generations in my wife's line. Nevertheless, it became abundantly clear that my wife's McHatton line had, upon migrating to America, made this slight change in their surname. I've also learned that other branches of this McIlhatton family from Ireland have migrated to Iowa in America without changing their surname. I'm still uncertain there's a connection to the Australian McIlhatton line, but the good news is there is certainly a connection to the McIlhatton family descendants from Belfast.

Had we been unwilling to think outside the box, we may have missed the chance to learn about the origination of this McIlhatton/McHatton family from the parish of Loughguile in County Antrim.

About two years ago, my wife and I took one related family history preservation step to video tape a discussion, by this same first-cousin. We taped several hours of her family recollections growing up, as we all had, in a small town, Elma, in eastern Grays Harbor County, WA. We are so thankful we undertook the effort to do that for, now, two years later; this very cousin is the one who has just died recently. — Charles Francis Murphy, WA, NAVLAWCFM@aol.com

The Odessa File

In 1972, Frederick Forsyth published his book *The Odessa File*; a fictional thriller about a freelance journalist trying to track down Nazi atrocities. In the course of his inquiries, the fictional reporter does research at a large

number of German military archives; describing the location and records available at each archive.

I was almost finished reading the book when it struck me like a dropped brickwall. Even though the story was

fiction, the locations and background were real. All of those archives and military records were actual places that contained real records. I re-read the book, not as a suspense story, but as a "how-to" book for obtaining German military records. I was able to contact those record centers and I received German military records with the same ease I am accustomed from the NARA and the National Personnel Records Center in St. Louis.

The Odessa File is important because that is where I got the details on 18 family members who were in German military units. If you had relatives in the German military, head for your nearest second-hand book shop and buy a couple of paperback copies of the book. Circle, arrow, highlight and mark the pages with yellow stickies, and get those records. — Ron Halbritter, CA

Led Up The Garden Path By The Census

Searching for my great-grandfather Thomas Murray, I came across an entry in the 1881 British census: Joseph Eggleston, Head, 56, Weardale, Durham, Coal Miner; Margaret Eggleston, Wife, 55, Weardale, Durham; Mary Eggleston, Daur., 17, Weardale, Durham; Ellen Eggleston, Daur, 13, Weardale, Durham, Scholar; Thos. Murray Lodger, Widowed, 23, Crook, Durham, Colliery Engineman and Margaret Ann Murray, Daur, 7, Crook, Durham.

From this information it appeared that Thomas had been married and that a seven-year-old Margaret Ann was the issue from this union.

I searched for a marriage in about 1873-74 (using Margaret's age as a guideline). I was somewhat puzzled though because Thomas would have only been 15 or 16 at the time; it wasn't unheard of to get married at such a young age but I just knew this wasn't the case with my Thomas.

I had not realized that this one 1881 census entry would take me up the garden path in one way but help me tremendously in another. As expected, I was unsuccessful in this search for the years in question but I did find a marriage for a Thomas Murray in the right area for 1880 just one year before the census. As can be seen in the 1881 census entry, Thomas was residing with a family of Egglestons. Could it be possible that he was residing with his in-laws I asked myself?

Using the General Register Office marriage reference I had for Thomas, I searched for a female Eggleston with the same registration details. It didn't take me long to find a Martha Ann Eggleston and thanks to the Durham County Council website I was able to purchase this certificate straight from the search results on the site.

From the details on the marriage certificate it was confirmed that they were indeed the couple I had been searching for and their marriage took place on 3 May 1880 in the Register Office in Auckland, Durham.

I then searched for Margaret Ann Murray's birth, again finding nothing in the years 1873 or 1874. However, I did find a registration for a Margaret Ann Murray in 1880. Could Margaret have been one-year old, not seven-years old in the 1881 census?

Querying the age of Margaret, I asked subscribers on a Durham-area message board if someone could check the original 1881 census film to find out if the cd-rom version of this census had been mis-transcribed. Within a day I had my answer. Yes,

	CERTIFIED COPY of an Pursuant to the		ENTRY OF MARRIAGE Marriage Act 1949					TH 3
	Registration District	Auckland						
'880. Marriage solemnized at the Register Office in the County of Durham in the District of Auckland								
When married	Name and surname	Age	Condition	Rank or profession	Residence at the time of marriage	Father's name and surname	Rank or profession of father	
Third May 1880	Thomas MURRAY	22 years	Bachelor	Joiner	Catholic Bank Crook	Joseph Murray	Farmer	
	Martha Ann EGGLESTON	21 years	Spinster	—	Mill Street Crook	Joseph Eggleston	Coal Miner	
Married in the Register Office						by Certificate Before me me:		
This marriage solemnized between us,	Thomas Murray Martha Ann Eggleston	in the presence of us,	Joseph Longstaff Margaret Cain		John Cary Herdy Registrar Thomas Dean Superintendent Registrar			

The marriage certificate for Thomas and Martha Ann.

Margaret was listed as being one-year old not seven-years old!

Next on the agenda was searching for a death registration for Martha Ann between May 1880 and April 1881. I found it within minutes using the Internet. Not having purchased this certificate yet I can only assume that she died during or after giving birth to her daughter Margaret Ann.

It was obvious Martha Ann was pregnant when she and Thomas married and it would appear that Thomas was trying to following in the footsteps of his older brothers by becoming a joiner (occupation given for Thomas on the marriage certificate). By 1881, though, he was a colliery engineman and in later censuses was working as a coke drawer. From this snippet of information, I would assume that Thomas was training to be a joiner and had to give this up once he found out that his beloved was pregnant. What a heart-wrenching story though, when just a few months later he became a father and a widower.

So even though I was led up the garden path by the 1881 census I did learn quite a lot about this couple just by digging deeper and persevering in finding them. — Jayne McHugh, jam001@cogeco.ca

Fond Of Fond Du Lac

I had been looking for the death dates of my husband Joe's great-grandparents Johann "John" and Amelia (née Bittner) Schumacher. I found them in the 1930 federal census in Fond du Lac, Fond du Lac County, WI, so I knew they died after that. If I could get their death dates I could send for their death certificates. These certificates should have their full birth date, possibly the location of birth, and possibly their parents' names.

I decided to write letters to Fond du Lac to see if they were buried there. Only two of the five places I sent self-addressed stamped envelopes and queries to responded, but one of them was the cemetery where they were buried. Not only did I get John's and Amelia's information, I also got information on his mother, Anna Maria (née Lesselyoung) (Schumacher) Grosswieser, who is also buried in that plot. — Jane Schumacher, WI, jjschu@itis.com

Going Global

Over the years I have been collecting genealogy information for my kids to have in the future. When I go to a cemetery I like to take a photograph of the gravestone to include in my database as another source. Many of the stones have fallen over, been destroyed or gone missing. This is going to be quite a brickwall for our grandchildren when they eventually try to locate where their ancestors are buried.

A few weeks ago, I was trying to find where my step-grandfather was buried because he has no stone. I contacted the man with the journal for the cemetery and he told me where my step-grandfather was buried.

What will happen if this journal is destroyed or this man dies? Who will be able to tell my grandchildren where he is buried?

My solution to this problem is very easy: buy a global positioning satellite (GPS) system. You can go to the cemeteries, find the gravestones and the unmarked sites, write down the coordinates with the GPS system and place the information in your database for future use. By using a GPS system, you can go back to the location anytime, even if the gravestone is missing. Depending on the GPS system, some have digital street maps which are very useful if you are looking for a certain street, as you simply type in the information and it will pinpoint the exact location for you, even giving detailed instructions on how to get there! — Mary Rosevear, NB

Sharing Leads To Solving — Genealogy Style

When I started the family tree, I got help from experienced researchers through the Internet. Eventually I began doing original research, using microfilm and traveling to courthouses and cemeteries. I post my finds on the Internet, as thanks to those who helped me, and to help those coming along behind. I also spend time tracing (and posting) collateral lines, hoping this will help relatives find me. I enjoy hearing from remote cousins and have received unexpected gifts as a result.

One was a scan from a Pitman family Bible sent by

This photo was sent to Jane Peppler by a stranger in Paulding, OH who stumbled upon her Burt family website. Jane's second-great-grandfather is at the far left.

a park ranger in Pulaski County, VA, which was lodged at her Wilderness Road Regional Museum. What an unexpected location! After generations of Pitman researchers had been unable to find mention of a young Uriah Pitman, born in 1735 (first seen marrying Ann Matson in Burlington, NJ, in 1762), this Bible includes: *"Uriah Pitman ye son of Thomas and Ann Pitman was born ye 30 day of July in ye year of our Lord 1735."* What a great lead; and a new trip in the making.

Another surprise was a call from a man who told me his sister had found their Burt family on my website — a branch rather removed from my own.

He said "I am not a genealogist but I ended up with this Bible anyway." He is sending information from the family Bible of Mark M. Burt (born in 1822 in Pennsylvania, married Elizabeth Emmick in 1849 in Marion County, OH) with entries back to when his branch and mine were one and the same.

Yet another surprise was an e-mail stating: "My grandmother was Nellie Viola Grimm, daughter of John Wesley Grimm... John Wesley Grimm's father was William Grim (born 1831, Baltimore County, MD). I have a family Bible from 1858, in which are written the names and birth dates for a number of the other Grimms that you sent me. Also, I have a picture album... Oh, I almost forgot, I have the certificate of birth and baptism for Isadore Wilson. You will probably want a copy of it also." I certainly did!

He also wrote: "From your e-mail address it appears you are just down the road from me," and so he was. We met and I made color Xeroxes of his many pictures, the family Bible and the baptismal certificate, which made possible the proof of a Daughters of the American Revolution line to Adam Fultz (Foltz), born in 1740.

Sometimes, sidetracked, I search and publish peripheral information. In the course of my search for the parents of Michael Wilson, born on 25 March 1812 (the father of Isadora Wilson), I put together a website for the Bachman Valley area of Carroll and Frederick County, MD and southern York County, PA, including tax maps, tax lists, census lists and all the information I could gather on neighboring families. Others submit information, and the site has augmented resources for researchers of that area.

While I have never found another researcher of my lost Wilsons, other tidbits have come my way. For instance, a man who purchased land adjoining the lands of my ancestor Conrad Heilman on Bachman Valley Road found my website while researching his historical right-of-way. He sent photos of stones engraved with Conrad's initials, still marking boundaries in the woods almost two-and-a-half centuries later!

It's obvious that when you've come to a standstill, helping others can offer chances to break through your own brickwalls. In many cases, it has been the efforts I have made outside of my own direct line which have resulted in the breakthroughs I cherish. — Jane Peppler, NC, jpeppler@duke.edu

Mack Came Back

My paternal grandmother was Annetta (McCaffrey) Meharg. I never knew her as she died seven years before I was born, but I knew all her sisters: my great-aunts Eliza Morris, Alma Bartlett, Gertrude Davis and their half-sister May Vannatter. These four were all sweet old ladies, very prim and proper, each with small families of their own. My dad was an only child and made sure we paid regular visits all through the 1950s and '60s.

At some point in time, growing up back then I understood there was an older brother to these girls, and he was known as "Mack" but he had disappeared somewhere out west at a young age. I never knew his real name until much later. These were the children of Ida Ann and Dennis McCaffrey; Ida was a daughter of Squire William Kelly of Glen Meyer, Norfolk County, ON. Squire Kelly

had been an influential landowner and local politician of the area in his day and left many descendants when he died in 1935 at age 93.

In discussion with my mother before her death in 2002, she mentioned that Mack McCaffrey had lived in Estevan, SK and had returned to Ontario for a visit during the 1950s. (The Estevan location was a bit of a red herring.) In several photo albums she left behind were many pictures of

William "Mack" McCaffrey in 1954 on a trip back to Ontario.

family members. Luckily, most were labeled and I could deal with them on that basis. However, the photo of one was labeled simply "William" and this became my mystery man. At my mother's funeral was Donna, a daughter-in-law of great-Aunt Alma. I phoned her a few months later to ask questions about the Bartletts and Gertrude as she had helped care for Aunt Gertie's needs a bit in her final few years. As fate would have it, I missed out; Donna had passed on all the McCaffrey pictures and papers a year before to the Kellys who had organized a family reunion.

One day while I was poking around on the Internet I got into the National Archives of Canada, particularly the War Enlistments. I entered surnames willy-nilly, including McCaffrey, and up popped a William McCaffrey, aged 34, having registered at Saskatoon, SK in January of 1918, next of kin was listed as Netty Maharg of Glenmire, ON.

Surely this was my Mack McCaffrey? The birth date sounded about right and the general location matched what I'd heard many years before, and Netty Maharg could be Annetta Meharg. Still, I needed to be surer. The next step was to try to find out more about this Kelly reunion, which I had missed the first time around. I had hardly wished it, when I received an e-mail from the organizers explaining there were copies of the Kelly family tree for anyone wanting one. Unbeknownst to me, they had my address courtesy of my mother a year before. I am right into family trees; I collect them, especially if my name appears in them. When I received my Kelly copy, there was William McCaffrey, oldest child and only son of Dennis and Ida Ann (Kelly) McCaffrey, born on 5 January 1884 exactly as reported on his war registration. I was on a roll now. I could match Mack's face to William's name.

A second Kelly reunion came and went in 2002, unattended by me — just too many commitments all at the same time. The Kellys decided I should have the box of McCaffrey papers, etc.; somehow I had to get it.

The 2004 reunion rolled around — double reunions on the same day but at least in the same town. I tore myself away and made myself known to as many Kellys as I could. I sought out the keeper of the important McCaff-rey papers. "Back at the house some-where, not sure where. I'll send them by way of Georgia."

On 15 August 2004, Georgia deliv-ered. In among the pictures, photos, funeral cards and obituaries were two crucial pieces of documentation con-cerning William "Mack" McCaffrey — a nice photo labeled "Uncle Mac" and a newspaper obituary from the *Herald*, dated 25 September 1957 for William McCaffery (note the alternate spelling). The photo showed Mack dressed in the exact same suit as the mystery man William wore in his photo. The obituary made a clear con-nection between nickname and given name, it explained about the Ontario visit of 1954, described how and when Mack had gone west, referred to his three living sisters in Tillsonburg, ON, and gave his home as Evesham, SK.

This was a man who left his birth place at age 25 to live far away among strangers, and returned to his roots once at age 70, spending a few weeks with his aging sisters; he had no fam-ily of his own, apparently lived alone — and died alone. His body was dis-covered and buried by neighbors with apparently no family in atten-dance. Today I know what he looked like, how tall he was; I have all his vital statistics, even his obituary as well as a transcription of his military registration.

Thanks to the National Archives on the Internet, relatives like Donna who save pieces of paper, families like the Kellys who keep good records and have reunions, plus some luck and coincidence of timing, and my own persistence, William "Mack" McCaff-rey has come back home. He may have lived an undistinguished life but he had an existence which deserves to be told. He may have been gone for half a century and it took many more years to bring him full circle back into the fold.

Today he lives in my photo album with his sisters. — Carol Morrow, ON

A Photo Finish

It is sad to see a grand old photograph without the names, dates or places.

Fortunately, 30 years ago, my father, David Amell Jr., who was in his 80s, took time with me to identify his collection with pictures back to the 1890s. There was a photo of his parents David Amell and Elizabeth Hughes; also the wedding pictures of his brothers, sisters and spouses. Those dates had been written in the family Bible. The collection included photos of cousins and spouses and relatives on his maternal branch.

However, a distinctive

The memorial portrait of Gilbert Amell and Lucy Beauchamp.

picture of two guys with hats and two gals would remain anonymous and a nagging mystery.

Soon, by some uncanny fate, a second-cousin invited me for a visit as he had just found something of interest. He had an old piece of cardboard with the skillful sketch of a couple etched in charcoal pencil.

Surprise, they were two of the same people in the curious first photo.

Second surprise, on the back of the cardboard was scribbled the important facts: "Gilbert Amell, McDonald Crs, 1902". His wife had died a few years prior. Thus the sketch had been copied from an earlier photo. The large sketch had been drawn as a memorial portrait. Such pictures in grand frames hung on a wall of many homes. A snapshot was taken of the sketch for comparison to confirm the identity of the same couple in the anonymous photo. Who were the other two people? When and where was the occasion?

Several years later the marriage record was discovered for Gilbert Amell and Lucy Beauchamp who were married on 7 October 1879 at St. Mary's Cathedral in Kingston, ON. The witnesses were her cousin Angeline Bertrand and his cousin William Turcotte. They had trekked over 60 miles from the rugged northern hinterland to the historic city. The cathedral was and still an impressive edifice.

Yours truly married there eight decades later unaware of the previous nuptials. Anyhow, no more lingering doubts about the pomp and circumstance for the memorable photograph long ago. — Bill Amell, ON, wdfa@nexicom.net

Other Family Members May Be Searching Too

The bonds between siblings can be hidden behind brickwalls, taking years to reconnect. The clues are often missing or misleading, sometimes intentionally or through ignorance.

I had finally broken through a brickwall after 36 long years of asking about and seeking two persons with whom I had lost contact.

On Memorial Day 2002, I met not only Joe and Lucille for whom I had been searching, but also found Barbara, Shirley and Connie.

My parents Bill Hajek and Mary Cross were married in Thermopolis, WY in January 1945. Bill had four children by a previous marriage (Barbara, Lucille, Shirley and Joe). Lucille, age six, lived with Bill and Mary at the time of their marriage. I was born in October 1945. Bill's son Joe at age five then came to live with us in 1947. Then Lucille went back to her mother in 1948. So that left Joe and me with Bill and Mary. One day, Joe suddenly disappeared while I was at school. I was told he went to live with his own family. I had never under-stood that Joe was my half-broth-er, only that he had another family. I had only his photograph, his school record and many lingering doubts. After Joe left us and returned to his mother, I was raised as an only child, having been led to believe that Joe was just a family friend. The years passed, my father died and my mother remarried. I then married and had children of my own. I enjoyed a huge in-law family, yet wondered who were my own family. I asked about Joe many times, but was never given any satisfactory answers.

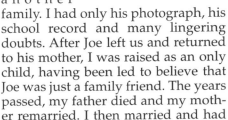

(L-R) Barbara, Lucille, Shirley and Joe as children. (Above) Connie, Lucille, Shirley and Carol reunited in 2002.

One day while going through a box of items that had been stored away, I found a *Ripley's Believe It or Not* newspaper clipping about my father. It told of him breaking a world record for 336 hours of continuous piano playing in New York City. Along with the news clipping, there was a copy of a radio interview script which ended his piano endurance record. In this interview a telegram was mentioned... that he had just become the father of a seven-pound girl born in Seattle, WA. The search for that baby (Lucille), born in 1939 six years before I was born, then began — along with a renewed search for information about Joe. I contacted a friend, who had found Joe through his military records and we found the birth record of the baby girl. The baby girl was not a first born so there were others! School records led to baptismal records for Joe, which gave Joe's birth date and place of birth. Joe's military records came back as "classified". I then gave up considering classified to mean top secret. Not so. Joe served as William Joseph Sheldon. Joe's birth-mother had remarried and her children assumed the Sheldon name, with one more child (Connie) to be born in 1948 shortly after Lucille returned to her birth-mother. Joe's step-father had signed for the underage Joe to enter the US Navy at age 17. So no official adoptions were on record, the trail become cold.

I was successful in locating two uncles, but one died before we could meet. The other had pictures and confirmed that Joe served in the Navy.

With the arrival of home computers, the Internet and genealogy websites, my half-sister Lucille was finally located. Lucille had posted a query on Genealogy.com asking for information about William Hajek because of health concerns. My daughter saw that posting, called me and the brickwall was finally penetrated.

Just before Memorial weekend in 2002, I called Lucille and at the end of a long telephone conversation, a reunion was set for that very weekend. That night of conversations and the subsequent reunion brought us to a decision to put a positive spin on the lost years. The lack of information and cover-up was our parents' doing. We, as children, had suffered enough through the many years of doubts, searching, wondering as we had all been deprived of a connection to family members.

Many lessons have been learned through the search for connection, most imports to never give up, to keep searching knowing that other family members may be searching too, and one day that brickwall will be broken down.

Joe said to me "I feel blessed that love and hope, with the help of God, has brought us together. We have truly been part of a miracle." — Carol Hajek Borgstadt

A Child Named Solomon

Dismantling one of my many brickwalls was tedious, but the reward was worth all the work.

The objective was to find the parentage of Matthew Bennett, who was my third-great-grandfather. All I knew about Matthew was that he married Ruth Hodgson on 13 August 1801 in Guilford County, NC. Except for two of his children, they were all named after members of his wife's family. Ruth was a Quaker and the records after the marriage were very good. Matthew died in about 1814 in Guilford. He had a son named Solomon; this was the only clue I had.

I searched all records in North Carolina that mentioned Solomon Bennett. A Solomon Bennett found in Montgomery County was a good possibility. However, land records were among the few records that were left after a courthouse fire. They did not show Solomon or Matthew Bennett owning property.

The next possibility came from *Abstracts of North Carolina Wills* by J. Bryan Grimes, which showed several Bennetts including a Solomon in Currituck County, NC. I kept this in mind for further research. In the meantime, while I worked on other ancestors in North Carolina and Virginia Counties, I kept an eye out for Solomon and Matthew. I did not have any luck in counties surrounding Guilford. However, while at the FHL on a research trip, I decided to check abstracts of Currituck County records in the book area.

Sure enough, there was a Matthew Bennett with a brother named Solomon. Matthew was the right age for my Matthew. The age was estimated using census records. His father was Moses Bennett and his mother Mary, which is the name of my Matthew's only daughter who was not named after anyone in his wife's family. The Bennett family was not Quaker. Matthew probably became a Quaker when he married Ruth. The monthly meeting records for the Quakers of that district were destroyed in another fire.

There were errors in the abstracts of wills from several sources, which made it necessary to get copies of the original wills. It is always a good idea to get the originals because of extraction errors. Using the wills and many deeds in Currituck County it was possible to find the ancestors of Matthew back five generations. There is one will that mentions a grandfather of one of the wives and a cousin with the cities of residence in England given, which will be useful for future research. Later deeds mention the original 1668 land grant of Benjamin Bennett, which binds the family together.

The land deeds and grants give the first names of the wives. The search to discover the maiden names has been unsuccessful, however. Searching deed, probate, and court records of the Bennett neighbors gave some possibilities, but no real proof. — Betty Herzfeld, WI, genealogist-milw@att.net

It's All About The Map

Biographies of various Martsolf family members in the histories of Beaver County, PA, gave conflicting and confusing information about the early years of my wife's immigrant ancestor, Diebold Martzolf.

One story said he settled first in Maryland then moved to Pennsylvania in 1838; another said that he first settled in Wrightsville, York County, PA, and then bought land in Manheim Township. Separate information we had claimed the youngest child of Diebold was born in Maryland. Another family researcher had found baptismal records for the two youngest children at two churches in Hanover, York County, PA. Hanover is only about five or six miles from the Maryland border. In addition, we located Diebold's older brother Henry in Abbottstown, Adams County, PA; several years after Diebold had moved to Beaver County.

However, we were unable to locate where Diebold Martzolf lived prior to settling in Beaver County, PA. We had searched deed records in York and Adams Counties, PA, and Frederick County, MD without any success. We also researched tax records for some of the communities around Hanover and Abbottstown, including Manheim Township, all to no avail. Although it was quite possible that Diebold had not owned any land, it was unlikely that he avoided taxation.

Diebold Martzolf's gravestone.

There was a story that, in around 1900, Diebold's son Philip visited the old homestead. At a recent Martsolf family reunion, we learned that during this visit a rough map was drawn showing the route from Hanover to the property where the Martzolf/ Martsolf family had lived. The map was in the possession of Philip's great-grandson and namesake, also named Philip.

The map is on a long strip of brown paper, and suggests that the property was east of Hanover. Unfortunately, not all of the landmarks were easy to identify. Also on the map are a few names of individuals who lived in the area in 1900, and one in particular seemed to be the current owner of the old Martzolf property at the time Philip made his visit.

A section of the hand-drawn map, showing where the Martzolf/Martsolf family had lived.

At the York County courthouse, we did a deed search for this individual and found a record for an 1855 transfer of property in Heidelberg Township. In the description of the property we found what we had been looking for. Among the list of previous owners was the following:

...and the said John Mumma Jr and Nancy his wife conveyed by their deed of August 16, 1832 to Dearwalt Martzolph and the said Martzolph and Eve Barbara his wife conveyed by their deed bearing date the 24 August 1836 to Christina Leichty and Doroth Leichty...

The list of previous owners also included the original land patent. For York County, PA, there are warrant maps done by Neal Otto Hively. With the deed information and the warrant map we were able to locate the exact location of the property owned by Diebold Martzolf.

The municipality was Heidelberg Township even when the Martzolf/Martsolf family lived there, but it was very close to Manheim, and they probably attended the nearby church in Manheim. — Regis Zagrocki, PA

Mary Keeps Getting Younger And Younger

Learning about my husband's great-grandmother was a challenge. I found her in the 1900 census and she was listed as Elizabeth M., age 34, meaning she was born in 1865/66. In a county history she was listed as Mary Elizabeth Stevens. On a daughter's death certificate she was called Maude Stevens and on her Social Security application she was called Maude Stevenson. On her sons' death certificate she was called Maude Stephenson and his Social Security application it was Mary Stevens.

Apparently she divorced her first husband and remarried in 1909 and was listed as Mary Sparr (first husband's name), age 26, same as her new husband! In reality, she was 43 at the time. In the 1920 census, she was listed as 36 and in 1930 she was 46. What is her true name and age? How do you find out?

Finally, I located another daughter, Martha Breed in San Antonio, TX. Living with her was Maude Pollard (Mary Elizabeth Maude Stevens/Stephenson's second husband's name) who was a widow. I then was able to obtain her Texas death certificate and verify things. She was born in July 1865 to Andy Stevens. She was listed as Maude on the death certificate. I have been able to go back and find her in the 1870 census and she was listed as Mary E. Stevens, age five.

In her obituary, her father's and brother's, she is called Maude. I have been able to conclude from all of this that she was born in July 1865 and when she married her second husband, who was 17 years younger, she just eliminated those 17 years from her age to make their ages the same.

She was probably born as Mary Elizabeth Stevens and sometime about 1910 she decided that she might like Maude better so started using that name. — Carolyn Peterson, CA, corksterr@sbcglobal.net

Great-Grandpa's Secret

As a child, I had always heard about my granny's mother dying young and leaving three children. My granny Clara Elizabeth Salter was raised by her mother's sister Mattie Ham.

I had never heard anyone in the family speak about granny's father.

As an adult, I began a family genealogy. When I asked questions about great-grandpa Salter, I was told all the family knew about him was the fact that he came from West Virginia, and had claimed he rode up the hill with Teddy Roosevelt. He would never talk about his life in West Virginia or his family.

My aunt and mother shared with me that Harry Montgomery Salter, their grandfather, was buried in Riverdale Cemetery's military section, in our hometown of Columbus, GA. Knowing he had served in the Spanish American War, my first step was to send for his military records.

When they arrived, I realized why Harry Salter had not wanted to talk about life in his old home. The records revealed that he was married when he left for the war. I have found nothing to indicate his wife had died or that

they had divorced, so great-grandpa Salter was already married to Minnie Allison when he married my great-grandmother! Harry and Maggie married on 30 May 1900 in Phoenix City, AL, just across the river from Columbus, GA.

He had mustered on 7 May 1898 in Charleston, WV and had traveled from Moundsville, WV, which was 254 miles away, in order to join the army. He was 29 years of age at the time of enlistment.

I was so excited, because I had found his hometown. I immediately searched the Internet for Moundsville, WV. I found an online census which had only one Salter family in the county. There he was! Listed in the 1880 census as Harry M., age 12. He was with his parents, Eli and Martha Salter. Since I now knew his parents' names, and the name of his hometown, my next step was to write to Marshall County, WV to see if I could find a birth record. I wanted his mother's maiden name. I was able to get the record, but it only listed his mother's married name. I sent for any other information they might have on this family. I received a death certificate for Martha Salter. While it did list her father as Edward and mother as Mary, there were no last names mentioned.

Meanwhile, I put inquiries on any message board I could find, asking if anyone knew this family. To my amazement, I was contacted by Jeff, whose ancestor was Ebenezer Zane Salter, brother of Harry Salter. He had a great deal of information he was willing to share. He said Martha's maiden name was Hadsell and she was the granddaughter of the famous patriot, Elizabeth "Betty" Zane, heroine of Ft. Henry, in Wheeling, WV.

Martha's father was Edward Hadsell who had married Mary Ann McLaughlin, daughter of Elizabeth Zane. I also learned Edward Hadsell was the grandson of another patriot,

James Hadsell, one of the first settlers in the Wyoming Valley, PA. James was killed in the Wyoming Valley Massacre in Luzerne County, PA in 1778.

I did find a cemetery listing on the Marshall County website which showed Edward Hadsell and Mary McLaughlin, buried in Buchanan Hill Cemetery, Moundsville, WV. I also found three Salter Children buried in the same cemetery. These children — William, Eddie and Ada — were shown as the children of E.W. and M.A. Salter. From census records, I knew these children were the siblings of my Harry.

I just had to see that cemetery! In October of 2001, my husband and I drove to West Virginia from Florida. I was able to find the cemetery and locate the graves. There they were. All in a row and located fairly close together. Edward, Mary, another of their granddaughters, Jane Riggs, and the Salter children. Willie and Eddie shared a gravestone. They had died in within a few weeks of each other. Ada's stone was right next to theirs.

Then I saw another stone right at the base of, and actually touching, Willie and Eddie's. It read "Mary M. Hadsell, died 10 December 1853." Mary was 27 when she died.

Mary was known to be the daughter of Edward Hadsell and Mary McLaughlin Hadsell.

While I didn't have an actual document to prove my Martha was a Hadsell, this, along with her death certificate, was enough to convince me Jeff had been right.

So, learning great-grandpa's secret led me to two new lines and two more American Revolutionary Patriots. — Anne Brown, FL, jbrown73@tampabay.rr.com

"Board" Meeting

My maternal grandfather's parents were Balint Nagy and Julianna Batari, both Hungarian immigrants. Although I hadn't gotten very far on either of them, I considered Balint my biggest brickwall.

I knew that Balint was living in E. St. Louis, IL before August 27, 1907, when Julianna arrived at Ellis Island with my grandfather, who was then seven-years old. The ship's manifest said they came from Patroha, which is in Szabolcs Megye (county), and that Julianna's mother, Mrs. Imre Batari, lived there. I wasn't sure for a couple of years if I had found the manifest for Balint, since the most likely record, in January 1905, said he was deported because of illness. But it was the only clue I had as to his date of birth, which indicated about 1870. I still have not found him arriving in the US at any other time or port, but he obvi-

Imre Batari (Uncle Imre), left, with an unidentified companion.

ously did; or he slipped through somehow in January 1905. I have since become convinced, however, that the 1905 manifest shows my great-grandfather.

The problem with Balint was that no one who was still living knew very much about him, and what they did know, did not care to remember. According to my grandmother, who has been a treasure trove of information on her Hungarian family, he was, to put it kindly, a "bad, nasty person" and "Why would you want to know anything about someone like him?" It seems that within a year or two after Balint, Julianna and my grandfather settled in E. St. Louis, another family member threw him out and gave him money to go live in Detroit. No one in the family ever heard from him again.

I went to the local FHC and ordered film from Patroha, Hungary. The church records contained baptismal records for more than a half-dozen Balint Nagys in the period 1865-75, but since I didn't have the names of siblings and wasn't sure about the 1870 year of birth, I didn't know which record, if any was correct. I tried looking for Julianna, since I had a birth date of 6 April 1877, but she wasn't there either. I also tried looking for Julianna in Nyiregyhaza, where she said she was born, but no luck.

I'd already posted what I knew about Balint and Julianna on the RootsWeb message boards some time

Julianna Batari Nagy Kiszely, Sandra Wincek's great-grandmother, around 1912.

before. One day I decided to take a look and see if anyone else had posted something on my family since then. To my (cautious) delight, I found another researcher who mentioned a Julianna Batari, born on 6 April 1879 — the same month and day, but two years different from my Julianna. There was nothing on Balint, but Veronica had researched the Batari family, who had lived in Gegeny, Szabolcs Megye, which is very close to Patroha. They lived there until after 1900.

I contacted Veronica, and she was doubtful that her Julianna and mine were the same, but she sent me a summary of what she had. Veronica's grandfather was Imre Batari, brother to Julianna, and their father was also Imre. Now I had (maybe) two Juliannas, same birth date and month, two years apart, both with fathers named Imre, and living less than 20 miles apart. Veronica was not convinced, but this was too much of a coincidence for me to ignore.

I went back to my grandmother, and told her what I'd found. When I mentioned the name, Imre, she told me about "Uncle Imre" (who she had never mentioned before). Uncle Imre was my grandfather's uncle, brother to his mother, Julianna. Imre actually lived with his sister's family for several years in Ingalls, MI, before dying on a poorfarm in the early 1930s.

That cinched it for Veronica. When I told her about the other details I had about Imre Batari, it matched the little bit she had. She had been looking for him for years, and never knew what happened to him after he and his wife divorced. Although we still don't have a death certificate for Imre (Michigan did not keep records of all poorfarm deaths), we do have a place and time frame.

As for Balint, matching my Julianna Batari with Veronica's helped me there, too. With the name of the town of Gegeny, I found the civil marriage record of my great-grandparents in 1897. It confirmed his birth date in Patroha. With that, I got the correct baptismal record, along with all of his siblings, and records going back three more generations.

This is all because of my posting and reading the postings of others on message boards. This is hardly a novel way to bring down a brickwall (or go around one), but for me, it is nearly always a part of the solution.
— Sandra Wincek, WI

In The Name Of Science

I received an e-mail one day from a lady I shall call Mrs. Linda. She was interested in finding out some information about her biological father. No one in her family would give her any information about him. She had been doing a little bit of research on her own and found her biological grandmother who was buried in a cemetery that I went to quite frequently to do look ups and was wondering if I would be able to stop by and take some photos and check and see if her father was buried there.

I wrote her back and let her know I would go to the cemetery and see what I could find. She gave me a list of relatives and dates. I found her uncles and grandparents but not her father. I e-mailed her the information that I had and told her that I was unable to find her father. I then decided to take it upon myself to investigate this matter further. I started making phone calls to every cemetery in Norfolk, VA without any luck.

I then decided to go to the central library and look for an obituary, figuring that I would be able to find the name of a cemetery or funeral home and then I could go from there. I did, in fact, find an obituary but it had no information whatsoever. It simply stated that her father had passed away on the date she had given me and the city he died in. I then called back to one of the city-owned cemeteries and asked them how I would be able to find where a person who died in Norfolk was buried and they referred me to the city health department. I then called the health department and the lady explained to me that the only way I would be able to find that information is if I ordered the death certificate but because the death had only occurred a few years ago, only the next of kin would be able to get the information.

I then explained to the lady on the phone that the daughter of the man I was looking for lived out of state and was going to be visiting shortly and would like to know where he is buried so she could visit the grave. I further explained that I had personally called all the cemeteries and since there was no information listed in his obituary, I was literally at a dead end. I was beginning to believe that he had been cremated and maybe his ashes were spread somewhere, hence there being no record of him anywhere. Explaining that she was doing me a favor, she then looked up his name. Within minutes the mystery was solved!

"I will tell you why you cannot find him," she said. "When this man died he donated his body to science."

Just like that, I had found out the information that this lady needed to know but unfortunately for her there is no memorial of the father she never met.

However, I learned a valuable lesson as a result of my investigation: Remember that from state to state the law varies on what information can be given out. Don't be discouraged if there doesn't seem to be any information, or the trail appears to run cold after they die. Try contacting the health department of the city in which the person died and you just might get lucky. — Bonnie Carriles, VA, krazyb73@aol.com

A Time Line As A Compass

I was interested in tracing my Hoover family in the New Castle, PA area back another generation, so I consulted the death certificate of my third-great-grandmother, Mary Jane Hoover Gaston. Unfortunately, the words "unable to tell" were written in the box for mother's name. I was later able to piece together the maiden name of my fourth-great-grandmother, Cornelia Evans, from her 1854 death notice in the local newspaper and the obituary of her husband over 40 years later. Cornelia had died less than two years after giving birth to Mary Jane in 1852, so information about Cornelia was lost to the later generations. I then felt it my genealogical duty to document more about Cornelia, particularly by finding her parents.

Beginning this search, I found Cornelia with her husband, Jared Hoover, and their two young sons in the 1850 Census living in Shenango Township, which had just become part of Lawrence County, previously Beaver County. Cornelia was listed as

having been born in New York, uncommon for people in the Lawrence County area at that time. I also found three deeds in the same time period where Jared Hoover was buying or selling property in Beaver County. I checked all of the Evans entries in the 1850 Census for Beaver County, but no one was listed as having been born in New York. I visited the Beaver County Courthouse hoping to find mention of Cornelia Hoover in an estate deed or will, but I found nothing. There was no orphans' court or other records listing her children as heirs after her death. I was at a standstill.

Frustrated with my lack of progress, I put the information I'd found so far in chronological order, creating a brief time line of Cornelia and Jared's life together. Looking at the time line, I realized that I should have been looking in Lawrence County, not Beaver County, for potential family members and possible court documents. Switching focus, I consulted all of the Evans entries in the 1850 census for Lawrence County for a possible match of birthplace in New York. Only two entries matched for New York: Warren Evans and Randall Evans. Based on age, Randall was likely Cornelia's father, and Warren could have been her older brother. Further research revealed that Warren Evans sold land to Jared Hoover. Also, both Warren and Jared were shoemakers in Lawrence County in the late 1840s, so Warren most likely introduced Jared to his younger sister, Cornelia. Research at the Lawrence County courthouse revealed the Evans wills and deeds I'd been looking for (incorrectly) in Beaver County.

Based on approximate birth dates

> On Wednesday morning, the 12th inst., Mrs. Cornelia Hoover, wife of Mr. Jared Hoover, of New Castle, aged about thirty years.

Cornelia's 1854 death notice from the local newspaper.

from the census records, I was able to trace Cornelia with her parents, Randall and Mary Evans, back through different counties in New York. Randall was a laborer, and the family moved every few years to follow available work.

I'm still on the hunt to find the maiden name of Cornelia's mother, Mary, who was born in Connecticut about 1784, as well as the parents of Randall Evans, born in New York about 1779, but the time line approach really helped me meet my goal to document the parents of Cornelia Evans Hoover. — Lisa Kerr Ilowite, NJ

Let The Professionals Handle It

I have been looking for my grandfather's family for several years. The only information I had was my grandfather's date and place of birth and the names of his parents.

My grandfather, Frederick Diamond, was born on 22 July 1889 in Philadelphia, PA. His parents were called Harry Diamond and Katherine O'Brien.

I was able to find my grandfather at the St. Francis Industrial School for Boys in Bucks County, PA in the 1900 federal census. The Archdiocese of Philadelphia has the admission records of the school and Frederick's record lists his parents as Francis Diamond and Catherine O'Brien.

I then went off searching for a Francis Diamond. The closest match I could find was the Philadelphia city directory, from 1908 to 1915, which lists a Kathleen Diamond, widow of Francis. Kathleen was pretty close to Katherine, but no proof that it was my Katherine.

My brickwall came tumbling down when I hired a professional researcher.

Although she found a Kathleen Diamond listed in a city directory, Christine Dorval wasn't sure it was the right person.

She found my grandfather's birth record which listed his parents as Mr. And Mrs. Harry Diamond, and the address where they lived. She also found Harry listed in the Philadelphia city directory and his death record, which has the cemetery he was buried in and other Diamonds he was buried with.

I still haven't found my Katherine, although there is one in the 1880 US census who lived in the same ward as Harry. I now have several other Diamond names to research and several leads to follow.

My advice is to hire a professional researcher in the area your ancestors are from. It is well worth the money. — Christine Dorval, ON

Directory excerpt:

Galbraith
" Earl (Nora), p t instr Westminster Hosp, h 118 Appel
" Edna R, h 1 Brighton
" Edwd (Cora), h 183 Duchess av
" Emma, 363 Cheapside
" Ethel, wks German, Eckert, 732 Queens av
" Evelyn J, clk Income Tax, h 379 Talbot, apt 8
" Frank (Ann), h 671 King
" Geo H (Laura), elect 849 Maitland h same
" Harry (Elsie), clk Cowan Hdwe, h 432 Clarence, apt 2
" Herman (Ivy), ins agt, h 868 Hellmuth av
" Isabel R, clk Income Tax, h 379 Talbot, apt 8
" Jack L (Betty), clk Granger-Taylor sub P O 15 London
" Jas R, 57 Euclid av
" Ken J, wks Kelloggs, 671 King
" Lorne, lab C S Hyman Co, 432 Clarence
" M Vivian, tchr Beal Tech, 517 William
" Malcolm (Amy), slsmn Silverwood, h 445 Central av
" Percy G (Eleanor H), h 271 Piccadilly
" Rachel, h 331 Wortley rd
" Robt L (Lacy), clk C N R, h 738 King
" Ronald H (Margt), dntst 214½ Dundas, h 104 Elworthy
" Ross P, wks Price Lmbr, 671 King
" Vivian, tchr Tech & Comm Schl, h 517 William, apt 2
" Walter W (Jean), stk clk T R Faulds & Son, h 86 Langarth
Gale, Annie (wid John), h 1238 York
" Arthur, lab Kelloggs, h 664 Grosvenor
" Arthur A (Ethel A), c o formn Bell Tel, h 768 Hellmuth av
" Benj, h 390 Princess, apt 401
" Bertha, clk Kelloggs, 664 Grosvenor
" Emma, h 97 Sanders
" F John, elect hlpr Johnson-Turner, 1238 York
" Gladys, wtrs Simpson's Lon Ltd, h 454 Quebec
" John, wks McCormicks, b 840 Queens av
" Lillian M, dist instr Bell Tel, 510 Adelaide
" Lorena M, clk Somervilles, h 599 King, apt 2
" Muriel B, clk Income Tax, 1238 York
" Oliver (Ida A), h 510 Adelaide
" Philip, 731 Nelson

Gale
" Regd C (Evelyn), drvr J A Brownlee, h 167 Wildwood av
" Shirley L, opr Bell Tel, 242 Oxford
" T Edwd (Margt), soldier, h 82 Sterling
" Thos E (Gladys), swpr Emp Brass, h 76 Sterling
" Wm, eng Ont Hosp, res same
" Wm J S (Violet), mach Hobbs Glass, h 731 Nelson
" Wm W, studt, 796 Maitland
" Wm W J (Christine), slsmn London Mtr Prod, h 798 Maitland
Gales, Louise (wid J), 77 Glenwood av
" Richd H (Hazel), pntr C N R, h 465 Hill
" Wm, h 77 Glenwood av
" Yvonne C (wid Chas), h 702 Hamilton rd
Gallacher, ndw, 108 St Julien
Gallagher, Betty, prsr Aladdin Dry Clnrs, 25 Partridge
" Dorothy, wks G Linkovich, 342 Adelaide
" Edwd H (Viola), slsmn Lon P M, h 210 Emery
" Floyd V (Olive), carp, h 34 Childers
" Geo (Eva), prs Penmans, h 26 Walnut
" Geo (Hilda), wks Genl Stl Wares, h 1054 Mabel
" Geo (Mary), mldr Wells Fndry, h 342 Adelaide
" Gordon C (Irene), wks Hydro, h 556 Richmond
" Helen, wks Geo Linkovich, 342 Adelaide
" Hugh, drvr Smithson's Transp, rm 724 King
" Jean, wks Victoria Hosp, 143 Wellington
" John J, cashr Lewis Sand Shoppe, h 345 Adelaide
" Kathleen, Mrs, 316 Horton
Gallagher, Lloyd S (Jean), (Gallagher Motors), h 290 Huron, Phone Fairmont 3754
" Loretta, nurse St Joseph's Hosp, h 867 Colborne
" Margt, fnshr Richmond Hosy, 304A King
" Margt (wid Jas), 629 Dufferin av
" Margt, hlpr House of Providence, 857 Richmond
GALLAGHER MOTORS
(S H and L S Gallagher, B MacLean), Mercury and Lincoln Sales and Service, Gasoline, Oils, Washing, Greasing, Storage, Tires, Batteries, Etc, Imported Antique Furniture, cor King and Wellington, Phone Metcalf 7080

Gems in Chancery Court Records

I started researching my great-grandmother's Bulifant family in 1980. From family information and several other records I knew that Susan Jane Bulifant, born on 11 July 1864, in Charles City County, VA, was the daughter of George A. Bulifant/Bullifant and Mary Virginia Spraggins.

Over the years I searched every census, will, deed, court order, tax record and Civil War record I could locate for information on the parents of George A. Bulifant. There are no church records extant for the family church before 1900. Every avenue I tried came to a dead end.

The 1840 census revealed that only two families in the surrounding counties had a male in that age bracket. One family was headed by Jane Bullifant (no older male in household) and the other by Furnea Bullifant. The 1850 census revealed that George was born in 1830, but he was not living at home at the time. I was able through extensive research to discern that only Jane's family was a good candidate for George as a child. Furnea's wife had died in 1818 and he had not remarried. The children shown with him were probably the children of his only daughter.

I expanded my search to include every Bulifant/Bullifant in Virginia, for as far back as I could go. I placed queries online to see if anyone else was researching this family. I received several answers and located a lot of additional data by sharing with others. Over time I was able to tie the other families together and carried the Bullifants back to 1670 in James City County, VA.

During this research I had obtained a deed in 1824 from John Bullifant to his four children; William J., Albert J., Flemming J., and Susan J. Bullifant. This deed further stated that the land he was deeding to his children was: *fifty acres where upon my father, John Bullifant now resides, (being the land left by my grandfather James Benge, deceased to my brother James J. Bullifant.)* That's a lot of good information.

From tax records I discovered that Jane was the wife of John Bullifant. If my conclusions were correct, then George was the son of John and Jane, Since George was born in 1830, it is obvious that he would not have been included in this deed. The 1840 census also included three other children not included in the deed; all born after 1824.

Various documents have George A. Bulifant with Flemming J. Bullifant together. George also owned land next to the "Oteys Plantation" owned by William J. Bullifant.

This was all wonderful information, but I could not tie George definitively to this family. Since I live in Oregon and any other records that might help were housed in Virginia, it was difficult for me to continue my search. I had become genie buddies with Pat, a Bulifant cousin, who lived near Richmond, VA. Pat was making regular trips to the county courthouse in Charles City for research on her families in the area, and offered to help out. She made many trips over the years and provided a lot of additional family data, but none on my George.

Then one day in 2001, Pat visited the courthouse and dug into a box of old chancery court records. There was one document there that was not available elsewhere. On 19 November 1846, George Bulifant, as an infant, sued for his portion of the sale of the land "that was purchased by John Bullifant, dec'd" and was to be distributed "the same among the heirs of John Firth, dec'd, and conveyed by said John Bullifant to his four children William J., Fleming J., Susan J. and

Albert Bullifant". This document placed George in this family as I had long suspected. It should be noted that there is no data on the other three children identified in the 1840 census.

Chancery court records includes law suites that pertain to equity cases. They might be referenced in the court order books, but all of the pertinent data might not be recorded and therefore not available on microfilm, if the court order books have been filmed. Other records are not microfilmed or neatly recorded in those big books in the courthouse either. The only way to get to them is to go to the courthouse and start digging.

If I had not shared my data with Pat, and developed a wonderful Internet relationship, I might never have broken down this brickwall.

None of us can do it all alone, so sharing is the best way to gain the information you might need.
— Carolyn H. Brown, OR, sidcarol@escapees.com

Regarding Henry

The paternal family of my great-grandfather Herbert Healey, was a mystery that has kept my aunt and I busy for years. Herbert's parents were very scandalous for their time.

According to family legend, Jessie Healey had to be persuaded to marry the mother of his child, by her father, a few years after the birth. This father happened to be a Civil War veteran and the first sheriff of a small south-western Pennsylvania borough called Arnold. The marriage took place in 1896 and by 1900 the couple was living in different counties. By 1910, Jessie and his first wife had both remarried and moved on.

Herbert passed away as a young father in 1948. His family and his father's family did not keep in touch. My great-grandmother made sure that the facts as she remembered them were passed on to her children. All that

we knew was that Jessie's father was Henry Thomas Healey and was born in Oxford, England on 21 May 1847. His wife was Jane Milk and they were married in England. His parents were Susan and James Healey. Sounded like a lot to start with. First my aunt found Henry's naturalization papers at the Carnegie Library. The arrival date and ship were not included in the information available. But he applied for citizenship in 1882 and was approved in 1886. Everything we knew about Jessie pointed out that he was born in the US to English parents. His approximate date of birth was 1873, from his marriage license. So we figured that Henry had to come to America before then.

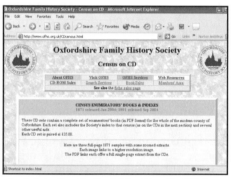

A visit to the Oxfordshire Family History Society website proved to be beneficial to Kim Policastro.

We stumbled across an entry in *A Genealogical and Biographical History of Allegheny County, Pennsylvania*, edited by Dr Thomas Cushing in 1889:

Henry T Healey — brick manufacturer, Homestead, was born May 21, 1847, in Oxfordshire, England, the only son of James and Susan (Johnson) Healey, former of whom now resides with him. Mr Healey was a carpenter by trade in England, immigrated to America in 1872, and was the first one to settle in Homestead after it was laid out in lots... and since 1877 he has been successfully engaged in the manufacture of bricks. His first wife, Jane Milk (deceased), was the mother of five children: Albert, William, Henry T, John A and Jessie. By his pres-

ent wife, nee Maggie Freeburn, he has four children: James, Edward, Susan and Alice. Mr and Mrs Healey are members of the Episcopal Church and he is a Republican.

The 1880 census for Homestead, Allegheny County, PA listed the Healey household as: Henry, carpenter, age 33, England; Margaret, keeping house, age 23, Ireland; Albert J., working in brickyard, age 14, London; Willie, at home, age 11, London; Henry T. Jr., at home, age 9, London; John A., at school, age 7, PA; Jessie (listed as daughter), age 5, PA; James, age 1, PA and Susan, mother, age 53, Oxfordshire, England.

Wow! Maybe all the facts Grandma remembered were correct. This is where a huge brickwall appeared and stayed for years.

I found an entry on the Ellis Island site listing a Thomas H. Healey, age 24, and a mechanic along with his wife, Jane M. also age 24. They were traveling with children, Albert J., age three, William, age two, and Thomas H., age one. They arrived aboard the *Alex Marshall* on 11 July 1871 from Liverpool. They traveled in steerage. From there I thought a look through the 1871 census might give me some more information. The family was in St. Mary Paddington, Paddington, London. Henry's birthplace was list-

Kim Policastro's great-grandparents Herbert Clair Healey and Cordelia Annie Dunmore shortly after their marriage in 1914.

ed as Witney, Oxford, UK. Great! Now I needed to find Susan and James Healey. I could find neither of them in the 1871 census. I knew Susan was alive. She was listed in the Allegheny County census in 1880. Maybe the father's name was wrong.

I found a great website called FreeBMD.com, sponsored by RootsWeb, and tried to find a birth record for Henry, thinking that the father had to be listed on his birth certificate and the mystery would be solved. I searched using his parents' names in connection with his and came up blank. Eventually I just used his birth date and last name, along with his birthplace. There he was. I ordered the certificate. Next, I checked for his marriage to Jane Milk. No such luck. I tried Henry Healey marrying a Jane in a range of years and there they were. Jane Matilda Mills married Henry Thomas Healey on 26 December 1867 in St. James Church, Shoreditch, Middlesex. Once again I ordered the certificate. One of them had to name his father.

In the meantime, I searched for a way to get a look at the 1851 census for Witney, Oxfordshire. I could not find it on the Internet anywhere. I asked a recently found cousin in England if he had any suggestions.

He suggested the Oxfordshire Family History Society website. For a fee, they would look up the entry for me. The fee was small so I went for it. A very generous researcher armed with everything I knew about Henry went hunting.

He came back to me within 24 hours with some news. Henry was listed with William and Hannah Healey in St. Mary's, Witney. He was listed as their child along with several other children, including another three-year-old boy named Mark who was listed as a grandson. This and the fact that Healey was spelled differently for several members of the household intrigued him so he went to the parish records for baptism. Mark was listed as the son of William and Hannah. Henry was listed as the son of Susan Healey. Susan Healey was listed as the daughter of William and Hannah. There was no James listed.

I waited the longest week and a half for the certificates to come from the General Registry Office along with the St. Mary's parish records. When they arrived I found that there had been no omission from the parish records. Henry Thomas Healey was born to Susanna Healey. No father was listed there or on the marriage record for the same Henry Thomas Healey.

By searching for Henry's beginnings, I learned not to blindly trust the written accounts in local histories but to use them as a guideline for my search. In the past few weeks we have made contact with a descendent of Susan's brother George and shared our new information which included Hannah Healey's maiden name (Harris) and the marriage date of she and William, as well as the names and birth years of all 14 of their children. We have learned that our family was adventurous. George left the UK for South Africa 20 years before Susan and Henry left for America. — Kim Policastro, PA

The Kitchen Connection

My heart sank when I discovered that my great-grandmother's name, Mary Elizabeth McDonald Kitchen, an immigrant from Eastern Canada, had never had her name engraved on the family gravestone, when she died in 1927. Perhaps the onset of the Depression caused this oversight, but it was never corrected in more prosperous times.

I scolded my father, saying that this was one more example of relegating women to second-class status in both family and world history. We collaborated to see that the name of Mary Elizabeth was properly added below her husband's name, Henry Clay Kitchen, who died in 1911. Their gravestone was one of a larger Kitchen family plot in a lovely section of Lowell Cemetery, MA.

The missing name spurred me on to research my female relatives on the Kitchen side of the family. Unfortunately, my grandmother, (the daughter of Mary Elizabeth), Ada Clayton Rollins died before I was born, so the Kitchen side of the genealogy was fractured — a brickwall.

Through constant nagging of my father's memory, I began to learn about the 'Kitchen Kids' — his first-cousins. One of his cousins, Elizabeth Kitchen, intrigued me, but was the most difficult to track down. My father had lost all contact with her, as she had become a world traveler, eager to escape the confines of her small town upbringing in Billerica, MA. One piece of information — that she had graduated from Simmons College in Boston — made me think that I could use this piece of the puzzle to finally solve the mystery. Luckily, Elizabeth kept in contact with her alma mater. Her name had changed with marriage, but the alumnae office was able to make the proper name connection. However, the alumnae office did not make things easy for me. If I did not phrase my questions in a certain way, with "yes" or "no" answers, then I would get no information. Fortunately, I broke the question code and was able to find she lived in Florida.

I took the plunge and wrote Elizabeth (Betty) a letter introducing myself, as her long-lost relative. She warmly responded and sent me pictures and stories about her large family (seven children) and an annual Christmas letter. We even met once in Cambridge, MA, and I was surprised to see she looked somewhat like my father — the Kitchen Connection. — Ann Rollins, WA, Foundation700@yahoo.com

Mom's Branches Have Roots

My brother and I went down to Dubuque, IA to research some of our Mom's branches of the family tree. We were especially interested in her Nicholas and Margaret (née Wagner) Heinz line. A brief family history written by our great-aunt Myrtle told us that her aunt Kate (née Heinz) Steckel Mueller, who died childless, had gotten all the original Heinz documents.

While we were in the courthouse looking for land records and wills, I said "Why don't we look for Aunt Kate's will? It might give us a clue as to what happened to those documents." We didn't find a will for her, but we did find a document to help us. In the probate files there was one for a Magdalin(a) Ley (her sister) trying to get guardianship of Kate and her possessions. We poured through all the documents and found out that she was successful. I knew through census records that Magdalin(a) lived in the house that her dad, Nicholas Heinz, built on arrival in Dubuque around 1859.

We decided to look for her will. It stated that her daughter, Lillian Loecke, got the house. We still had at least one generation to prove the house was still in the family. We went to the Stout-Carnegie Public Library and found they had a phone book that listed people by address.

One of the handwritten notes from Jane Schumacher's great-aunt Myrtle (Heinz) Fox.

We found the entry, but there was no phone number listed. Since we wanted to see the house anyway, we went there and knocked on the door.

No one was home. So when I got home I wrote this person a letter explaining who I was, and what I was looking for. Eureka! This person was my cousin and she had most of the original Heinz family documents. She also knows another cousin who has done extensive work on the Fogarty line, which had married into the Heinz family. As soon as we can coordinate our schedules she will come down to see my brother and me to share what she has. Likewise, we will share what we have with her. — Jane Schumacher, WI, jjschu@itis.com

Jerry's Expanding Family

After discovering that my maternal grandmother, Kate, had several siblings I didn't know anything about, most of whom survived to adulthood, married and had children, I began a frantic search for their grandchildren and great-grandchildren. Considering my own age, I didn't expect that any of their children were still living. I had an almost-immediate brickwall breakthrough that located my grandmother's sister's son's widow who put me in touch with some of my cousins. Still, I hoped to find others.

No one I got in touch with knew anything about Kate's brother Jim's family. No one had names, addresses or phone numbers. So I launched a telephone search on the Internet for people of the family surname in the state where my great-grandfather had raised his family and where I had found some of my cousins.

Not many names surfaced, which could prove either good or bad: good in that there was not a huge list; bad in that none might be related and I might be butting my head against another brickwall. Most phone calls produced nothing. Finally, one produced a very tentative "maybe", but probably not, as her husband was the only son of an only son and didn't have any cousins, aunts, uncles, and so forth. But she gave me their e-mail address and I sent some information about my grandmother's family, including everything I knew about Uncle Jim (which was almost nothing).

Back shot the reply, "It is possible". The next day brought an even more excited reply, "After checking through materials, Jerry hardly slept a wink last night. He didn't know he had any cousins anywhere!"

So it turned out that Jerry was Jim's great-grandson, my second-cousin once-removed. True enough, he was an only child, as was his father, but his great-grandfather had eight siblings who had families, and his grandfather had a number of siblings too, although most of their whereabouts, etc., were unknown.

Bob Hartsell's great-uncle Jim, who also happened to be Bob's cousin Jerry's great-grandfather.

This was one case where the person found was even more thrilled than the person who found him, as I had already found some of my cousins and knew others existed, whereas Jerry thought he was "all alone in the world" except for his immediate family. A subsequent personal visit with Jerry and his family cemented our relationship and we continue to e-mail on a frequent basis.

Once again, it was the Internet that enabled me to find Jerry and connect him to his lost family — a family he didn't even know existed! — Bob Hartsell, AR, u4eah@hsnp.com

Guidance From Beyond

My research of my grandmother's family seems to be filled with nothing but brickwalls. I have almost no documentation and no older relatives alive, but sometimes childhood memories, even vague ones, are one of the best tools. Every step of the way has been filled with stumbling blocks, but a childhood memory is the amazing story of my research.

Shortly after I started my research a year ago and wasn't having much luck, I woke up out of a sound sleep in the middle of the night with "Webb City" in my thoughts. Keep in mind, the only time I heard of this was when I overheard a conversation between my mother and grandmother when I was a little girl. My grandmother told my mother that one of her relatives (I didn't remember whom) was married to a man named Webb who had started a large drugstore in Florida. I never thought of that conversation again until my dream woke me.

I got out of bed and got on the Internet immediately and entered "Webb City". Much to my amazement, I found several articles about a James Earl "Doc" Webb from Tennessee who had bought into a small drugstore in St. Petersburg, FL in 1925; then bought out his partner; and then proceeded to form a huge conglomerate consisting of 70 stores that spanned seven city blocks. This was one of the first "super" stores in the US. The stories the articles told about this phenomena were utterly fantastic. This was a Florida tourist attraction, and people from miles around came to see this spectacle clear up into the 1970s. St. Petersburg even had a musical *Webb's City* which has been performed in recent years.

Finding the articles still did not answer my question as to what connection Webb was to my grandmother's family. I tried a Webb message board forum and corresponded with the wife of James Earl Webb's grandson, but although she told me James Earl Webb had had three wives, none of the names rang a bell with me.

In the meantime, I tried a Linde message board and found a message which looked like it might pertain to one of my grandmother's sisters. The man who had written the message listed the town in Florida where he lived. So, on one of the sites on the Internet which I don't think is available anymore, I found the same name in the town in Florida, with an address and telephone number. I called the number, and lo and behold,s this man was the grandson of my grandmother's sister! During the conversation we had, he told me that his father's sister was James Earl Webb's first wife; so she was the daughter of my grandmother's sister and was my grandmother's niece!

Even being inexperienced and new to genealogy research, I am already asking myself if our ancestors are "guiding us and helping us along the paths of discovery". Maybe they are the answer to our brickwalls? — Georgia Kruse, rockingranny@comcast.net

Get To Know Your Local Library

Public libraries in the US and Canada have been great resources for my research over the years. Some libraries have staff that only do genealogical research. One librarian in Ontario supplied me with census information, birth records and book suggestions. They will also look at city directories.

I was trying to locate descendants of my grandmother's cousin. My mother had a general idea of where she lived. I asked the librarians in that town for an obituary for her. Although they didn't have it, they did have an obituary for her daughter-in-law (same last name). The obituary had the names and hometowns of her children listed. I found addresses for two of them and wrote letters. I have been corresponding with her grandchildren for a few months now. They have the same stories about their great-grandmother that I do for my great-grandfather (who were brother and sister)!

I try to remember to send a contribution to the library if they don't charge a research fee. Public libraries can be an invaluable research resource, but are sometimes overlooked.

Get to know your local library; you'll be amazed at what they can do for you! — Carolyn Harmon, IL

Finding My French Roots

When I started researching my family tree, I had some facts and stories that had been gathered by my mother after 20 years of research.

For instance, we knew that her father's family, the Kienlens, had come from Alsace-Lorraine. We knew the year that they had immigrated, but could not get them back across the ocean to France. We were definitely standing in front of a brickwall. I had just started researching on the computer and found out various things about the town that they were from:

Gabrielle and Judith at the Ecomusée of Alsace in Egosheim, Alsace, France.

Hussen in Alsace. There were no websites for it, but by looking on various sites that pertained to Alsace, I had gleaned some small bits of information.

I went to a website with a phone directory in Paris and decided to give that a chance. I found 10 Kienlens. Four of them had e-mail addresses. I decided to e-mail the four and send the other six letters with self addressed, stamped envelopes. I didn't hear from any of the letters, but two of the men with the Kienlen surname contacted me.

One had nothing, but the other one told me about a cousin of his, Gabrielle, who was researching the Kienlen line in France. She was an ex-school teacher and she did not have e-mail, but he gave me her address and I decided to mail a letter to her. I included all of the research that I had done to that time. I also included some family pictures and sent it off. About a month later, I received the answer which far exceeded my expectations. Gabrielle had been doing research on the Kienlen line for about 20 years and she sent me a tree, taking my line back to about 1500. She was, it turned out, my mother's third-cousin. She said, that she usually didn't send such complete answers, but since I had sent her so much information that she didn't have she would have felt guilty, not replying in kind.

We corresponded for about two years, then my husband and I made a trip to Colmar where we finally met Gabrielle, who took us to the various family towns, cemeteries and homes and set up a party with the current Kienlens who were now living in the area, and I met some of my French relatives. I acquired invaluable information, and also made a friend of my new cousin. While we were there, Gabrielle took us to an outdoor museum that was set up like a French town in the 1500s, the Ecomusée of Alsace.

We have been writing for about five years now and she fills me in on things that are happening in Alsace, as well as how her life is going. I am so glad that I took the time to break through this brickwall. — Judith Henderson, CO, BlkUni42@aol.com

No Stone Unturned

For 30 years I have searched for the place in Germany from where my great-grandparents, Anton and Bertha Boesch, emigrated. My grandfather died when my father was 10 years old and almost nothing was known of his father.

According to the Dayton city directories, it seems that he was no longer living with his wife in the late 1870s and then disappeared from the city shortly thereafter. It was said that no one would talk about "the scandal" and his place of birth was lost by the time I began researching the family almost 100 years later. His naturalization papers indicated that he was from Baden, which did not seem to be a big place until I began looking at all the small towns there were in the area.

In the 1870 census, his oldest son was listed as Charles, followed by his younger brother and two younger sisters, all born in Baden (my grandfather wasn't born until after the census was taken that year).

Who was Charles and why had no one ever mentioned him? For years I searched the 1880 census in Dayton to try to find the family. Finally, the 1880 census index cd-roms arrived and I could search for every person and every possible variation of the name Boesch.

I found Beartha Basch and two children, one of whom was Charles Miller, on a farm in the county. Great, I thought, he changed his name to Miller and now I will never find him and any clues that his information may reveal.

On I trudged until I found an index to the *Gedenk-Blatter: Sonntags-Beilage zur Daytoner Volks-Zeitung* (Sunday Memorial Supplement to the *Volks-Zeitung* newspaper in Dayton, OH). This paper asked families of deceased Germans in the area to send a portrait and an obituary to be printed.

Only a few were submitted each week and they did not encompass the entire German community. It listed some of my more distant relatives as having printed obituaries. I do not read German, but I utilized some of the free translation websites available and I figured I might be able to get additional basic data on them. I also noticed that there were three Charles Mullers listed and thought I might give them a shot to see if my Charles Miller might have an obituary. Even if he was my relative, how was I ever going to know it with such little information about him? It was a very long shot.

When I got to the library, I photocopied the articles from the microfilm and brought them home. Since time was short, I only copied one of the three obituaries for Charles Muller. When I got home and started sorting through my information, I was ecstatic. The one Charles Muller obituary that I had copied referenced his mother, Bertha Bösch, and gave his place of birth as Mahlberg.

FamilySearch.org

I immediately went to FamilySearch.org to see if there was microfilm available for Mahlberg, Baden through the FHL. I ordered two films, one was the Catholic Church baptismal records, written in old German script and the other was an ortssippenbuch for the town; an ortssippenbuch is a lineage book for the area.

I was able to find my great-grandparents and an additional four generations back. As it turns out, Bertha had been married previously to Apollinar Müller, and Charles had not changed his name, but was my great-grandfather's step-son. You've got to love census takers!

In one month, I have found hundreds of ancestors that I have been searching for going on 30 years.

Serendipitous? Yes. My advice is to keep turning over all of the rocks to see what is there; sometimes it pays off in a big way. The next questions are where did Anton go when he left his wife and children? Did he return to Germany or migrate somewhere else in the United States?

Guess I need to turn over some more rocks! — Martie (Boesch) Callihan, OH, mcallihan2@mindspring.com

Where Was Grandpa Born?

Finding an overseas birthplace is probably the toughest brickwall a genealogist faces.

First, one must find a hint in a later record. Hint is the keyword, as most records will not be very specific. The passengers list of the vessel *Canada*, sailing from Havre, France to New York in 1883, states that my husband's grandfather, George Augst, came from Alsace.

His Hamilton County, OH naturalization papers in 1888 note him as "native of Germany." His birthplace in a census record is given as France. Although his death certificate in 1927 wasn't any more specific in regard to his birthplace (Germany), it did give his date of birth as 26 January 1866, and his father's name, the same as his. The 1930 census record for a son of George listed Alsace Lorraine as his father's birthplace.

With this information in mind, I turned to the Internet to see in which Alsatian villages I could find the sur-

name Augst. I found it in Woerth, Bitschhoffen, Niederbronn, Mertzwiller, Weitbruch and Schweighausen.

On my first trip to the FHL in Salt Lake City in 2003, I found myself pleasantly surprised with the ease with which the films could be found and replaced. My mission was to locate the birth record for George Augst in 1866. I had no luck in Woerth, Bitschhoffen, Niederbronn or Mertzwiller. In birth records for Weitbruch I found a George Augst born in October 1866, whose father was George Augst. I ended my first day of research wondering if I found the right one, since that was nine months later than the birth date I had for him.

On my second day at the library, I viewed records for Schweighausen. Although I am unable to read another language, it is fairly easy to recognize names and dates in these records no matter if they are in German, French or Latin. *There it is*! The right name, the right date, and the young woman at the library help desk was able to translate the rest of it for me: "son of George Augst and Madeleine Gruss."

Working my way back through family history, I found the 1865 marriage record for them, which gave the information that the groom was 35, a widower, and the son of Philippe Augst, 68, and Christina Bald, 64. It also revealed that Madeleine, age 26, was the daughter of Jacques Gruss, who died on 19 February 1847 in Mertzwiller, and Anna Margaretha Freytag, who died on 16 March 1864 in Mertzwiller.

This information lead to more birth, marriage and death records — enough to add several more generations to this branch of the family tree. — Marian Huber Dietrich, OH, marian_dietrich@myfamily.com

Clues In Religious Traditions

I was researching my grandmother's maternal line of Brainins, which is a Jewish family. My grandmother remembered when and where her mother's parents, Mendel Hertz and Rose Braining, had died, so I thought it would be straightforward to obtain copies of their death certificates. But I could not find them in indices, and the city of New York could not find them when I tried to order the certificates.

This brickwall stayed around for a while until I met some cousins from that side of the family. The husband was my blood relative. I learned his full name, Murray Howard Pollack, his birthday, and the fact that he had been named after his (and my grandmother's) grandfather (my second-great-grandfather), Mendel Hertz Brainin.

Death certificate of Mendel Hertz (Morris) Brainin.

Eastern European Jews have a tradition of not naming a child after a living ancestor. For my cousin to have been named after his grandfather, that meant Mendel Hertz had to have passed away before he was born. But the date my grandmother had given me for his death was after my cousin's birthday.

I had not considered that my grandmother could be wrong because she had been so positive about the dates. But I backdated the year Mendel Hertz was supposed to have died until the death fell before my cousin's birthday and reapplied for his death certificate. This time I was successful. I then reordered my second-great-grandmother's death certificate by backdating the date by the same number of years and received it also. My grandmother had been close — the month and date were correct, but not the years. Because I was able to determine what the problem was, I have taken this family line back one additional generation on each side.

Look for clues in the traditions of your ancestors' religion, and never take someone's word as absolute if you can't find verification. — Janice Sellers, CA, janice@seismosoc.org

Long-Lost Cousins

I had begun to despair of finding some of my cousins. I had learned that my grandmother, Kate, had eight siblings who lived to adulthood, married, and had children. I had almost miraculously found several groups of them, but others eluded my quest.

Kate had a brother called Hunt, who married and moved to Canada. One of Kate and Hunt's nieces, Alda Lucille, also married and moved to Canada. All this took place in the early 1900s, years before I was born. And I never heard my grandmother or mother speak of any of these family members.

None of my conventional methods had produced a shred of information. In an e-mail, I mentioned this to my cousin Barb, granddaughter of one of Kate's sisters. Soon Barb replied that her husband, doing some genealogical work of his own, had run across a man in Canada who could be related to our family. She sent me his name and e-mail address.

His name didn't register, as it was not the family surname I was seeking. But when I made contact with him, he turned out to be Alda's grandson, thus he had a different surname. But he was, indeed, my second-cousin once-removed.

Furthermore, he told me that Hunt's family was living in the same city. In fact, Hunt's daughters-in-law, widows of his two sons (in their late-eighties and nineties) were still living there, as well as all their children and most of their grandchildren, nearly 50 people in all. He furnished basic contact names and addresses, and letters started flowing, resulting in some phone calls as well.

Bob Hartsell's great-uncle Hunt.

After nearly three years of correspondence and phone conversations I was able to travel to Canada in November 2003 and visit most of my cousins there. In addition to a number of individual family visits during some of the days I was there, on a Sunday afternoon, 40 of us gathered for a big get-together — a reunion of sorts.

Just as I had never heard of Hunt's and Alda's families until I got well into my search on that branch of the family tree in 2000, none of them, except for Alda's grandson who is deeply involved in genealogy, had heard of my branch or the other branches from Hunt's and Kate's siblings. He had a great deal of information on many family members, not only descendants of my grandmother's siblings, but many more distant cousins, as his research extended much further up and out than mine. However, Hunt's family knew essentially nothing of the information Alda's grandson had, as they live in different parts of a huge city, had not maintained close contact, and did not share his interest in genealogy or family history.

It was not only deeply fulfilling and satisfying to me to meet so many of my cousins, but also it was a marvelous, warm get-together-for them as well as for me. Each of Hunt's sons' families maintains fairly close contact with their own group, but the two groups don't get together. So this occasion not only brought together most of both of these groups, but also Alda's grandson's family, as well as me being included, representing Kate's family.

And all of this because the husband of one of my cousins happened to run across someone while he was doing his own genealogical research, and I happened to mention to that cousin that I had been unable to locate any of our cousins in Canada. Computers are marvelous family-finding instruments!

Not only did my computer help me to make contact with my Canadian cousins, but also it enabled me to make contact with my

Japanese/American cousins in Hawaii. But that's another story. — Bob Hartsell, AR, u4eah@hsnp.com

Coincidental Carters?

I have finally found my George Spencer's baptism. I always thought that because my George married Martha Ridgeway in Sheffield, Yorkshire, that he was from Yorkshire or because they had a daughter in Derbyshire that he could also be from Derbyshire.

As he married after 1861 and died before 1871, I couldn't rely on either census to help with a birthplace. A check of the 1861 British census for Sheffield also drew a blank.

George was 48 and a widower in 1864, when he married Martha Ridgeway, making his birth year about 1816. His occupation was listed as carter, as was his own father George. The only George that fit this birth year was one listed in the IGI as being christened in 1817 in Austerfield, Yorkshire, to a George and Mary.

When I received my 1861 British census cds for Derbyshire, I came across an entry for a George Spencer, 16 years old, a carter, from Everton, Nottinghamshire. What are the chances of three Georges being carters?

Fortunately, I also have the 1861 census on cd-rom for Nottinghamshire so I checked the Everton entries and what did I see? A George and Mary residing in Everton from Austerfield. Not only that, but I found a widowed George, aged 42 in Harwell, born in Everton. Ages in census can often be wrong so I'm not too concerned about that.

Now, the Austerfield, Yorkshire threw me but a check of the Nottinghamshire Family History Society's baptismal cd came up with the following entry:

AUS 7/20/1817: George [son of George and Mary] Spencer.

Apparently, Austerfield is on the border of Yorkshire and Nottinghamshire, hence the reason for the different county in the IGI entry and the cd-rom entry.

If it wasn't for that link to an occupation I would more than likely still be searching and still trying to climb over a brickwall that went up ages ago. — Jayne McHugh, jam001@cogeco.ca

The Steneker Family

Since I began my research on the Steneker family, I have not been able to find the parents of Hermanus Hendrikus Stene(e)ker. He was my wife's third-great-grandfather. All I knew was that he married his wife Annetje Carels (age 28) in Amsterdam on 9 February 1777. His uncle, Abraham Van der Tuyn, stated on that date that his parents were deceased.

According to the census of 1947, the population in the Netherlands was 9.6 million. Only 184 individuals in this census had the name Steneker or Steeneker and 83 of these individuals resided in the northern provinces of Friesland and Groningen.

Since there were so few individuals with the name Ste(e)neker, I decided to include in my research all individuals carrying that name. The two main genealogy societies in the Netherlands (the Dutch Genealogical Society and Central Bureau for Genealogy) provided me with many birth, wedding and death announcements from the last 150 years.

In addition I gathered additional information from FamilySearch.org and the websites of GenLias and Tresoar, until my database of the Ste(e)neker family had grown to 850 individuals representing some 300 families, in addition to the data of my wife's family.

During my research I met a gentleman who had researched one of the Friesian branches of the Steneker family. The progenitor of this branch was Hendrik Johannes Steneker, who worked with his father Johannes in the peat moss industry in Friesland. Hendrik Johannes married a Dutch girl and settled in Friesland. His father Johannes eventually returned to his place of birth, Voltlage, Germany, and assumed the original family name of Steinke.

Johannes Steneker/Steinke was born in 1737 in Voltlage, Germany and was the oldest son in a family of eight children. The parents, Diedrich Heinrich Steinke and Margaretha Elisabeth Brockschmiedt, died in 1753 and 1756 respectively. At age 19, Johannes became responsible for all the siblings ranging in age from three to 18. One sibling was Herman Heinrich Steinke, born on 3 February 1747.

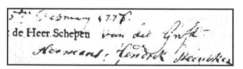

Hermanus Hendrikus Stene(e)ker's signature on the 1777 engagements document (above) can be read as Ste(e)neker... but also as Steinke.

Herman Heinrich Steinke is likely the same person as Hermanus Hendrik Ste(e)neker, for several reasons: his age is similar to that of his wife, Annetje Carels, his signature on the 1777 engagement documents can be read as Ste(e)neker but also as Steinke, his oldest brother Johannes Steneker/Steinke took care of Hermann Heinrich as a youngster and likely took him to Friesland, where he was employed most of his life. Herman Heinrich is literally translated from German to Dutch as Hermanus Hendrikus.

To prove that Herman Heinrich Steinke is the same person as Hermanus Hendrikus Steneker, I am now researching the family background of his uncle Abraham van der Tuyn in Amsterdam and hope to confirm that Hermann Heinrich Stienke and Hermanus Hendrikus Ste(e)neker are one and the same person. — Peter Hanhart, AB, phanhart@telusplanet.net

Switchboard.com

My major as yet undemolished 40-year-old brickwall is proving the circumstances and ancestry of my great-grandfather, David Freimeir Crampton (1842-1912).

At the same time, my branch of the family had lost contact with the family of Helen Mary Kyner, David's wife and my great-grandmother (born in 1848 in Anderson, IN, died on 8 February 1875 in Norfolk, NE). After Mary died, at age 27, David abandoned his three children, including my grandmother, and took off for the mines in Colorado. Family contact between the Sleepers and the Kyners was virtually non-existent in the intervening 125 years.

In the summer of 2003, I was re-reading the now-out-of-print autobiography of my grandmother's uncle James Henry Kyner, called *End Of Track*, a volume as notable for what it does not say as for the information it reveals. After reading the book, I did an Internet search on the married name of James Kyner's daughter whom I had met nearly 40 years previously. She had been living in her father's historic home in a Washington, DC suburb.

Her name showed up, though many years deceased, in the municipal website of the town where she had been mayor. However, more interestingly, mention was made that her daughter, who shared her given name, had succeeded her as mayor.

The daughter has an uncommon married surname which I entered into Switchboard.com with only the qualifier of "MD". That turned up a listing in St. Leonards, MD with a telephone number. A call connected me with a very friendly second-cousin, once-removed, who ultimately furnished me with a cd-rom connecting over 500 Kyner cousins.

My cousin and I have established a cordial relationship and I have the pleasant task of getting to know many new relatives. — Richard Sleeper, OR, Dick@Sleeper.us

Eastins On The 'Net

My father-in-law had done the genealogy on his surname Eastin about 30 years ago by going to court houses and libraries in different states.

When I started doing my family line he showed me all the information he had on his side. I started going on the Internet to see if I could find more than what he had. I couldn't believe all the information I found on the Eastins.

I was able to go back to Thomas Eastin born in about 1725 in England; died on 14 June 1793 in Albemarle County, VA. I took the information I had and made a website with all my names and dates on the Eastin sur-name and couldn't believe the people that e-mailed me.

My father-in-law didn't have any photos of his grandparents or great-grandparents. I didn't think I would find any either but I started searching and talking to people that had some of the same ancestors.

I received an e-mail from a lady in Florida who said she had photos of his grandfather and a photo of his great-grandmother. I found out this lady knew my father-in-law when they were children and was related to him. I took all the information she had on his family and showed him but it took him awhile to remember her. I asked her if she would get copies and send them to me and she did. I gave some to my father-in-law, who talked about how he had never seen them or knew them. My father-in-law was excited to see what his ancestors looked like and he started comparing them to relatives. I couldn't believe I would ever find a photo of any of his ancestors from the Internet.

Sarah Priscilla Bohannon, wife of Columbus Calmes Eastin. One of the photographs shared with Darlene (Arbogast) Eastin's family due to her hard work on the Internet.

I now know there are relatives out there that might have some photos of your ancestors. Try making a web-page and add a posting of your sur-name in a genealogy genforum, this is what helped me. — Darlene (Arbogast) Eastin, OH, Darlene913@aol.com

The Captain And The Marchioness

As my biological father never recognized me as his daughter I concentrated all my efforts in successfully documenting the genealogy of my foster parents, all from Uruguay. When I arrived in the US more than 40 years ago, along with my few precious possessions loaded in a 45-lb. suitcase, came a sheaf of now-yellowed paper which contained all the information my foster mother's prodigious memory produced.

It was not until recently that I made the decision to investigate my paternal roots. It all started with a letter to my paternal aunt in Montevideo, Uruguay, explaining who I was. She lovingly answered, surprised that a niece existed and so far away. Active correspondence followed and she started to share information with me on the family tree.

Along with information on immediate family, she sent a story handwritten by a deceased ancestress which told about the Spanish Captain José Cipriano Guasque with whom a Spanish Marchioness eloped. She was taken to his ship inside a rolled tapestry (her jewels wrapped in a shawl), carried by her servant, Juana. They had children born in different countries.

This romantic story piqued my desire to investigate them. This aunt, after she was able to give me all the information she remembered, fell into a cycle of senile dementia or Alzheimer's.

The IGI had an entry for a Joseph Guasque, baptized in Liverpool, UK in 1828. The record showed that his parents were the Captain and the Marchioness and gave the name of the Reverend and the witnesses. A later check into the British Isles Vital Records Index showed the Reverend's name along with his wife's and her father's name, one of the witnesses in the baptismal record.

I located and photocopied the maps of the street where they lived (near the harbor) and that of the church. At that time it seemed I was at a dead-end. I joined several message boards where I posted: *Conoces a Guasque?* (Do you know a Guasque?).

Four cousins answered: one from Italy and three from Brazil. They shared information and recommended getting in touch with other Guasque-surnamed families in the electronic White Pages and the Internet, which I did. I contacted everyone listed and explained my venture. Everyone gladly responded and I organized a cyber-reunion. Cousins who had not gotten in touch with each other for 10 and even 20 years were reunited and a spirited and jocular group of 22 families was formed.

I made a master e-mail address list and all agreed to send their messages to the entire group so everyone would have access to comments, photos and documents. We became a large family and great friends. They knew by then that I was going to write a booklet with all the information gathered and that it was going to be sent to each of the 22 families. Contributions started to come and the booklet quickly grew to be a book and I was soon inundated with copies of obituaries, data and family photos.

While visiting the FHL in Salt Lake City, I perused two Brazilian books, *Registro de Estrangeiros* (Register of Aliens), which showed two entries to Brazil by the Captain, in 1828 and 1838. What a find! I asked a member of the group in Rio de Janeiro to go to the National Archives and obtain photocopies of these two entries. The records were damaged by water and time, so it's hard to read the photocopies but the first one for 1828 is priceless: it mentions the Captain's name, 48 years old, born in Cartagena, Spain, accompanied by his wife Maria Cabeza (Cabeza de Vaca), and three small children: Exaltagao, Oscar (didn't know about these two) and Joseph-José, the one baptized in Liverpool, eight months old. The Captain's ship was a British Indiaman and he was at the service of His Majesty George IV. He was in Brazil to establish a business and they were all staying at the Hotel Imperial, etc.

My Personal Ancestral File software data has grown considerably and consists of 1,944 individuals. I have burned 23 GEDCOM cds and each of *The Guasque Lineage* book includes a copy. This book contains copies of all gathered information, maps, photographs, poems, music sheets, paintings, obituaries, e-mails, other Guasque surnames in the world, IGI findings and most importantly, the investigative process and accessed archives. It is written in both English and Spanish and most of the e-mail messages are in Portuguese.

Although I have recently mailed the books, the Guasque saga is not yet finished. The Library of Congress has copies for loan of an English register of ships and seamen which contains captain and crew names, names of ships, etc., from which I hope to glean further information about the Captain. Wish me luck! — Renée Roldán-Gadea Canals, NC

FreeBMD Success

When I began studying my Welsh ancestors, I knew very little. I decided to start with my great-grandfather, David Smith, as I had at least learned his place and date of birth, and the name of his first wife, Margaret Davies, who had died in 1892 at the age of 42. I also knew he had had two other wives and another son, Basil.

My first breakthrough came in the form of David's funeral card (1926), on which the name "Alice" appeared. Since David was 76 at his death, I assumed Alice was wife number three. The card came to me in a treas-

ure trove of family photos (sent over the years to my grandma from her sisters in Wales) which an aunt by marriage had kept for over 50 years and which no one knew she had.

When I downloaded a 1901 census page, I was astounded to find five Smith children, but no Basil: Hilda, Cuthbert, Brindley, Alice and Dorothy. The first two were born in Bromyard, Hereford, the others were born in Cwmtillery, Monmouthshire.

FreeBMD.com

Using Alice's approximate age and birthplace, I did a FreeBMD search through RootsWeb.com for all Alices born in Ringwood, Hampshire during the period 1860-65; there were 13 of them, none who had married a David Smith. I then found five marriages amongst those Alices, and, bingo, one of them — Alice Bevington, formerly Colbourne — had married a David Smith in 1895, but in the wrong place.

I found Alice on the 1881 census working in Worcester, just a few miles from Bromyard where a large Colbourne family was living, as it happens, in the next estate cottage to where my grandfather Price and his family were.

I also found Alice's marriage to Henry Bevington, from Worcester, in 1887, their entry on the 1891 census in Brecon, his death in the third quarter of 1894 in Cwmtillery, and a birth for an Alice Mary Bevington in the fourth quarter of 1894. Ergo, Hilda, Cuthbert, and Alice were Bevington children, Alice having been born after her father's death.

David and Alice's marriage certificate proved my Colbourne research. They must have slipped away to Newport for the weekend to marry.

But where was Brindley? And who was wife number two? And where was Basil?

I finally made contact with the only descendant of David Smith still living in Blaina, Monmouthshire who told me Brindley was the son of one of David's siblings and that the name of his second wife was Rachel Hone. I knew Brindley was not a sibling's son, due to the 1851-91 censuses.

I searched unsuccessfully for Rachel Hone for months. Finally, Brindley's birth appeared on FreeBMD and I sent for the certificate. His father was David and his mother was Rachel, all right, but Rachel Thomas, formerly Jones, not Hone.

The marriage of Rachel and David had been on FreeBMD all along, in 1893 in Crickhowell, Brecon. Brindley was born quite a few months "early" and Rachel died suddenly three months later. Basil appeared on FreeBMD in 1902.

Solving this puzzle has been one of the most rewarding and interesting genealogical journeys I have taken. — Jojo Smith, AB

Diligence Of Clerk

Preparatory to driving through an out-of-the-way area in my state or across a number of states, I've learned to turn to my computer. My genealogy software permits me to do a complete search of entries pertaining to places of death and/or known burial sites.

Thus, when time permits on a trip, we can frequently factor in a stop to the library to look for obituary columns as well as cemetery books provided by the city or the local genealogical society.

My husband and I were in Missouri during 1999 and we knew there was a lot of mystery about our son-in-law's grandmother. A search of the 1920 federal census found she'd been enumerated on 20 February 1920, so 1920 was the starting date to learn something about her death.

We stopped at a state office to order a death certificate, but were informed that since we weren't closely related to the deceased, we weren't permitted to do so. With an application form in hand, we filled it in to the best of our knowledge and sent it to the grandson to complete. After several weeks, in July, the response came: "The certificate requested is not on file." Not listed? Why not? More mystery.

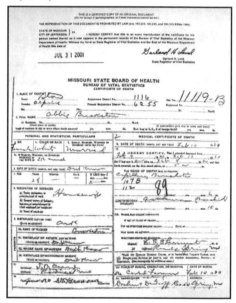

Death certificate for Abbie Curd, who was buried under her maiden name, Abbie Buckston.

Still unfulfilled and frustrated two years later, we urged our son-in-law to go through the application process again. In August 2001, Jim phoned us with the good news. He had the death certificate in hand. What was different this time? Our son-in-law's grandmother, Abbie Curd, had been buried under her maiden name, Abbie Buckston (also known as Buxton). Surprisingly, she'd died at the age of 28 after a 10-day illness of capillary bronchitis on 10 February 1920, just 10 days before she was to be enumerated. The census was retroactive to January 1 of that year when she was still alive.

It took a discerning, diligent clerk to look for a first name and confirm it with the surviving husband's surname. It also supports the old adage; if at first you don't succeed, try, try again. — Marjorie Stoner Elmore, CA

Extended Families Traveled Together

I guess that initially everyone is primarily concerned with tracing their father's family and even then concentrating on the father's family name. Once I had that line firmly established and traced back to England in the 1500s, I began to try to flesh out my family tree. No one in my family claimed to have any knowledge beyond a few generations.

My paternal grandmother's parents came from Arcola, IL and supposedly William H. Holland and his wife, Anna Hazen, were both born there. With William Holland, I was fortunate enough to find his father, George, born in Indiana and his father born in Ireland, probably Northern Ireland. However, with Anna Hazen I seemed to be getting nowhere. I checked every Hazen family site with queries about any Anna born in Illinois during that time period. Nothing showed up that matched.

There were several Annas and even a couple of Anna Hazens, but none fit exactly. One was born in Illinois but at the extreme southern end of the state with no known connection to the area I was researching. At that time I became familiar with a

few of the census sites available online. I found a 1900 census for Arcola, IL with William and Anna but it showed that Anna was born in Indiana, not in Illinois. There was also a difference in the age of what I thought she should be and what was recorded on the census. I looked for an earlier census of the same area and found an Anna Hazen as a daughter of Loring Lusk Hazen. Loring had several children living with him. Again the dates were not consistent, causing some confusion. However, she was in the right place and I didn't want to eliminate her as a possibility. One of her brothers was James Waldo Hazen and that name started ringing bells. I could not recall where, but I had seen that name before. Since I could not remember, I placed that name aside and continued my search.

I had assumed the genealogical duties from my aunt who was ready to pass them on following the publication of her short family history on the Worden family. She had told me that my paternal grandmother was raised by her grandparents in Louisiana because her mother, Anna, had died at a very young age soon after giving birth to her third daughter (my grandmother). Her father had been a Baptist minister. I also had learned that my great-grandfather Holland had visited Louisiana several times to learn about rice farming. Of course, I could not find any relatives in Louisiana. Everyone I had discovered came west into Indiana and Illinois and then down into Arizona. Well, here we were at a brickwall.

Some time later, I learned through an online Hazen family forum that a book, *The Hazen Family In America* by Tracy Elliot Hazen, was one of the best and most reliable sources to the history of the Hazen family. Unfortunately, there were very few copies available and they cost a lot more than I wanted to spend. However, I discovered, through a friend, that because I was a member of the McCracken County Public Library, I could access, at no cost to me, a paid website that had a copy of the book online. I visited the site and began a slow page-by-page study of the book. At the time I didn't think to look in the index for Loring's name. That would have saved me quite some time.

Eventually, I found what I was looking for. On pages 435 and 436, Loring Lusk Hazen was described, listing his Hazen ancestors, his first marriage with children, his second marriage with children, and, what I had been searching for, Anna.

Anna was born in Tobinsport, IN and died in Arcola, IL. It even listed her husband as William Holland and named one of three children, my grandmother's older sister, Lotta Belle. Her brother, James Waldo, was also listed. Loring was a Civil War veteran, a Baptist minister, and he had researched rice farming. Another daughter, Bertha Maria Hazen Creviston was listed as residing in Jennings, LA near Lake Arthur.

Slowly it was all coming together. At this time I had discovered that extended families and friends often traveled together and settled in the same areas. I did a 1910 census check of Jennings, LA and found Loring Hazen and his wife. These are the ones who raised my grandmother. As a fruit grower and rice farmer, he was the one my great-grandfather, William Holland, had visited in Louisiana to learn more. Also at that time, it dawned on me where I might have seen James Waldo Hazen's name. I checked at an online listing of Oak Grove Cemetery in Weiner, AR near where my father was born, and there he was. He obviously had traveled from Illinois with his brother-in-law to keep the family together.

Months later, I called my aunt to tell her of my discoveries. She was thrilled that I was doing something

with her mother's side of the family. When I shared with her that one of my real clinchers was the fact that James Waldo Hazen was buried right there in her home town, she replied. "Oh, Uncle Jimmy, yes I put flowers on his grave for Memorial Day."

Information on Loring and Anna Hazen, from The Hazen Family In America.

She had known that connection all along, but had failed to share it with me and I had not asked the right questions. By remembering that extended families often traveled together, I was able to find the Louisiana connection, which matched our family stories, and verify the correct Anna Hazen. — Robert Worden, KY

Who Is The Man In The Neck Scarf?

After my father passed away in 1998, my wife and I were looking through his possessions and found a box of pictures and other family related items. A large old photograph of a distinguished-looking gentleman was discovered wrapped in brown paper with a note taped to the outside asking "Who is the man in the neck scarf?" We had never seen it before nor discussed any unidentified photographs with my father. Now, of course, we couldn't ask him what he might know.

Memories fade with time, so we immediately embarked on a project to identify this mystery person. After consulting clothing-style books, we ascertained the man's clothing was from the early 1800s. Photography wasn't invented until the late 1820s and only came to America at the end of the 1830s. The photograph was obviously from an even later period because it was a large print and matted. There were no indications of who had taken the photograph either.

Since there might still be someone alive in my family who could identify the individual in the photograph, we made several copies and sent them off to relatives and others asking who he was. All the replies came back negative.

We even postulated the photograph might be of a relative dressed in period clothing. This meant it was going to be even more difficult to identify. We didn't know where to research next and had now hit the proverbial brickwall.

Since we travel in a motor coach most of the year, we frequently do genealogical research on-site. After a particularly full year of material gathering on Bradish and collateral lines, we stopped by to share what we had with my cousin, Juanita and her husband.

We hoped some of the material would supplement her book on the descendants of my ancestor, Robert Bradish. I was showing Juanita a chapter we had scanned into our computer from the *History of Oneida County, New York*, published in 1878, when she suddenly exclaimed, "There's your boy!"

In our haste gathering material to be analyzed later, we had missed the small but identical portrait of Dr. Alexander Coventry at the beginning of the biographical section. Alexander was born on 27 August 1776 near Hamilton, Scotland and died on 9 December 1831 in Oneida County, NY. This man was my third-great-grandfather and I had a photograph of him! Or did I?

It turns out that Alexander Coventry was the mysterious man in the neck scarf.

If Alexander Coventry died in 1831, how could this photograph of him as a young man have been taken before the widespread use of photography?

We took the photograph to an expert in old pictures and learned what we really had. It was a photograph of a black-ink print from an engraving of Dr. Coventry done on steel or copper. The mystery was finally solved thanks to our commitment to identify the portrait, researching collateral lines and the sharp eyes of my cousin. — Peter Bradish, TX, bradish@attglobal.net

It Pays To Be Determined

My great-grandfather, Julius R. Ford, served in the Civil War and that was pretty much all I knew about him.

While we were on vacation in New York State, we visited the state archives in Albany, as I wanted to look up the 1865 veterans' census. We were surprised and happy to find Julius' parents' names including his mother's maiden name and his full name (Julius Ransom Ford) along with the other census information.

Julius' pension paperwork from the NARA had no information regarding his date of death. Because his checks were sent to Ohio, we could ascertain that he was living near his brother in Ashtabula County. Ohio State Archives' death certificates start with 1908, so they were of no help, the Conneaut County Health Department had no information on him and the Ashtabula County Genealogical Society could find nothing on him either, so I went to the libraries. The Conneaut library assistant came up with an obituary which read as follows:

J H Marsh was called to his farm south of Cherry Hill yesterday by the sudden death of Julius R Ford, an old soldier who had made his home on the Marsh farm for 8 yrs. The deceased was seventy-six years of age and leaves a son in Ashtabula and two sons and two daughters in NYS.

I then went onto Google.com and searched for funeral homes in Conneaut, OH. From there I just picked one, the Marcy Funeral Home, and called that number. Lo and behold, they were the same firm that handled Julius R. Ford's burial in 1906! Their records revealed that he was 76 when he died and was "killed by cars" on 30 July 1906. The entry above his name was of another man killed at the same time, same day, and same place.

I don't think a lot of people know about the New York state veterans' census of 1865. I'm sure many use libraries but for those who don't, this shows how helpful they can be. Simply by doing an Internet search for funeral homes and a phone call resulted in more about Julius which was true and made his life story more interesting. My family tree certainly became enhanced. — Brenda Ford Miller, FL, Brenfm@tampabay.rr.com

Pay Attention To Your Instincts

When I started researching the Hollenback family, I kept coming across genealogies that claimed that the descendants of John and Elizabeth (Stanborough) (also spelled Stansbury) Hollenback had all been lost.

I found all kinds of erroneous data on the Internet. Some claimed that Elizabeth was born and died in Virginia. Some of the information has John dying in Virginia. The more I read, the more I became intrigued with this couple. The reality is John Hollenback was born on 24 May 1755 in Jonestown, Lebanon County, PA as the youngest child of John and Eleanor (Jones) Stout Hollenback and died on 22 August 1797 in Wilkes-Barre, PA. John was the younger brother to the well known Matthias Hollenback a survivor of the Battle of Wyoming, and often referred to as the Astor of the Susquehanna. Elizabeth was born in Virginia in 1747 and died in Owego, NY at the home of her son, John, on 2 January 1831. Both are buried in Wilkes-Barre, PA.

I knew a lot about Matthias but what about John and his wife Elizabeth? I read numerous histories about Luzerne County, PA and discovered that John and Elizabeth Hollenback did have two sons, John and Matthias. The younger Matthias was often referred to as Matthias II in order to distinguish him from his famous uncle. What about their descendants? From these same history books came a biography about Elizabeth's father which stated they had moved from Tyrone County, NY to Wilkes-Barre in the early 1770s. John and Elizabeth were married on 23 July 1778 in Lebanon County, PA, three weeks after the Wyoming Massacre. John and Elizabeth had been living in Wilkes-Barre and, just prior to the massacre, John led his sister Mary Ann Hollenback to safety down river to their former home in Lebanon County. It is my firm belief that he also led his future wife, Elizabeth, to safety as well.

Catherine Hollenback Comeau in a Wilkes-Barre cemetery.

In other genealogies, I found that John's eldest brother, George, and his wife Hannah (Barton) Hollenback had 17 children. Surely that must be a mistake and the more I researched it, the more I was convinced it was a mistake. Some of the dates did not seem to line up and I just knew something was amiss. Also, two of the sons were named John, one born in 1775 (my third-great-grandfather) and another John born in 1780, both who lived and that would be much too confusing for any family. John Hollenback Jr. (born in 1780) died in Owego, NY on 12 June 1847.

Knowing he left a large fortune to my second-great-grandfather, George W. Hollenback, I tried to find his will at the courthouse. It was listed in the register but was not at the courthouse. Then I searched for the obituary. The obituary stated that his business was being run by his nephew, George W. Hollenback (in fact he was a cousin, once-removed) and that he was survived by one brother, Matthias Hollenback of Wilkes-Barre. If he had been a son of George and Hannah he would have had many surviving siblings, not just one. And since his brother lived in Wilkes-Barre, surely this must be the son of John and Elizabeth.

It took more digging but I finally found the will I had been looking for, not in Owego, NY but in Wilkes-Barre, and it clearly states that he left his Wilkes-Barre property, formerly owned by his parents, John and Elizabeth, to his brother Matthias.

In the cemetery in Wilkes-Barre we found John and Elizabeth's gravestone and next to them are their son Matthias Hollenback and his wife; clearly parents and son. Elizabeth (Stanborough) Hollenback left a will as well. She inherited her father's mill and she, in turn, left it to her son, Matthias Hollenback II.

What about descendants? John and Susan (Welles) Hollenback never had any children which answers the question as to why my George went to live with his wealthy elder cousin and eventually became his trusted business partner.

What about the younger brother,

Matthias? The family lot in the cemetery had more burials of the family of Matthias.

Now the story gets rather strange. All genealogists have stories to tell about strange things happening while doing research. This is one of those occurrences that make you realize that you should always pay attention to those little odd happenings. I'm not going as far as to say the spirits are out there watching, but just pay close attention and follow those inner instincts.

We were finishing up our day at a large cemetery in Wilkes-Barre. We had found all the Hollenback lots, photographed the gravestones and were packing up to leave. I love walking in cemeteries and we were just walking around enjoying the general calm. As we walked down the hill towards the car, I was struck by the sheer beauty of a stone marker off to the left up a rather steep hill. It looked like a Grecian statue. Behind the statue was an open book and on the book names had been carved. But unfortunately all the letters had been obliterated by time. Upon close inspection, however, my husband managed to make out the last four letters of the name; "back". The name had been carved in an arch with the K being nearly halfway down the edge of the book, so it must be a long name. We photographed it from several angles and headed for home.

Once we got home we downloaded the photos onto our computer and were able to force in a few letters. The word "John" was in the middle and the numbers ??81 and 24. The ??81 must be 1881 and the number 24 could be a date or an age. I wrote the caretaker but never got a reply.

Then I found out that the Northeastern Pennsylvania Genealogical Society has an index for that cemetery so I wrote to them asking for all the Hollenback records they had. None matched my mystery stone.

Several years later, a genealogy came into my hands that showed one possible match. A woman married a man by the name of John Doyle, MD. She was born on 14 February 1857 and died on 12 February 1881; just two days shy of her 24th birthday. I then wrote to the NE Pennsylvania Genealogical Society asking for any Doyle records they might have. Now I know what the stone reads. The stone reads "Catherine Hollenback, wife of John Doyle, MD, 1857 — 1881, aged 24".

The barely legible grave marker for Catherine Hollenback Comeau was discovered purely by chance.

Since then, I have done more research, found obituaries and other information that proves that my John and Elizabeth, in fact, had many descendants and they are no longer lost to posterity. Catherine Hollenback was their great-granddaughter.

Pay attention to your instincts and follow your senses. — Catherine Hollenback Comeau, FL, cats14818@yahoo.com

Looking For Grandpa

While growing up in East St. Louis, IL in the late 1930s and early 40s, I was always told that my grandpa, Homer Weaver, died in 1910, shortly after my father was born. Family was never talked about and it was not until after my mother died in 1997 that I found pictures of my grandparents, Homer and Martha Reid Weaver.

After finding these photos and a little information, I became interested in family history. All I had to start with was the names of my grandparents and the names of my grandpa's parents.

In 1998, I began my search and it took me to California, Ohio, Kentucky, Tennessee and Pennsylvania. I found information on my Weaver Family as far back as 1569 in Switzerland but I could not find Grandpa.

After meeting a first-cousin, Daniel, we decided we would work together and concentrate on finding him. Grandpa was a big brickwall that we desperately wanted to climb.

While in Salt Lake City at the FHL, Daniel found Grandpa in the 1930 federal census listed as an inmate in the Oklahoma State Prison. With more diligent searching we were able to find that Grandpa had been sent to prison in 1929 for life for the murder of his second wife, who was not my grandmother, because they had separated some years before. Grandpa died in prison of heart problems in 1939. If it was not for the federal census, Daniel and I would still be searching for Grandpa. — Homer Weaver, IL, hhwcw@accessus.net.

An Analytical Method Of Resolving A Brickwall

My wife's maiden name is Tottman and tracing this name led to a village in northern Essex called Castle Hedingham. Along the way we discovered that the family name was also spelled Totman and that the two spellings were used quite randomly.

When we looked at the pre-1750 parish records for Castle Hedingham, apart from the difficulties in reading, the family was quite difficult to sort out. There were repetitions of first names of fathers, sometimes wives' names were given and sometimes they weren't. Finally I decided to transcribe them all into a Microsoft Excel spreadsheet. I had columns for the year of the event, the month and day in one column, child's first name, father's name, and finally, the mother's name. I had separate columns for baptism and birth dates because some entries gave the baptism date and others the birth date. I also kept the year in a separate column because the next step was to use the data sort feature since I wanted to sort the entries in chronological order.

I then sorted by the father's name, year and date to see what the list would look like. From disorder there now appeared to be some semblance of order, so I inserted rows between each group of fathers. I assumed that a child was born about every two years, for about 20 years, and it was possible to split, say, the John Totmans, into separate groups. I now had a semblance of order and it was possible to see that there were different families.

My next step was to make a list of all of the marriages, and again, making some assumptions, I was able to insert marriages into appropriate places. Fortunately, after 1700, the wife's first name was also given, and as a result it was easy to verify that some marriages fit the group of names. I then listed the burials and matched them up. Once everything was sorted and organized, I now had the early parish record entries grouped into families and was able to identify which families were in my wife's line.

Another way of using Excel spreadsheets is to analyze IGI data downloaded from the FHC computers as GEDCOM files. I have software that will convert these files into Excel, which can then be sorted and organized as required. For instance, a downloaded file of identical surnames can be sorted into parishes or by parents' names, so that families can be identified. — Robin A. Fairservice, BC, R&B.Fairservice@telus.net

Never Underestimate The Power Of County Bulletin Boards

Joseph and Pierra Christian Campbell emigrated from Tennessee to the Republic of Texas on 22 December 1841. They settled first in Nacogdoches County, then emigrated to San Saba County in about 1856. Pierra died in San Saba on 10 September 1862. I had searched every cemetery in San Saba and the communities surrounding San Saba, but could not find where she was buried. Finally, I submitted a query on the San Saba County GenWeb. (Should have done this at the beginning.)

After several weeks, I received an e-mail with the words "I found her!" In my query I only gave the name and death date, but the writer had included all the information on the grave-

stone and it was a match. Several months later we visited San Saba and met my correspondent at the entrance to a ranch. We drove across a cattle guard and through a pasture and finally arrived at the Smelser Cemetery.

To my surprise, this small cemetery, which is on private property (in the middle of nowhere), was fenced and beautifully maintained. I had finally found my second-great-grandmother's resting place.

Gravestone of Pierra L. Campbell at Smelser Cemetery in San Saba, TX.

I would never have found it had I not put a query on the county website. This is only half of my brickwall. The other half is finding Joseph's final resting place. He moved to another county after her death. I located him on an 1880 census, but nothing more. Maybe I will get lucky again. — Joan Petty Bounds, TX, jbounds@dbstech.com

Cockney Connection

When I took up genealogy in 1994, I decided to search first for the birth of my grandfather, George Henry Ward, because, although I knew nothing about his family, I had a solid clue to his identity, for he was immensely proud of being a true Cockney, "born within the sound of the Bow Bells." I already had his 1899 marriage certificate, revealing that he was 25 in 1899 and the son of George Ward, a school keeper. This one will be easy, I thought — how wrong I was!

The civil registration birth indexes revealed several George Wards born in London in the relevant period, but no George Henry. Nevertheless, I ordered birth certificates for the likeliest Georges, but none had a father named George. I widened my search to Greater London, but still no luck, and eventually I hired a researcher, who found George Ward, son of George, a carpenter, baptized in Shoreditch in 1874. Ah, I thought, here he is at last! But my researcher could find no birth registration for this child, and I could not prove he was my grandfather.

So for years thereafter, baby George Henry remained in limbo, no more than a twinkle in the eye of the City of London.

With the release of the index to the 1881 British census, I tried again, looking for six- to eight-year-old George or George Henry. None fit the description. I combed the 1891 census in the area where he later married, but couldn't find him or his father. However, I did find his future wife, Eliza Fuller, living with her parents, Isaac and Sarah, and her brother Firman.

When the 1901 census came online, I was elated, because by then George Henry was a married man with a six-month-old daughter, Winifred (my mother), born at 74 Bickerton Road, London. This gave me several reference points to search from.

My search on the 1901 census for George netted about 60 possibilities, but since the initial search doesn't give marital status or family relationships, it was hard to decide which image to call up. I ordered two or three, but none fitted. Next, I tried baby Winifred and found three born in London, but again none turned out to be correct. More money down the drain! As for Eliza, there were far too many results to make an informed choice. So, in case the Wards and Fullers might have been neighbors, I searched for Eliza's brother, Firman Fuller.

His unusual name was a bonus, and I easily found him, living with two unmarried sisters at 74 Bickerton Road, London — the very house where baby Winifred had been born, and, as it turned out, where she was still living. There, too, were her parents, the long-lost George Henry Ward and his wife, Eliza! It had been my misfortune that the entire Ward family was missing from the census index, but my great good fortune to find them in the same house as brother Firman.

I scanned the image eagerly for George Henry's birthplace, and was astonished (not to say disenchanted) to discover that he was not born in London at all, but a good 40 miles away in Gillingham, Kent — where, it

1901 census entry for George Henry Ward and family.

later turned out, his childhood was also spent! My Cockney grandfather was no Cockney after all.

I will never know for sure why he so persistently declared that he was. I can only conclude that, having worked in and loved London for nearly half-a-century, he had become so much a Cockney at heart that the truth of his birth had faded into insignificance in his mind.

There are two morals to this tale: first, don't take anything you're told as gospel, not even the teller's own birthplace! Second, if you're stymied by mistakes in the 1901 census index, try looking for relatives who might live nearby. I knew nothing of George Henry's siblings, but my lead to Eliza's brother paid off handsomely. My luck had changed at last! — Barbara Lynch, BC, pblynch@telus.net

Seeking Sally

For eight years, I searched for my third-great-grandmother   Sarah "Sally" Brown, born in March 1790 and died at the age of 105. I have two photos of her — but little information except her son's name Wadsworth Brown — my second-great-grandfather. I was told she lived her entire life in Granby or East Granby, CT. I visited the towns twice, as well as Simsbury and Canton, two other towns nearby. I checked town records, obituaries and town newspapers at the state library, census records — everything I could think of — to no avail.

The family Bible listed Sarah and Wadsworth, and penciled in next to Sarah's name was "Newell" — which I assumed was her husband's name. I spent over a year chasing Sarah and Newell Brown — all the way to Meigs County, OH. A roll of film ordered from the FHL showed ordinances of the church being performed on Sarah and Wadsworth in Canton, CT,

through information given by a seventh-cousin once-removed from Sarah in the 1920s. Still, I couldn't find more details on Sarah. Trips to various town facilities frustrated me with the lack of information on Sarah's origin and husband.

A year ago, out of frustration, I revisited the Granby town hall — to no avail again. A town clerk suggested I contact a local genealogist who helps run a small, private genealogy society in Granby. I made an appointment for the next week, and gathered my notes and things to show her.

I brought a copy of one of the photos of Sarah and of Wadsworth for her to keep in her files. As she greeted me, she told me she had located a little something for me. She handed me the missing obituary and I almost fell over. It had a sketched picture of Sarah "Aunt Sally" on it — the same picture I was holding as the photograph to give to the genealogist! You can just imagine the excitement we both had when we realized what we had there! Now we were sure we had the right person.

The records she produced, which seemed to be unavailable at the town hall, showed no husband and mentioned her four "illegitimate" children in the birth records. No husband was mentioned anywhere and the first two girls had different last names. Sons Newell and Wadsworth were also listed with no fathers noted.

This wonderfully helpful genealogist, on her own time, did more research into this line and I now have Sarah's line back many generations. There are one or two missing pieces to link her to the earliest Browns in Windsor, CT in the 1600s. With the help of several of her genealogist friends, my brickwall was starting to crumble, and quickly!

This experience taught me three things when faced with a brickwall: Ask if there is a local genealogy society in town or a local genealogist to speak to. Next, find out exactly where various towns in the area came from and what towns were originally part of another town — or even more than one at various times. I thought I had done this — but not back far enough to know that Windsor (where Sarah was actually born) and Bloomfield were in the equation. Strangely enough, I know both towns very well, but never realized the connection. Finally, check out church records in the various areas. I could have saved myself years of frustration if I had only followed these paths! — Barbara Stevens, CT, genealogybarb@snet.net

Multiple Marriages Provided The Clue

Back in the 1980s, before my use of the Internet, it was a painstaking process to find family information. And now, even with all the online databases, it is often difficult to put all the available clues to their best use. My solution to the question of where my husband's great-grandfather, Josephus Richardson, was born on 20 August 1855 was solved because we'd remembered the family story that he had been married at least three times.

My husband's grandfather, William Henry Harrison Richardson, was born to Josephus and his first wife, Jennie Hill, in Indianapolis, IN. Marriage applications for Marion County, IN do not exist for 1878; however, a marriage license has been copied from a microfilm. It does not include information on where the bride and groom were born.

However, a search for Josephus' subsequent marriages did provide birthplace information on one of them. When Josephus Richardson applied for a marriage license to his second wife, Jessie Edith Mayo, he indicated he was born in "Virginia, Mottocourtt Co.," (the clerk must have had a difficult time deciding

how to write Botetourt; in fact, it took some time for me to decide what was intended). He also indicated his parents as Joel Richardson and Amy Carrol.

Later, I was able to verify his parents' marriage in *Botetourt County Marriages, 1770-1853* (1987): "Richeson, Joel & Anna Carrell — 11 Nov 1852; license only; age pro by William Carroll." (Don't let spelling variations deter your search!)

Josephus Richardson's application for a marriage license.

Incidentally, Josephus' third marriage, to Catherine Murray (he divorced Jessie) in 1914 (which also ended in divorce) did not indicate Botetourt County; it only listed Virginia.

It pays to check any and all marriage applications that include your ancestor's name. You may even pick up some other details as Josephus' applications did, e.g., the year his first wife died and the year of his divorces. (He married and divorced his second wife twice!) Wish I had known him! — Joan Griffis, IL

Ad In Local Norwegian Newspaper Locates Family

All I knew about my grandfather was that he was from somewhere near Oslo, Norway. An aunt had an old business card of his that said Eidsvoll on it. We felt he was probably from that town which is near Oslo in Akershus County.

I found him and his parents and siblings on the 1865 and 1875 censuses on microfilm. They lived in a crofter or servant's home, on the large Frilset farm called Frilsetaasen. The Eidsvoll (also spelled Eidsvold) church records were destroyed in a fire. We were going to Norway in 1988 to visit family on my grandmother's side of the family in North Trondelag. One of those relatives suggested we put an advertisement in the Eidsvoll newspaper. We put in the photograph of my grandfather Ole Henriksen and one of his sisters who also came to America. We asked if there were any descendants of a sister who remained in Norway and whose name was Hilda Henriksen.

Two weeks before we were to leave for our trip, our advertisement was answered by a man who was a retired local postman and interested in genealogy. He knew the area well and knew the family of Hilda Henriksen.

Two weeks later we met all of the family and were taken to the farm home, a husmann's place or servant's home, on the large Frilset farm, where Ole was born. People in Norway

Bev Nelson's grandfather, Ole Henriksen, and one of his sisters.

rarely moved very far away for generations and often still live in the same area. It is most likely someone in the area will know of your family, even generations back.

If you put an advertisement in the paper there is a good chance you may hear from someone who knows your family. — Bev Nelson, WA

Connecting The Dots

When we were children we all did connect-the-dot drawings where you use a pencil to discover what object is defined by the numbered dots. In genealogy, you not only have to connect the dots but you have to find them first. You never know how many you might find or where or what picture they will create. Brickwalls arise when there are not enough dots evident.

My wife's maternal grandfather, George Doyle, was a mystery to us. He died in northern New York when my mother-in-law was very young. She did not know his birth date, birth place, his marriage date or his death date. The few living relatives seemed equally vague in their knowledge. We knew his name was George Joseph Doyle and his parents were John Doyle and Margaret Barr and that George died in the mid-to-late-1920s in Ogdensburg, NY and that he was Catholic.

I started chipping away at this brickwall long before the Internet was available and when my travel budget was not-existent. I searched various US census listings for Doyles. Doyles were plentiful, especially Johns and Georges, but this particular family was very elusive. I requested a search of birth records from both the state and the county and gained nothing. Similarly, I requested a search of death records and found nothing. Such frustration resulted in little effort for several years.

When the Internet became available to me, I resumed my assault on my brickwall. Online access allowed me to perform detailed searches of the 1900, 1910 and 1920 census records using improved indexes. I found the Doyles in the 1900 and 1910 censuses, but after much searching I was unable to find any of them in the 1920 census, yet I know they lived St. Lawrence County at that time. The census records yielded details that were useful but still plenty of mystery remained.

What to do? Common responses to such problems include trying to think outside the box and try something new, looking for new sources, reviewing every detail you already have, renewing your efforts to cover all of the conventional bases, using query boards, contacting living relatives and giving up. I decided to try all but the last one.

I searched and posted on several of St. Lawrence County and Doyle surname bulletin boards. Nothing. I wrote to living relatives. Still nothing. I started compiling data on all Doyles and Barrs in St. Lawrence County from census information hoping to tie things together. Looking at neighbors and geography yielded nothing useful.

My review of existing information revealed notes I had taken years before when a relative took me on a cemetery tour. I had little recollection of this long-ago tour and the relative was now deceased. I had made a detailed description of the burial place of George Doyle and his wife but there was no stone on the grave in the Catholic cemetery. The cemetery knowledge led me to assume what church would have been involved in his funeral. I sent letters to a Catholic church in Ogdensburg for marriage or death information. This yielded marriage and death information on George. I was then able to obtain an obituary for George and then for his father, John.

The problem of the Doyles missing in the 1920 census still puzzles me. I did note that the Barrs were enumerated on the same day that George Doyle and Margaret Barr were married. Were the Doyles missed because they were busy with wedding preparations?

Revisiting all of the Doyle family groups I had detailed from census records, I was quickly able to connect the proper families and determine the relationships of four generations of Doyles back to Owen Doyle who emigrated from Ireland. Now to tackle finding where Owen originated and when he came to the US. My speculation is he was part of the Potato Famine exodus, but that is a new wall.

It sometimes takes a long time to find an adequate number of dots and get them connected but when you do… you soon find you need more dots for the next generation! — Greg Wight, TN, eggwight@msn.com

In Search Of Uncle Robert

My brickwall was an obstruction to finding my great-uncle, Robert Presland.

My grandfather was Arthur Augustus Gibbs and he was married to Sarah Louisa Presland. Sarah had a brother named Robert Presland. He would be an uncle to my father and a great-uncle to me. I could not find his birth registration; however, I hoped the censuses might provide the elusive answer.

The 1871 British census did not show a Robert Presland but it did show an address for some Preslands in Great Yarmouth, Norfolk at 99 Theatre Plain. Thomas Presland as head, married age 36, a painter, born at Bury St. Edmunds, Suffolk, and Sarah Presland, wife, 36, also born in the same place. However, also listed was my father's mother, Sarah (Louisa) Presland, nine-years old according to the census. It also included her brothers, James and Alfred, but no Robert Presland.

The 1891 British census did show a Robert Presland, age 19, and his sister, Sarah Louisa Presland, age 27, at 9 Row 117, Yarmouth. Then I discovered a boarder at the same residence by the name of Arthur Augustus Gibbs, my grandfather.

When requesting a birth registration from a researcher in England for a Robert Presland, his age subtracted from the 1891 census to give me a date of 1872 — I was told the following: There is a Robert Prestland (with a T), boy, his father is T. Prestland, occupation: painter, mother is Sarah Prestland (formerly Chinery) — address: Theatre Plain, (Great) Yarmouth, registered on 30 January 1872.

I told the researcher that this must be my uncle Robert. But the researcher said "No, it's Prestland not Presland." I said all the facts seem to fit like the address, the parents, etc. So I purchased the copy and I am more than satisfied.

Birth entry of Robert Presland (incorrectly listed as Prestland).

However, just to be sure, I looked up the 1901 British census and found Sarah Ann Presland (formerly Chenery), 66, head-charwoman, grandmother of Cecil Gibbs at 20 Row 113, Yarmouth; James Presland, 33, son, single, housepainter and Robert Presland, 29, son, single, market porter.

Success is achieved by sleuthing through the data and putting the pieces of the puzzle together correctly!

Unfortunately, I have not yet found what happened to Arthur Augustus and Sarah Louisa. — Ken Gibbs, ON, ken.gibbs@sympatico.ca

Reviewing Old Information Really Paid Off

I am researching my mother's family. I found an index showing her grandfather's marriage record. I sent to the county clerk for a copy. After several weeks, I received the marriage record. It had been tri-folded with the marriage license showing. Of course, I was so excited to get this; I immediately filed it in a document protector in my family binder.

After hitting my brickwall, I spent an afternoon going back reviewing.

Imagine my surprise when I turned the plastic page and noticed the writing on the back! There were their parents' names and places of birth. What a gold-mine. I still don't know how I missed it but reviewing old information really paid off. — Kathy Robarts, FL, grob44@gte.net

What Goes Around Comes Around

I started researching my paternal side of the family because my grandfather had died when my father was just six-years old. As a result, my father couldn't tell me anything about him.

I spent a lot of time trying to find out where he was interred and since he was from Brooklyn, NY, I decided to take a shot in the dark and call around to all the cemeteries to see where he was buried. However, I did stumble upon a McCandlish family plot in a cemetery in Brooklyn. They would only let me know that there was one there but wanted me to pay $28 per person for the information, and there were five people in the plot. I was disappointed. I know that my name is not a common one but I didn't want to put out over $100 unless this was, in fact, my family, so I started making inquiries to people who did look-ups.

Luckily, I came upon an angel who went to the cemetery and took a photo of the gravestone. She wrote me back listing the names of my ancestors: Jessie (great-grandmother) James (great-grandfather) James (great-uncle) Helen (great-aunt) and Jenny. I'd never heard of a Jenny in our line before so I made calls to my father. "Nope, she can't be related,

I've never heard of her," he said. My uncle also said the same thing. I am thinking she had to be related, otherwise, why is she buried there and if she isn't related, then who is she?

So began my four-year journey to figure out who this person was. From the information on the gravestone, I knew she was born in 1905 and died in 1925. I scoured the Internet using various search engines, censuses and even looked in the Ellis Island records because I know my great-grandparents had come through there; but still couldn't find this mysterious Jenny. I then did a general search through the McCandlishs and found a Jane. (Many times Scottish ancestors had many variations of names like Jenny, Jean and Jane — they were all the same.)

It stated clearly that Jane was going to Brooklyn to be with her father, James McCandlish (I knew this was her because I recognized the address) and noticed that unlike my grandfather and his brother who were born in England, she was born in Pennsylvania. I had realized that she was a sister of my grandfather. She had died young. I wanted concrete evidence of who she was so I started hunting down records. I wrote to the office of the Register of Wills in Pennsylvania and asked for a copy of her birth certificate and got a response that stated they had no record of her there. So I

Dear Ms. Carriler:

This is to acknowledge receipt of your letter dated April 14, 2004. We researched our records and couldn't locate Jenny McCandelish. I would need more information. If you have a date of death then maybe it could help us search broader.

If I can be of any further assistance, please fell free to contact me at the telephone number provided above.

The letter (top) Bonnie Carriles received from the cemetery informing her that there was no formal record of a Jenny McCand(e)lish buried there, despite the fact she had a photograph of the grave (bottom).

decided to write to Brooklyn to a church where I had found that my family frequented and they had no records of her either. I then wrote to the Municipal Archives of the City of New York to request a death certificate. That also came back with no record. I then decided to write again to the birth records office to find out some information and again got nothing. I then contacted the cemetery and got a nice person who would only tell me the funeral home that performed her services. I called them hoping to find something and got nothing.

After two years of searching, I decided to take my chances and write to the cemetery again to see if they would help me. They stated they had no records of her being there. If I hadn't had the photograph of the actual gravestone in my hands I would have believed that this woman never existed. I had exhausted all of my resources, and pretty much gave up all hope.

I then began researching my maternal family in Chicago and asked a lady to do a look up for me and she ended up referring me to another woman who goes to the NARA every so often to look up information. I wrote to her to get some records on my Italian family but Jenny still haunted me. So I asked her if I could make an unusual request even though I knew she only did Chicago requests but thankfully she obliged. I sent her the background information, as well as detailing the difficulties I was having trying to get some kind of evidence that this Jenny had actually existed. Through her hard work, I ended up with my documentation. She managed to find a death certificate for Jenny which had all the necessary information that I needed to place her in our tree.

I have been lucky enough to find wonderful volunteers to help me in my search. I think a lot of times I could not do this without the help from others. Of course, when I started out I wanted to do everything myself. However, I soon realized that it isn't possible. And everyone knows, what goes around comes around.

I believe that one of the best resources genealogists have are each other. — Bonnie Carriles, VA, krazyb73@aol.com

Even If You Think An Idea Won't Be Fruitful, Give It A Try

I knew that a great-grandfather of mine, Dennis McHugh, who lived in Summit Hill, PA, had a sister, Josephine, who moved to San Francisco some time in the 1870s or 1880s. My great-grandfather actually died out there when he went to visit his sister.

I had very small obituaries on both of them from the *San Francisco Chronicle*, which gave no information other than the dates of death. I had also contacted the funeral home in San Francisco, but they had no further information. My assumption was always that his other sisters and brother had all stayed in Summit Hill. Over the years, I searched the church records and census records, but could never find them.

One day, while surfing the Internet, I saw an address for the cemetery where I knew the sister was buried. I decided to take a chance and write to the cemetery association to see if they had perhaps some little bit on these two people buried there. I never expected to get anything back.

A month went by and to my surprise I received an envelope full of information. It seems the sister had eight lots and from the information recorded on who was buried there, I was eventually able to find out that all the family, with the exception of my great-grandfather, went west.

I was able to track down a lot more information from obituaries that I was then able to send for, but the most important find of all was that the mother of this family had also gone west with them and she died in 1910. I was able to get a copy of her death certificate which recorded the names of her parents and so got one more generation back. Since this family was Irish, getting that information was a treasure.

If I hadn't taken a chance, even though I expected nothing, I would not have received such a treasure trove of information. I did have to pay $25 for the material, but it was well worth the price. — Pat Shirock, PA

He Was There All Along

One of my brickwalls involved the family of my great-grandfather, Daniel Moul (originally Maul; also found as Moule/Mowell/Mowelle). Some 42 years ago, when I was a novice researcher using information from relatives, I started from where Daniel died and followed him back in time. I obtained Civil War pension records, searched censuses, vital records, etc. Eventually the search for this family led to York County, PA, where I found birth records for two of Daniel's siblings. Daniel's brother John was born there, and I had John's birth date. After finding a christening record for John, I looked for other children of the same parents in York and surrounding counties and found only Daniel's sister, Catherine, in the same parish as her brother John.

I knew from Civil War papers and other sources that Daniel and some other family members had lived in Ohio. So I looked for Maul/Moul names in federal census records for Ohio. On the 1850 census, I found a

family in Franklin Township, Franklin County, OH, headed by Christian Moule (male, age 45) with 10 others, ages four to 27. The 27-year-old was Kesiah, a female, perhaps Christian's wife. Among them were names I recognized: Mary, John, Daniel and Henry, but the other six were unfamiliar to me. I did not find a family headed by Heinrich (Henry) Moul whom I knew was my Daniel's father.

Louise Nelson's great-grandfather, Daniel Moul.

I assumed that perhaps Christian was a brother or cousin to Heinrich as there were a number of Maul families listed in that Ohio census. And I knew from other experiences that it was quite common for many branches in a family to use similar names for their children. I could find no records for Christian Moule, male or female.

Further research in Franklin County revealed that Heinrich's wife, Christiana, remarried in 1852. With continued research in that area I found more information about Daniel's brother, Emanuel Moule and family. A marriage record for Emanuel Maul and his wife is included in his Civil War records, but I have not yet found it in York County, PA records. There still were not enough clues to put him in my family, although later I determined that he was my great-uncle. He had appeared twice on the 1850 census, once with his wife and child, and also with his mother and siblings.

About 25 years after first finding the Christian Moule 1850 census record, I returned to researching this family. That 1850 census record kept nagging me. I had seen the name Christiana as Christian, presumably with the A pronounced "ah". So I decided I would take another look. There crumbled one brickwall. When I looked at the gender column, I discovered that the census taker had apparently erased F for female and changed it to M for male. All those years I had my great-grandfather's family and didn't know it. I have since been able to add a few more facts about the family in Illinois, Indiana and Ohio.

So, as has been said many times before, carefully examine records, take good notes, look back over your notes often, and revisit some of the records if there is any chance that there might be a mistake.

Now, if I can only find the birthplaces of Heinrich's other children, and more information about Heinrich and Christiana. Breaking through one brickwall often leaves you facing another one. — Louise Nelson, UT

A Tale Of Two Janes And One Fred

A small picture labeled "Fred Osgood Half Uncle to my Father" was a brickwall for longer than I care to acknowledge as I was compiling a family history, *Finding Our Family In Fryeburg, Maine.*

This picture was among a large stack that I inherited from my late great-aunt, who was not always accurate in her details. I really wanted to include "Uncle Fred" in the family tree, but the question was which branch?

The mystery about him increased when I found, in the library of the Fryeburg Historical Society, a sizable file of newspaper clippings for Frederick Blanchard Osgood, with one stating "He was the son of Maj James [my third-great-grandfather] and Jane Harnden Osgood... and was born in this village [Fryeburg] in 1851" and, "Mr. Osgood was an uncle of the late Maj Winchester Osgood, who fell in 1896 fighting for the Cubans."

Boston Daily Globe.

FRIDAY, DEC 6, 1901.

Death of Frederick B. Osgood.

FRYEBURG, Me, Dec 5—News of the death of Frederick B. Osgood of North Conway was received here today. He died suddenly at Lowell. Mr Osgood was a prominent attorney of the Carroll county bar. He was the son of Maj James and Jane Harnden Osgood, a cousin of the late James R. Osgood and was born in this village in 1851.

He was a graduate of Bowdoin college in 1875. He was a member of the New Hampshire legislature several terms, was county solicitor for Carroll county two or three terms and was one of the directors of the North Conway loan and banking company.

Mr Osgood leaves one brother, Edwin S., and a sister, Mrs James M. Weeks of Chatham, N H.

Mr Osgood was an uncle of the late Maj Winchester Osgood, who fell in 1896 fighting for the Cubans.

Obituary for Frederick B. Osgood as it appeared in the Boston Daily Globe.

It happened that just a few days earlier we met the great-niece of Winchester Osgood, who was a grandson of James Osgood and his first wife. My curiosity was really aroused — I had to determine whether Uncle Fred and Frederick Blanchard Osgood were the same person!

I was using the book *A Genealogy Of The Descendants Of John, Christopher And William Osgood*, published in 1894, as a guide to my Osgood ancestors. It stated that "Maj. James Osgood married, second, Jane Henderson, of Denmark, Me." This book listed only the ten children of the Major and his first wife, including my second-great-grandfather, but no one named Fred. Jane's maiden name of Henderson had been repeated in some hand-written family genealogy which a cousin had passed on to me. I had no record of any children from that second marriage, but the Fryeburg file of clippings led me to the conclusion, with some effort, that they had four children, with Uncle Fred being the youngest, and the fourteenth child of Major James Osgood.

The answer to the question of the correct name for his second wife appeared in the transcribed Fryeburg marriage records which stated "Jan 31, 1844 Marr. Intent. Mr. James Osgood of Fryeburg and Miss Jane Harnden of Denmark. Cert. granted July 16, 1844."

Uncle Fred and Frederick Blanchard Osgood were the same person, and Great-Aunt Hattie was right in saying Fred Osgood was a half-uncle to her father. — Emma Osgood Jones Hann, OH, wdhann@wcnet.org

Get All The Birth Certificates You Can

Always obtain all certificates for family members that you can. This can fill in details regarding relationships, geography and place names.

Several of my Irish ancestors lived in places that are not shown on maps.

Newtown Saville is a group of three townlands in Clogher parish, County Tyrone. The townlands are Dunbiggan, Lisnarable and Tamlaght. The McGinn family lived there and it was impossible to decipher which of the three townlands my McGinn family called home. The land records would list names by townland but on their civil registration records the McGinns always listed their home as Newtown Saville. I had several death certificates, baptismal records and birth records but all listed Newtown Saville as residence. The land records showed that there were McGinns at Dunbiggan and Tamlaght in the appropriate time frame.

It was not until I received Ally McGinn's birth certificate from 1870 that her place of birth was listed as Tamlaght, and not Newtown Saville, that I had a better idea of my family's location. — Kevin Cassidy, NE kmct@earthlink.net

An Answer Found Because Of An Article I Wrote

I broke through my brickwall in an unusual way. I was told a certain ancestor was Indian. There was no proof, just a very strong family legend. Her name was Elizabeth Barbara and she was married to a George Kunfer of West Penn Township, Carbon County, PA.

I searched for years trying to come up with her maiden name. I looked in church record books for Elizabeths born in the time frame, but could never make a family connection. I had just about given up when I answered the plea of the editor of *Penn Pal*, a little publication of Palatines to America, for someone — anyone — to write some articles. The editor was in desperate need of fillers. I am neither a historian nor professional genealogist, but he was willing to let me submit some articles.

After my first article on our local historical society appeared in print, I received a phone call from a Mr. Donat. Mr. Donat lived in my area and was one of the very few people who could translate early German script wills into English. While talking to Mr. Donat, he asked me which families I was researching and when I mentioned my dilemma with Elizabeth Barbara, he said I should hang up and he would call me back. He believed he had just translated her father's will. I was dumb struck! Could it be possible?

It was. Her father was Philip Jacob Shellhammer and she and her husband were mentioned by name in his will. Time and location also fit. I never did prove the Indian connection, but to have discovered this whole new family was wonderful indeed. And to imagine it came about because of an article I wrote. — Pat Shirock, PA

Bumpy Road Ends In Success

My research on my great-grandfather John Osborn Mars, was down a "bumpy road". From census records, I knew he was born in Tennessee. I finally found guardianship of him, a sister and brother, all minor children of William Mars in Wayne County, TN. Each was with a separate family household. The guardian of my John Osborn Mars was William Galleghley. I later found Galleghley was his stepfather as he had married William Mars' widow.

Finally in 1982, I noticed a full-page query from David Bunton, of Fayetteville, AR in a *River Counties* magazine about his relatives John Osborn Roberts and wife, who had 13 children. The first child was Sarah Elizabeth "Sally" Roberts who married first William Mars and then

William Galleghley in Wayne County, TN. This gave me a maiden name for William Mars' wife. From this finding, I made a trip to the Wayne County courthouse.

John Osborn Mars.

Among my findings was the will of John Osborn Roberts. In this will he mentioned his daughter Sarah Elizabeth, wife of William Mars. This showed me my great-grandfather was named after his grandfather, John Osborn Roberts. — Irene Barnes, MS

Rescued By Militia Rolls And Church Records

I had traced my Jackson line back to Gwinnett County, GA when my brickwall appeared.

A sketch in Flanagin's *History of Gwinnett County* said William Jackson married Sarah Smith and came from South Carolina to Georgia, where he died in 1849. Census records showed that before 1830, their children, one of whom fit my ancestor, John, were born in South Carolina. The 1820 census for Fairfield County, SC seemed to be them, but led nowhere. I made contact with a distant cousin in

Georgia who said that the family legend was that William was an orphan and Sarah was of Dutch descent. This same legend also mentioned Sarah's Dutch Bible.

No other evidence of them in South Carolina surfaced, even after much effort, until a book of Georgia militia rolls for the Civil War was published, showing L. Jackson, age 52, physician, residing in District 444, Gwinnett County, GA, enrolled in the militia on 14 December 1863, and giving his birthplace as Lexington County, SC. This was like opening a logjam, as this was undoubtedly Lemuel, first child of William and Sarah and brother of my John, whose family was listed in the 1850 census next to that of Lemuel and their widowed mother, Sarah, in that very same district. Lemuel was a schoolteacher then, but was shown as a physician in the 1860 and 1870 censuses. William Jackson

Gravestones of William and Sarah Smith Jackson in Prospect Methodist Church Cemetery, Gwinnett Co., GA.

was also listed just three households away from John Smith in the census of 1810 for Lexington County, SC.

My effort now was vigorous, though the problem still appeared insoluble due to a great paucity of records, most of which had been lost in the Civil War. Fortunately, however, this section of South Carolina, northwest of Columbia where the Saluda and Broad Rivers join, and earlier called Saxe-Gotha (now mostly in Lexington County), was initially settled primarily by German and German-Swiss, beginning around 1740 and the Lutheran churches tended to keep careful records. One of their later churches was St. Michael's Lutheran. Their old records were pre-

served, showing William and Sarah Jackson as members from its beginning in 1813 until at least Easter of 1816, when they moved just north and fit an 1820 census listing in Fairfield County.

Those church records gave family data, showing Sarah Smith was born on 19 February 1793. This matched exactly with the date on her gravestone in the Prospect Methodist Church Cemetery, Gwinnett County, GA, where she was also shown as the wife of William Jackson. Her parents were given as John Smith (born on 20 April 1770) and Elizabeth "Kencler" (Künzler, born on 11 May 1772) who married on 8 March 1792.

This family and church data explained why two grandsons of William and Sarah were named John Kenzler Jackson and William Luther Jackson. William and Sarah's daughters, Mary Ann and Elizabeth, were found to be names of two of Sarah's sisters and her mother. Sarah's old Bible in Dutch, or German, had probably come from her parents, as she was their first child. Her Künzler line arrived in South Carolina in 1737 from St. Margrethin, canton of St. Gallen, Switzerland. — Don R. Jackson, MO

How I Saved Myself From Chaos

It has been over 35 years since I was infected with that incurable disease known as genealogy. Like most ailments, it arrived slowly and inconspicuously. But it grew and soon began to consume me with a passion, which allowed for fewer and fewer outside activities.

As time went by I found that I was drowning in heaps of notes on bits of paper and Xerox copies taken from reference books from libraries I had visited all over the country. My list of ancestral names was growing and I was creating a mass of material which needed to be categorized if I ever hoped to find anything.

First came accordion folders, soon replaced by loose-leaf notebooks. Today, I have about 50 loose-leaf files organized by family name. Each family name is sectioned off by Xeroxed copies, mail correspondents and family group sheets. At the head of each family group sheet section is a tree chart beginning with the daughter's name (where the name daughtered out) and including the generations of that name as far back as I have been able to go.

I am a member of the Mayflower Society, the Connecticut Society of Genealogists and the New England Historical Genealogical Society. I found that I could maintain a personal typewritten list of queries for my brickwalls and pop them into the query sections of those periodicals at regular intervals, (always maintaining updates gleaned from any responses I might get.) All well and good, and then, about 20 years ago, along came the computer, and eureka!

It took me a little over a year to input all the information I had gathered into my Personal Ancestry File program. And then along came e-mail and the Internet. What a wonderful advance. I find that if the Internet is used much like one would use the IGI (i.e.: as a pointer and with a grain of salt) it can be a fantastic tool, and what wonderful clues you can get.

If it's time for a new reorganization, the following tips can help: I keep a database file alphabetized to my family names, which contains all

e-mail responses to my queries.

I also maintain and keep up to date a file of about 50 queries for "my end of liners" and brickwalls which I toss onto the genealogical bulletin board query pages at regular intervals.

I keep a set of short GEDCOMS for major family lines, which can be uploaded as needed. I find that most family lines only last for four to seven generations before they daughter out so I have a ready made set of over 50 descendants charts that can be uploaded upon request, the same applies to a set of family Ahnentafels.

I also keep a database, by family name, of names and addresses of those who have written me so that I may refer others following the same line.

I scan all pages of Xeroxed material from library genealogical reference books and keep these pages in a special file under family name headings. Pertinent parts can then by copied and then added to the notes sections of my Personal Ancestral File database.

After all is said and done, why is it that since I am so well organized, I still can't relax but must keep up the constant search for those elusive and frustrating ancestors? — Frank Bouley, NJ, FBouley@prodigy.net

Sometimes Oral Traditions Really Are True

I was chasing up my second-great-grandmother's (Almina Webster Scribner) line, and chasing downwards at the same time (Noah Staples and Rutha Bradford), trying to prove a Mayflower William Bradford connection. I'd been working on this line for decades.

I knew that Mina's maternal grandmother was born in Kingston,

MA, and that her maternal grandfather was from New Gloucester, ME. I found they had moved to the hinterlands of Maine, in Franklin County and in particular, Flagstaff, where he was involved in farming and lumbering. Almina was said to be born in Eustis, ME, and died in Framingham, MA.

Through various documents and censuses, I determined the families lived in various places over the years, including:

1778 New Gloucester, ME

1805-19 Flagstaff, ME (children's births)

1815 Bethel, ME (according to *Early Settlers of Weld, ME*)

1815 Weld, ME

1821 Augusta, ME

1838 Iddo Jr. and Rutha Staples marriage in Eustis or Sumner, ME

1850 Jackson Plantation, ME

1860 Eustis Plantation, ME (census)

If you're familiar with Flagstaff, you'll know that it was flooded and no longer exists. Records from any of the area towns such as Eustis are difficult, if not impossible, to find. There are no records in Eustis prior to 1892, and the state archives turned up nothing. Local historical societies didn't have records that were helpful in obtaining proofs.

But the 1870 census connected my second-great-grandmother and her parents; I was fortunate. And I was lucky enough to find transcripts of the Stratton Upper Cemetery in Eustis online while doing a general search for the family name, where listed were my fourth-great-grandmother, along with my third-great-grandparents.

Although not a brickwall any longer, thanks to online resources, I was eager to get photographs of the gravestones and to find out any other information I could. Eustis is a long trip from anywhere, and traveling there was not an option. I used the Internet to search Eustis for anyone with the family name of Scribner, and then wrote the two people who turned up in the results. It was a long shot, but for the cost of a stamp, more than worth a try.

Well, to my surprise, I received a letter back with photos of the gravestones — my cousin had trampled through the snow for me — as well as a typed family genealogy that contained information that was not extant elsewhere. Bonanza! Not only did I get more data, but I connected with a very nice man whom I'm pleased to call "cousin".

As an aside, my grandmother, Ruth Bradford Wells, had always been told by her father that she had a Bradford Mayflower connection and called her "Rutha" although her birth

Panoramic view of Stratton Upper Cemetery in Eustis, ME, the location of the Scribner family gravestone (inset).

certificate was Ruth. She always thought that it was a diminutive pet name. It wasn't until I received the photos of the gravestones that it was apparent that her father had really named her after his grandmother, Rutha. And Rutha was named after her mother, Rutha. What I thought, and the transcribers thought, was Ruth A. Scribner was really Rutha Scribner.

Ruth Wells — 1917.

I wish my grandmother was still alive to learn that and see that I proved the Mayflower connection, too! I learned that sometimes oral traditions really are true. — Perry Lowell, perry_lowell@hotmail.com

Tony's Continued Quest

The query placed on Ancestry.com's website in December 2000 read:

Need information on Gilbert Hastings born between 1910-1920 who lived in New York City in 1935. His mother's name may have been Rose.

The reply almost one year later on 22 October 2001 read:

I think the Gilbert Hastings you are inquiring about is my cousin. His moth-er's name was Rose. Both are deceased. Can you tell me what your interest is? Perhaps we can be of assistance to one another. Gloria.

Before I did the researchers' happy dance, I convinced myself that this was probably another dead-end. We had followed many leads in recent months to locate Tony's (not his real name) father only to be disappointed over and over again. However, I felt encouraged, and typed a reply.

Gloria was told my friend's adoption story and I gave her some details without revealing his identity. He had already suffered disappointment and I didn't want to add to his anxiety until I had more information in hand. Gloria was a little skeptical at first to give me much, but she e-mailed me a birth date that matched the birth record my sister found in Fayette County, WV. She gave death dates for Gilbert, his mother Rose, and a sister, along with place of burial on the same lot with Rose's father in Cabell County, WV. She also said Gilbert had served in the Merchant Marines during WWII.

A request was sent to Vital Statistics for death certificates for Gilbert and Rose. I also e-mailed the West Virginia newspaper for copies of obituaries. With the arrival of the obituaries via snail mail, we noted that in addition to being a Merchant Mariner, Gilbert was a member of the Veterans of Foreign Wars (VFW). Another letter was sent to the VFW address obtained from the Internet. In three days, the commander telephoned me with the information in their files, plus he promised to send necessary forms to apply for papers detailing Gilbert's service. Those forms arrived in good time and we sent them on with copies of his birth and death certificates to Washington, DC.

Our application was acknowledged within the week, but then we had to patiently wait for the government to locate, verify and copy the records. It was with great joy several months later that I telephoned my sister to tell her a packet of information had arrived — almost 50 pages detailing Gilbert's service from 1930 through WWII. Included were several pictures of Gilbert, and best of all, his US Merchant Mariner's document with picture identification.

The facial resemblance left no doubt now that we had found Tony's birth-father. I could barely contain my excitement as I copied the pages and mailed the originals on to Tony. A discharge from the Coast Guard was also included.

Upon seeing the papers and pictures, Tony was easily convinced that this truly was his birth-father, and he decided to telephone his birth-cousin, Gloria, to make her acquaintance and to thank her for the useful information she had shared. Hopefully, they will be able to meet face to face someday. In the meantime, they have sent photos and information back and forth. We have also been able to extend Rose's family back several generations.

Once again, diligence and patience paid off for Tony. He now knows who both his birth-father and birth-mother are and can enjoy the friendship of cousins on both sides. He also has a record of some of his ancestors to pass on to his descendants. — Barbara Sutphin Witwer, PA

The Two Anna Pikes Of Haverhill

According to the *Descendants of Job Tyler* since 1619, Anna Pike married Job Tyler on 21 June 1786 in Haverhill, MA. In the town records she was listed as Nancy, which is a nickname for Anna. Also in the town records was an Anna Pike who married Moody Noyes on 24 January 1793.

There was an Anna Pike born to James and Anne (George) Pike on 21 February 1765. Several sources have assumed that the Anna Pike born to James and Anne (George) Pike is the Anna Pike who married Moody Noyes.

Nancy (Pike) Tyler had a child named James Pike Tyler which made me think that she might be the daughter of James Pike; the problem being how to prove it. I thought that there might be two Pike families in Haverhill but could only find the family of James. I then looked closely at James' family and could see a big difference in the age of the children, with Nancy being the youngest. Her eldest sibling was Simeon Pike. Simeon was killed at the Battle of Bunker Hill in 1775. He was old enough to have married and fathered a daughter slightly younger than Nancy [Anna]. Since he died at the Battle of Bunker Hill, I decided to order the records from the Daughters of the American Revolution.

Indeed, the records confirmed that Simeon had married a Mary — unclear on first name — and had a daughter Anna who married Moody Noyes. That would mean that Nancy who married Job Tyler indeed was the Anna who was the daughter of James Pike. — Carolyn Peterson, CA, corksterr@sbcglobal.net

The Mysterious Middle Name

I was born in 1946 and christened Stephen Barr Dilks. My father was christened Sidney Barr Dilks.

Since I was a small child, I have asked my parents the origin of my middle name. My mother just said, "Well, I think it was a family name, and I liked it." My father just said, "Dunno." (He must not have liked it, because he started using the middle name of Harold in the 1930s, a source of all kinds of confusion when he was drafted into WWII.)

When I began doing genealogy in the 1980s, one of my goals was to find out where the name came from. I assumed that because my father's mother was of German (Pennsylvania Dutch) origins, that the name was probably in her line somewhere. Well, I found Hains (Hahn), Eplers (Ebler), Wursters, Alberts and Muellers, but no Barrs!

So I went back to my father and said, "Dad, do you have a copy of your birth certificate?"

"Yes," he said. "It's in the lockbox. But it won't help you any. I didn't have a birth certificate when I was born. I had one created when I went into the Army."

In effect, he named himself and it showed the same name as above. Ok, now what?

I had long known that there were Barrses in his ancestry. His maternal grandfather was William Barrs Croshaw, the son of John Radford Croshaw and Mary Barrs. Could this be the source of the middle name, somehow truncated?

Dad's father, Oliver Croshaw Dilks, had emigrated from Thornton, Leicestershire, UK to the US in 1893, as a young man. None of the rest of his family came to the US, but a brother went to Toronto. The remainder of his family stayed in England.

I knew that Oliver had brothers named Titus, Croshaw, Thomas, William and Sydney. Some of this information came from the 1881 census, and some from monumental inscriptions in Thornton.

Time passed with no revelations. But when the Public Record Office opened up the 1901 British census in 2001, I was one of the first in line (well, really online). After what seemed like months of technical problems getting access, I was finally able to see the census of Leicestershire.

So, with bated breath, I entered my search criteria: "Titus Dilks (Oliver's father) in Thornton." And…. nothing!

"Geesh", I thought, "after all this." I was pretty sure that the family had

not left Thornton because of gravestones and church records. Also, I knew the pub was still in the family into the 1930s.

So, still staring at the screen in disbelief, I thought for a few minutes. Hmmm, Thornton is not that big. Maybe, just go through it street by street? I also wondered if it would work to search by Titus with no last name.

Name and Surname of each Person	RELATION to Head of Family	Condition as to Marriage	Age last Birthday of Males	Females
Charles Henry Massey	Head	M.	36	
Annie ...do	Wife	M		33
Reginald Orme ...do	Son		6	
Arthur Charles ...do	Son		2	
Henry Lawrence	Servant	S	19	
Job Wood	Servant	S	51	
William Massey	Head	M	83	
Maria ...do	Wife	M		82
Titus Wilks	Head	M.	56	
Mary ...do	Wife	M		56
Titus ...do	Son	S	26	
Elizabeth ...do	Daur	S		25
William Croshaw ...do	Son	S	20	
Sydney Barrs ...do	Son		15	

Titus Dilks as listed in the 1901 British census (sixth name from bottom).

So I keyed in Titus, waited a few seconds, and on the screen, I saw "Titus Wilks." I opened the image and it was my family. It had been incorrectly indexed. In this census, all the middle names are recorded. God bless you, census taker!

Listed with Titus and all the remaining brothers and sisters is Sydney Barrs Dilks! Obviously my father was named after his uncle.

My brickwall fell with a lot of perseverance, and a little ingenuity! I have since heard that as much as 30 percent of the 1901 census has transcription errors. The lesson here is to keep pursuing when the results you get are inconceivable. — Stephen Barrs Dilks, VA, sbdilks@attglobal.net

Payback Is Great

I helped a wonderful young man from Canada with his family tree here in New York State. He often told me to let him know if he could help me. I figured Canada is quite large and he wouldn't be able to, that is, until he mentioned he is from Ontario.

My grandmother, who died very young, left six children who didn't know much about her. All I had to go on was the name of Murphy.

Certificate of Baptism ✝

ST. ANTHONY OF PADUA PARISH, CENTREVILLE, ONT. CANADA
KOK 1N0

Name ANNE MARY MURPHY

Place of Birth

Date of Birth DEC. 28th, 1890

Date of Baptism JAN. 4th, 1891

Father's Name William Murphy

Mother's Maiden Name Caroline Mellon

Sponsors { Redmond Mellon
          Mary Anne McMahon

Sacrament administered by Rev. P. J. Hartigan

Confirmed October 26th, 1902.

Married

I certify that the foregoing has been correctly copied from the Baptismal Register of the above Church this 11th day of February 1980

J. Y. Lamarche

A certificate of baptism showing both the Murphy and the Mellon names.

This great man in Canada lives within walking distance of the National Archives in Ottawa and sent me many records of the Murphy family and of the Mellon family (which was my grandmother's mother's maiden name).

Do unto others is the best thing in the genealogy world. — Carol Michaud, NY, cmichaud@dreamscape.com

By Helping Others, You May Be Helping Yourself

The Donihoo family of my paternal great-grandmother was intriguing to research, to say the least. Making sure that I stuck to the facts instead of heading off in flights of fancy could be difficult at times. Such was the story of one of the daughters, Laura, who had been 16-years old in 1835 when the family migrated to the banks of the St. Clair River in St. Clair County, MI from Rockbridge County, VA.

According to family lore, her father John, a slave owner turned abolitionist, was a strict father, insisting that his daughters marry only the best. *The Genealogy Of The Descendants Of John Walker Of Wigton, Scotland* by Emma Siggins White, published in 1902, makes mention of the man who won Laura's heart and her father's approval: Captain Jacob Andrews. This was confirmed in the St. Clair county clerk's office, where in careful script, Laura and Jacob's December 1843 marriage was recorded. However, their love was to be short-lived. The Walker record stated that Jacob died in Racine, WI in 1851 and that Laura died shortly thereafter in 1852.

Had Jacob and Laura relocated to Racine? In answer to my query, the University of Wisconsin-Parkside sent me the mortality schedule for 1850. Jacob Andrews had died of cholera in that city in August 1849. On a slightly different note, I was researching a two-masted schooner built by Laura's brothers on the family's St. Clair River farm in the winter of 1848. The basis for this research was a letter preserved in a distant branch of the family detailing the schooner's construction. I turned to various museums and researchers dedicated to Great Lakes history and discovered the vessel was the *A.H. Newbold* and that Jacob Andrews had been its captain. I was also sent a newspaper clipping that the *A.H. Newbold* had run aground on the rocks near Racine. Surely there was a connection to Jacob's death there.

Racine, however, had no probate record and neither could I find one at the St. Clair County Court. There were no death records at that time and no cemetery record of either Laura or Jacob could be found. Neither could I locate Jacob's heritage, other than that at the time of his marriage he was living in Newport, (now called Marine City), MI. Reluctantly, Jacob and Laura's story was put aside without any real hope of learning more.

About two years later, a woman contacted me via e-mail regarding her ancestors; the Andrews/Androus family of St. Clair County. Early pioneers in the area, they arrived in the 1820s, shortly after the County was organized. My correspondent had some information about the family she sought. Apparently, the father, whose name she didn't know, had died shortly after arrival and the mother, Sally, had remarried a Mr. Hill. She also knew that Sally Andrews Hill was buried in Oaklawn Cemetery in Algonac, MI, a town in the southern part of the county about 20 miles from my home. I did not think that I could be of help, but I offered to visit the cemetery and take a photograph of Sally's gravestone and send it to her. On a beautiful October day and with the help of cemetery records, I located Sally's grave. I took the pictures, and, feeling somewhat foolish, spoke my thoughts aloud: "Sally, are you Jacob's mother?"

Since the local library was nearby and on the outside chance it might yield a clue or two, I decided to pay it a visit. Sure enough, there in a file drawer I found an index for early St. Clair County probates, extracted by the Daughters of the American Revolution many years earlier. I eagerly looked for Andrews and was rewarded with a file number for Jacob Andrews, husband of Laura and son of Sally Andrews Hill. Case file number in hand, I went back to the St. Clair County Probate Court. This time they quickly located the file. With great anticipation I read that Jacob had indeed died in Racine, WI, "about the 7th of September, 1849," and his wife Laura continued to live either with, or near, her parents. Her death must have been rather sudden, as her petition to the court on 6 October 1851, was superceded by her mother-in-law's petition on 6 March 1852, stating that "(Jacob's) widow Laura has since died." And there, tucked in the middle of Jacob's file, was another file! This belonged to Joel Andrews, who died in January 1826. The realization slowly dawned. Joel Andrews was Jacob's long-lost father! The papers showed the proper spelling of the Andrews name to be Androus, as Laura's signature attested.

The complete story of Jacob and Laura Donihoo Andrews/Androus will probably never be known. Jacob Andrews, captain of the schooner *A.H. Newbold*, was likely overseeing repairs to the vessel when caught in an epidemic and was buried in an unmarked grave. His young wife waited in vain for his return, only to die suddenly herself. Their story is much clearer now, due to information hidden in out-of-the-way places. In helping another, I had surely helped myself. — Suzanne Wesbrook Frantz, MI

Keeping Up With The Joneses

Recently, I decided to research further my elusive Jones family line. As you may think, with the surname Jones, this research was going to be difficult. Family stories are told to usually contain a grain of truth, and my story is no different.

My second-great-grandfather was said to have left Ireland under somewhat dubious circumstances, and changed his name to Tom Jones. Whether it is true or not is still unknown, because not much is known about Tom or his wife Lulu. No vital information, except further stories that he is buried in a small church cemetery in Doe Run, St. Francois County, MO. Being in St. Louis, and about an hour's drive from there, I enlisted my wife's service, and off we went to find if this story were true.

Once in Doe Run (after driving through it once and doubling back) we stopped at the gas station and asked if they knew of a small church cemetery in those parts. Lucky for us the attendant knew where the cemetery was, and directed us not far from where we were.

Pendleton Cemetery, above, in Doe Run, St. Francois County, MO, where Lulu Jones is buried, right.

Upon arrival at the church, with the cemetery behind it, we went in to determine where the graves may be. After speaking to the pastor, we learned that the old cemetery had no book listing burials. Though on church land, it was a public cemetery and anyone could bury their loved ones there. It was also one of the oldest cemeteries in the county. And even if it did have a listing, many markers

were either in poor shape, over grown, or vandalized and moved.

This would not suffice; I did not drive that far to give up without looking. So my wife and I went stone by stone through the small cemetery. But even though it was small, in the Missouri summer humidity it made for rough work. After walking through the entire cemetery, finding many family groupings like Link and other, non-related Joneses, we came across some names that were familiar. There, four plots from the edge of the cemetery, where the wire fence barely held back the overgrown woods, were the stones for my great-aunt and her husband, Earl Raby and Letha Jones Raby. Next to those stones was a marker that was weathered beyond reading. And next to it was a stone for Lulu Jones…

My search proved satisfying, though it only marked the first brick being knocked from the wall. Though I began with the hunt for information about Thomas (my best guess, the unreadable stone), it turns out that I gained a birth and death date for Lulu from her gravestone. Taking this information, I was able to determine a time for a search of obituaries, of which one was found. I saw many of the family names of which I had heard previously, adding validity to the obituary as the Jones I was looking for, and learned more information about the family and Lulu (including a death date for Tom!). Also, I was able to see that she did not die in St. Francois County (where I had been searching); she died in St. Louis while visiting my line which moved from St. Francois County. Now I was able to search for her death record, and that was found as well! Her son gave the information on the certificate, and listed her maiden name and her parents' names!

Mrs. Lula Jones
8-10-45 Lead Belt News

Mrs. Lula Jones was born in Elvins, Mo., August 12, 1873, and passed away in St. Louis on Thursday, August 3, 1945, aged 71 years 11 months 20 days.

She was the widow of Thomas Jones, who preceded her in death 23 years. She is survived by five children: Mrs Bessie Fostemeyer of Clinton, Ark.; Mrs. Letha Raby, Mrs. Clara Call, Herman and Irvin Jones of St. Louis; also sixteen grandchildren, six great-grandchildren, other relatives and friends.

Funeral services were held Saturday afternoon at the Boyer Funeral Home, conducted by Rev. George L. Britt. Interment was in the Pendleton Cemetery at Doe Run.

Obituary for Lula Jones.

From both of those resources I learned that she was born and lived in the St. Francois County area her whole life. I also discovered that I need to travel back to the small cemetery and walk some more. As it turns out, many of the family groups in the cemetery were her kin, since her maiden name was Link!

Now, I did not accomplish much of my main goal of learning about the elusive Tom, but I was able to learn more about his better half and fill in many missing details from my research.

Some family stories do start with a grain of truth, and may even be true, but don't be shortsighted to the possibilities that those stories will lead in new directions of research. — Patrick Jones, MO

Phone Payoff

I knew very little about the Kepharts, other than what my mother had told me about them. My mother was given her Grandma Kephart Hess' middle name of Jane. Nancy Jane Kephart was born in Clearfield County, PA and had married Alexander Hess there — before records were required. I had found them in the 1850 US census, and had a group sheet of their family. I knew only the basics and had put them on the shelf for further study while I worked on my other lines.

Back before the popularity and availability of phone cards, a Chelan Valley Genealogical Society member told of his great success of finding relatives by phoning people with his last name in the state where his ancestors had lived. I envied his success, but was too cheap to try.

Then one day I had nothing to do. I looked in the phone book for family names, trying to work up the courage to call a stranger. Wright and Bennett were out of the question since there were so many of them. I tried another family name, Litz, and talked to a very pleasant man whose ancestors came to the US in 1869. Too late, no direct connection appeared to be there.

Encouraged by his positive reaction, I looked for the name Kephart. There were several listed! I called one. When a man answered I said, "Are you related to the Kephart Family of Clearfield County, PA?"

Imagine my thrill when he answered, "Yes, I am. But my sister does the genealogy. You should talk to her."

I called her, got a name and address of the family genealogist with the intention to write as soon as I got home, which I did. A month later I received a book of Kephart genealogy, going back to Adam! More than that, I received information of the Hess family, too. All from a phone call — free at that! — Bettie Kenck, WA, benkenbp@crcwnet.com

It's A Family Affair

My brickwall was the lack of information about my paternal great-grandfather. My father (1913-80) was orphaned by age 12 and raised by his mother's family. My grandfather (1892-1924) was six-years old when his own father died and my father was 10 when his father died. My father had studio portraits of his grandfather and vaguely remembered being told by his father that he was a namesake of his grandfather, that the man has been a minister, a Baptist or Methodist and that they lived in the area of Wyalusing, PA. Unfortunately, I know nothing about my granddad's childhood.

My father took my mother, brother and me on numerous Sunday drives to the Wyalusing area to glean information about his father's family, with no success. Then, unfortunately, my own father died and it was left to me to find out about my great-grandfather.

My grandfather's death certificate verified his father's name but listed a "wrong" mother's name. Armed with only my great-grandfather's name I decided to pursue the church connection. Because of the large number of Methodist churches in northern Pennsylvania, I decided to start there.

I wrote to the Commission on Archives and History of the Eastern Pennsylvania Conference of the United Methodist Church. Two days later I received a reply and was asked to contact the Central Pennsylvania Conference Archives and Drew University General Commission on Archives.

From them I received photocopied pages describing my great-grandfather's life (1840-99), church postings, his wife's correct name, the precise location of his grave and even his official church portrait, which is exactly like the one I have. My father was indeed his namesake. I drove to the cemetery, found the stone, and documented it with photos. My paternal great-grandfather came from England, married in Connecticut, had churches in Florida where my grandfather was born, and died in northern Pennsylvania from whence my granddad and father came.

With a little research, thankfully, my brickwall has morphed into a tangled skein which can finally be unraveled. — Cora Cramer, GA, cscramer@aol.com

That's What Genealogy Friends Are For

I have discovered over and over again that new-found genealogy friends are one of the best answers to knocking down brickwalls.

Years ago, my mother gave my oldest son the original passport of her great-grandparents, Gottfried Macco (Godfrey Mock, Americanized version) and his wife, Johanna, who had emigrated with their two sons from Germany in 1853. When I started genealogy research a little over a year ago, I hinted to my son that I would like the passport, thinking he would give it to me, but instead he sent a photocopy which was too difficult to read. Then, he took his digital camera and zoomed in on each section and made a cd for me. I struggled off and on for almost a year with an English/German dictionary, trying to decipher the old German script on an almost unreadable old passport, with not much success.

Recently, I found a fifth-cousin once-removed from a different line of my family. It just happened that his wife is German. I mentioned the passport to her and the difficulty I was having; and she offered to help translate it. I sent her a copy of the cd; and she not only worked on it herself, but also sent it to her mother and sister to work on. They were able to interpret all of it except for the most critical information: the maiden name of Johanna and the name of the town where the immigrants were born and lived. They were able to tell me that it was in Neckarkreis County, Wuerttemberg, Germany and that the town started with the letter G.

Last year I obtained a copy of Marie Mock Selby's death certificate, a daughter of Godfrey and Johannah Mock. On the death certificate, my grandmother stated that Marie's mother's name was Johanna Flinchback. Then, I discovered on several censuses in Ohio that her brother, William Flinchback, had immigrated several years after the Mock family did and had settled in the same town in Ohio. On the 1900 census, William and his sons changed their name to Flinspach. I didn't pursue this change in name at that time.

In sorting through a blizzard of unfiled papers recently since my German friend translated the passport, I found a printout of someone else with the name of Flinspach. I went on the Internet with the name of Johanna Flinspach. I hit pay dirt!

I not only found my second-great-grandmother, Johanna Friedrika Flinspach, born on 9 November 1816 (same as birth date on passport) but also her parents and grandparents in the town of Grossgartach, Neckarkreis, Wuerttemberg, Germany. The German name for Flinchback was Flinspach! I'm sure

that eventually I will find my second-great-grandfather in the same town. (There were three Gottfried Macco men listed in that town, but with the wrong birth date.)

Once again, new genealogy friends have helped to knock down my brickwall. I am discovering that even if a person is not a blood relative, they will go out of their way to be helpful. I am finding that I will work as hard, if not harder, to help a perfect stranger find a relative or an ancestor. What a wonderful spiritual satisfaction that is. I believe we genealogy addicts are a special breed! — Georgia Kruse, rockingranny@comcast.net

Lost In Translation

I hit a brickwall very early on the research of my great-grandfather of Irish descent, George Bishop who came to Quebec from Boston, MA. There was little information on him, but I knew he had married Olive Leroux. I did not know the date or which parish, or town for that matter. Many long hours were spent pouring

The George Nelson Bishop family of St. Zotique, Quebec.

over many church records to no avail. I put him aside for several months while I researched others from my Quebec roots.

Going through various French records, I noticed parish priests used their discretion on the spelling names, sometimes changing the original name to one that was almost unrecognizable. It then occurred to me to look for George under the surname Levesque, which is the direct French translation for bishop. Sure enough, there he was: the record stating "Georges Levesque married to Olive Leroux.". It sure was satisfying having that brickwall tumble down. — Johanne Brown, ON, ericbrown@alumni.uwaterloo.ca

Sources Revisited

In the early 1950s, my mother met her birth-mother after having been raised by a foster family from about the age of three. Mary Hayes Denny told mother some of her background and named some family members. She died in 1959, so mother only had a couple of contacts with her and none with other members of the Hayes family.

After my mother's last illness and death in 1992, my sister and I had the responsibility of clearing out the homestead in West Virginia. We noted that mother had saved many obituaries, memorial cards and other newspaper clippings. Although there was no order to them, we placed everything in shoeboxes to be looked through later. There was much history contained in all this. What a find!

Eventually, I entered much of the information in my database. Beginning to do more research, I found it most difficult doing it long distance. Many queries were mailed out seeking information. Not to be discouraged in the process, I would check at public libraries and historical societies in Pennsylvania hoping they

might have available sources.

During a visit to the Pennsylvania State Library in Harrisburg, I first saw the 1880 census for West Virginia in print. Wow! Recorded in Mason County were the parents of my second-great-grandfather who were both born in New York. I later found that Benjamin's father was Samuel Hayes, and then the IGI listed the marriage for Samuel Hayes and Eleanor Amsberry or Almsberry in Chautauqua County, NY in 1818. Much correspondence flowed back and forth between Pennsylvania and New York without success. Queries in historical society newsletters offered no replies. New-found cousins in West Virginia knew nothing more. Hayes message boards offered nothing new. More frustration and no answers!

USGenWeb Project.

And then a light went on in my head: go back to RootsWeb.com and the USGenWeb Project for West Virginia, Mason County surnames where people are researching and try Amsberry. It would certainly be worth a try since the Hayes surname had led to another cousin. Within days a "cousin" in Nebraska responded and mailed me a cd with about 1,700 descendants and kin along with some pictures. She also included a copy of Eleanor's pension file for Samuel's service in the War of 1812. Cousin Ruby said that Eleanor Amsberry Hayes moved from West

Virginia with some of her children and her brother's family to Marion County, IA, after the death of Samuel. She lived there until her death in 1879. Although we had not been able to find a burial place for either Samuel or Eleanor in West Virginia after many cemetery inquiries, I just never thought of her going west like many others in the 1850s and 1860s.

Gratefully, another brickwall has fallen down. Never, ever give up! — Barbara Sutphin Witwer, PA

Read Over Those Old Letters And Files!

About once every three years or so, re-read over all the letters and notes you have saved and filed. It is not unusual for some item in an old letter, one that may be 20 or 30 years old, to contain a tidbit of information that you can now fit into data you have recently found.

I had a letter written by my mother's cousin in which she stated that my mother's great-grandmother, named Mary, came to America with a son and daughter-in-law. This woman had flaming red hair, had just one dollar to her name when she died which was to be used for a Mass and that her son made her casket. The information was added to my computer program and filed away.

I also found a list of the persons buried in the "old" cemetery. There was no record of a Mary Pankratz, but that name was added at the bottom of the list as a probable name. From another source, the archives in Prague, I had the name Franciska Pankratz as the mother of my second-great-grandmother.

Now I had two names for the same woman. And my mother's cousin actually knew her. When I was reading over these old letters and files, I

found the name Francis Pankratz in the cemetery list with the correct age and the correct parentage, as per the archives. I have both notations in my computer, but not feel quite certain that the correct name is Franziska.

That name comes from two sources — Prague archives and a cemetery list — both of which are more reliable than the memory of an elderly woman. — Beverly Vareka, WI, gapos@uwalumni.com

Two For The Price Of One

When I first began researching my family I almost gave up immediately. My father's line is Hall, and my mother's is Smith.

I knew my maternal grandmother (who died when Mom was young) was Lena Smith who married an Askew. She knew very little about them. Her parents contacted influenza when she was a toddler, and she was shipped out to relatives. Mom died just as I began my research.

Her sister, my aunt, was older and was able to give me a little information. She did know that they, Samuel and Rosalie Smith were from Canada, moved to Massachusetts, then Connecticut, where they died. She wasn't sure in what town they were buried. I searched and searched for Connecticut Smiths to no avail.

While at my local FHC one day, I announced "I quit", I was so frustrated. The director was in and asked if he could help. "Yes, if you can find Samuel Smith in Connecticut". He asked when they died, and then told me about the Charles R. Hale Collection. He went on to explain that this project recorded every gravestone inscription in more than 2,000 Connecticut cemeteries, through 1935, "And it's indexed," he said.

With this new information, I sent for the index that contained Smith. Do you have any idea how many Smiths are buried in Connecticut?

I found four Samuel and Rosalie Smith inscriptions. I sent for those films, and on the very last one, was Samuel Smith with his military unit for the Civil War, but it was in Vermont. That threw me a curve. But, next to him was his wife Rosalie. Buried next to them was Lena Smith Askew, their granddaughter. Bingo!

Next, I checked on Ancestry.com to see if there were pension records for him. No Samuel Smith.

Knowing to keep checking, I checked under his wife Rosalie. Still no luck, so I tried Rose and up popped Samuel Smith.

I sent for his records and received 21 pieces of information.

Death certificate for Samuel Smith.

A description sheet with all his enlistment information, and a description of him, a copy of their marriage record, which listed both parents; a list of all children living or dead, his death certificate, her death certificate and a request for reimbursement for burial from two of their married daughters.

I try to tell as many people who will listen about the Charles R. Hale Collection and the importance of pension records.

That was four years ago, and my line at that time was nine people. It is now at more than 1000 and growing! — Dale Hall, CA, gramft@earthlink.net

So Many Avenues To Travel

When I was young, my mother and grandmother told me a story about my grandfather being a foundling left on the doorstep of a widow and her widowed daughter by the name of Brown (pseudonyms have been used instead of the real names). They adopted him and renamed him John Allen Brown. When he was about seven-years old, supposedly, his birth-mother tried to kidnap him and that was when they discovered that his birth name was Phillip Jones.

I recently began research on my family. I wrote to the county where he was born with the approximate birth date and the two names. The information I received was inconclusive and the adoption records in the state were sealed. Since then, I have learned that the state did not have legal adoptions at the time of my grandfather's birth.

I put the information on genealogy message boards and heard from two separate researchers. One helped me to find the widowed mother, Sarah Brown, and the widowed daughter, Susan Wilson, on a census. The daughter ran a boarding house. As the researcher pointed out, at the top of the next page of the census was a James Allen, boarder which was the same last name as my grandfather's middle name.

I began to doubt the story told me all those years ago. Could Susan Wilson and James Allen have been his parents and the mother and daughter just made up the other story? Considering this was in the 1800s, it could be a strong possibility because of the shame involved in having an illegitimate child at that time.

Another researcher thought that maybe James Allen was just helping with the foundling and they gave the child his name as a middle name. She suggested that if my grandfather had wanted to know more information, he would have tried to find out. Why didn't I just leave it alone? I'm sorry, but it is very important to me to find out the true story. (Plus, I'm like a bulldog; I never let loose!)

A genealogy message boards directory on Cyndi's List.

Recently, I obtained a copy of his death certificate in another state. It stated that his father was David Brown and his mother was Sarah with an unknown maiden name. An earlier birth date was listed and I again wrote to the county to see if they might have a birth certificate either under the name of Brown, Jones or Wilson for that earlier time period. I never received a reply from them.

I had written to Social Security for a copy of his original application. I finally received that and it stated that his parents were David Brown and Sarah Johnson (maiden name). I also found that David Brown had been in the service and killed in action prior to the date my grandfather was born. So, the saga goes on. Will I ever have all of the answers? If I have my way, I

will find them. I am new at this, but am learning. I have knocked down a lot of brickwalls in my pursuit of the answers, and have developed different scenarios to try and arrive at the truth. There are so many brickwalls, but genealogy has so many avenues to travel. — Georgia Kruse, rockinggranny@comcast.com

Who Was Uncle Fether?

My brickwall was searching for the descendants of Ernst Rosenthal (born on 9 August 1824). He was a brother of my great-grandfather Friedrich Rosenthal.

Ernst and his wife, Sophia, immigrated in 1854 before they had children and they lived on a farm adjoining Friedrich 's in Washington County, WI. The 1860 census lists Ernst, age 35, Sophia (his wife), age 34, with a five-year-old named Sophia. He did not appear on any more census lists in Washington County after 1860. Friedrich also appeared on the same page in that census with his second wife, their two young children and the three children from Friedrich's first marriage, whose names are also listed on a page in Friedrich's German Bible. Friedrich had been widowed in 1854 when the youngest, named Sophia, was born. She was five in the 1860 census. These five-year-old Sophias were evidently cousins. (Friedrich's Sophia married Joseph Swoboda of Chippewa County, and they raised a family there).

It took some time to locate Ernst after he disappeared from Washington County, and I found him in Chippewa County quite by accident while researching Swoboda descendants. An elderly granddaughter of Sophia Swoboda mentioned the only Rosenthal that she could remember as ever knowing was an old man living with her grandparents. They called the old man "Uncle Fether" and he lived in a one-room house and ate his meals with the Swoboda family. A 1900 census search to locate the Swoboda family in Chippewa County found: 1900 Rosendal Anest, an uncle, age 74, born in August 1825 and in 1910, Rosandol Amse, age 86, widowed. This was the Uncle Fether that the Swoboda granddaughter had remembered from her childhood.

The 1870 census revealed Edward Rasendoll, age 44, with Sophia, age 43, and Sophia Junior, age 16; and in 1880, Earnest Rosenthal, age 56, and wife, Sophia, age 55. I felt that the information from one census to the next was close enough to indicate that this was the Ernst that I was looking for and that he had moved to Chippewa County. Therefore, Ernst and Uncle Fether were one and the same.

Next, I searched Chippewa County marriage records for Ernst's daughter, Sophia, who was 16 in 1870 and no longer at that household in 1880. With a married name for her, I could then trace her offspring. While I was at it, I would also look for a marriage record for Sophia and Joseph Swoboda who had also probably married in Chippewa County during that time period. I found one record. That was for the marriage of Sophia Rosenthal to Joseph Swoboda on 24 November 1876. Sophia's parents were listed as Ernest and Sophia Rosenthal. I was dumbfounded at that revelation. I had always been told that Sophia Swoboda was a sister of my grandfather, therefore a daughter of Ernst's brother, Friedrich. This marriage record indicated that Sophia Swoboda was Ernst's daughter rather than his niece, as I had originally believed. And yet the census record of 1900 confirmed that she was, indeed, his niece. So which was she? His niece or his daughter?

After puzzling over these discov-

eries for a few days, I came to the conclusion that there must have been only one Sophia — that Friedrich 's and Ernst's Sophia was one and the same. The marriage record to Joe Swoboda giving her parents' names as Ernest and Sophia Rosenthal, along with the 1900 census giving Ernst's relationship as uncle, was the basis of my conclusion. Sophia evidently named Ernst and Sophia as her parents for the marriage certificate; or perhaps the certificate was filled out by someone who thought that they were her parents because she lived with them and their surnames were the same. A check for Sophia's death certificate gave her father's name as Frederick Rosenthal as I had originally believed.

Sixteen-year-old Sophia appears on the 1870 census in Chippewa County with Ernst and Sophia, but there is no Sophia appearing in the Washington County household of Friedrich during that same period of time. I have no information for the intervening years between 1860 and 1870. It is not known when Sophia made the move, but Ernst must have moved up there between 1860 and 1862, because further research revealed that he purchased 120 acres of homestead land in Chippewa County on 28 April 1862.

The 1860 census for Washington County showing a Sophia, age five, living in Friedrich's household as well as Ernst's household seems to contradict my theory that there was only one child named Sophia. But I wondered how likely it would be for them both to have daughters of the same age with the same name. Upon the death of his wife, Friedrich was faced with having to care for a newborn baby in addition to his other small children, the oldest of whom was not quite seven; he also had his farm to tend with its crops and livestock. He remarried a little over a year later, but, in the interim, that first year of a baby's life is critical, and Friedrich needed someone to care for it. His brother and sister-in-law lived on the adjoining farm, and, to all indications, they were a childless couple. They may have been the perfect solution to help raise Sophia. Babies were often named for a witness at their baptism; so it is possible that Ernst and Sophia, were baby Sophia's godparents; and godparents are charged with the care and upbringing of the child if its natural parents can no longer care for it, I thought that little Sophia may very well have gone back and forth between both households, and it may be that both named her to the census taker.

Ernst's obituary states that he passed away at the home of his niece, Mrs. Joseph Swoboda, and that he was survived by a brother and several nieces and nephews. This is further evidence that he had no children of his own since no children or grandchildren were listed as survivors.

As for Uncle Fether, perhaps he was "Uncle/Father" to Sophia and "father" sounded like "Fether" to the grandchildren. — Sharon Rosenthal Lemley, WI

Check Your Spelling

My great-grandfather Beck was the last of my ancestors to immigrate to the US. The 1910 federal census listed him as Fred Beck, age 40, emigrating in 1892. His birth date in March 1870 was confirmed by several other sources, with his first name being given as Fred or Fredolin in his obituary, death certificate and cemetery record. The date of emigration indicated a possible entry via Ellis Island. A search for Fred Beck on the Ellis Island website resulted in multiple hits, but none matched the age and date closely enough for my comfort level.

Unfortunately, Fred died in an auto accident in 1918; three years before my father was born and my father could not recall any mention of his grandfather having arrived at Ellis Island. However, my father did recall having seen a variant spelling of his grandfather's first name as Fridolin. A search for Fridolin Beck on the Ellis Island website resulted in only three hits, one of whom arrived on 16 March 1892 at the age of 22, on the S.S. *Virginia*. From there I was able to pull up an image of the ship's manifest as well as a picture of the ship itself.

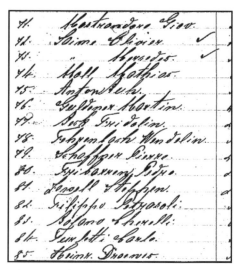

Ship manifest for the SS Virginia, *dated 16 March 1892, listing Fridolin Beck as a passenger.*

When faced with a brickwall, especially involving immigrant ancestors, it is important to consider alternate spellings of both first and last names. — Mary Lou Inwood, OH

What's In A Name?

When I started my research, I didn't know my grandmother Flora Alice Channell's mother's name. My grandmother's mother passed away when she was three and her father remarried. My grandmother never knew her birthmother's maiden name because they wanted her to think her father's new wife was her mother. As a result, my grandmother passed away never knowing her real mother's ancestors.

On a visit to West Virginia, I went through some family books and pictures looking for names. I was able to discover that Flora's mother's last name was Ware. However, I still didn't have her mother's full name, so when I came home I went onto the Internet and typed in her father's first and last name, with relevant dates and where he had lived, along with her mother's maiden name.

I was shocked with what I came up with; I discovered my mother and father shared some of the same ancestors. My mother and father's ancestors came from Virginia and West Virginia; the same areas they had grown up in. I discovered my ancestor, Richard Dickie Ware, born 1760, was related to me from both sides!

My brickwall solution is to take thorough notes and glean every last bit of information from your old family books; also, examine every last family photograph for relevant names

Darlene (Arbogast) Eastin's grandparents from both sides of the family: (L-R) Solomon Wade Arbogast, Flora Alice Channell, Mary Ruby Snyder and Guy Hubert Ware.

and dates on the back. Lastly, be sure to look on the Internet for information and important details regarding your family names. Most importantly, don't be surprised with what you come up — you just might be shocked! In fact, by using the Internet and a family tree software program I was able to go back to the 1500s on one of my ancestors from Germany. I put all my information together and put it on the Internet on my web page with all the links to other websites that helped me along the way. — Darlene (Arbogast) Eastin, OH, Darlene913@aol.com

The Joseph Barkers Of Essex County

Joseph Barker has been a brickwall for about five years. I had traced him to Spencer, Tioga County, NY. He had married Phoebe Dodd either in New Jersey or Pennsylvania. Both the Dodd family and Barker family settled in the Wyoming Valley area of Pennsylvania in about 1785.

In 1796, Joseph wandered north a little and was one of the earliest settlers in Spencer, NY. According to the town history "he was orphaned at a young age and had a cruel guardian and ran away to fight in the revolution". I figured this was a clue for my research. I also found a cemetery record that indicated he was born in 1763. I found a Revolutionary War record, dated 1779, for a Joseph Barker, age 16, from Chelmsford, MA. Chelmsford is in Middlesex County, so I checked all guardian records for a Joseph Barker. Unfortunately, I found none. I also checked a couple of databases for Joseph Barker, born in 1763, in Massachusetts, as well as the family history.

I found three who were born around that time in or near Essex and Middlesex County. One went to Nova Scotia with his family when he was a child. There was one who was in Middlesex County (same county as Chelmsford) who married and had a large family that was well documented. The third one married and settled in Salem.

I decided that Massachusetts was not that large of a state, so I checked for a Joseph Barker in guardian records for the entire state and found none. In the meantime, I rechecked the various databases for Joseph but found the same thing, the three Josephs were all accounted for. I put my information away, and after about a year I decided it was time to review my data.

This time, I decided to assume that perhaps he was not orphaned which would mean studying the Joseph born in 1763, who was the son of Lydia Gutterson and Moses Barker of Methuen. I also looked close at the marriage records. Indeed, there was a marriage record for Joseph in Salem, MA. I started thinking and said to myself, wait a minute; Joseph lived in Methuen, which is 30 or 40 miles from Salem. I decided it was a little far to travel for marriage in those days. I checked further and there were two Joseph Barkers in Essex County, MA, very close to the same age. There was one in Salem and one in Methuen. Upon studying the Methuen family I saw that they had moved to Chelmsford around 1770. Indeed,

Joseph Barker of Salem married and settled there. The other Joseph Barker from Methuen had moved to Chelmsford and fought in the Revolution and along with the rest of the family, had left the area for New York state shortly after the Revolution. — Carolyn Peterson, CA, corksterr@sbcglobal.net

A Clue In The Cemetery

My husband, Joe, and I went up to Fond du Lac County, WI, hoping to find information on his second-great-grandfather, Peter Shoemaker (Schumacher), such as when he died and where he was buried. We knew he died between 1865, when he mustered out of the Civil War, and the 1870 federal census when his wife and kids were living alone. We knew some of his kids were baptized and married at St. Michael's Catholic Church near Forest, Fond du Lac County, WI, so we thought we would start there.

No one was at the church when we got there, but the cemetery was open so we looked through it. No luck there, but when we stopped at a nearby gas station they suggested we try the large cemetery in Holy Cross, WI near Forest.

When we went walking through the cemetery we found a Peter H. Shumacker with dates on the gravestone and a Peter H. Shoemaker with no dates right behind him. Peter had a son called Peter. I figured this was a good possibility that this was the father and son of my husband's. I wrote to the graveyard caretakers to find out if they had any information on the two graves. No luck there.

I then decided to write for a death certificate using the dates on the gravestone. The parents' names and the burial location told me that this was the correct one. I still have the question of when Peter Shoemaker, Sr.

died, but at least I'm pretty sure I know where he is buried. — Jane Schumacher, WI, jjschu@itis.com

Spot The Difference

Both my parents passed away many years ago and I inherited a wooden box of old family photos. Not knowing to do with these photos, I put them in a photo album and put them away. Some of the relatives in the photographs I remember and others I recall my mother explaining who they were and when the photograph was taken.

Recently, while working on my family tree, I decided to use some of these old photographs to scan into my computer program.

My mother's oldest brother Jack (John Delmage) died on

Sophia Delmage and son Jack (John) Delmage, at the family home in London, ON, in March 1940.

2 April 1940. Jack had only been married 10 days when he passed away. He had been a soldier in the Canadian Army and his funeral included a full military service with the body taken to the cemetery on a gun carriage. I recalled hearing stories about him.

Another brother of my mother, Donald Delmage, was also in the army. I knew there was a photograph of him in the photo album, so I decided to scan a photograph of him into my computer. After checking the photo album I was a little confused.

There was a photograph of Donald with my grandmother, (Sophia Delmage) and another photograph of Donald in Germany and although the face looked similar, there was something odd about the two photos. While scanning the two photographs, I enlarged the images and started to study the faces more closely. They looked like two different people. Who was in the photo with my grandmother?

I had assumed it was her son Donald. While looking at the left hand in one of the photographs, I noticed a wedding band. This could not be Donald because he was not married until June 1959 and my grandmother passed away in May 1959.

The soldier in the photo was Jack and all this time I had a photograph of him.

Only by noticing the wedding band was I able to solve the brickwall. — Carole Nickels, ON, anickels@sympatico.ca

Use Those Indices, Maps And Databases

Family tradition in the Sims family held that Mary Jane Sims and her sister Elizabeth were born in Quebec, near Montreal, to parents Andrew and Elizabeth (Bell) Sims. The Ontario census records verified this as both women were listed in more than one census year as being born in Lower Canada (now Quebec). My challenge was to find their baptismal records, probably recorded in a Presbyterian Church register.

My first stab at trying to find these records was to contact a genealogical association in Quebec and ask for a search. The search that the researcher conducted did not produce any information of value. A query in the association's journal did not produce any results either.

I assessed my brickwall again. The challenge lay in the fact that the family arrived in Quebec after 1830 and had moved on to Ontario by 1839 so census records were of no use in trying to find a geographical starting point for this family. I decided that I should try to find siblings or relatives of the family since family tradition also held that some of the family members stayed in Quebec near Montreal. It seemed logical that I take the male names of Andrew's children and search using them. Where would I start my search, as Quebec is a big province?

Since I needed to narrow my search, I went to the Lambton Room of the Lambton County Library in Wyoming, ON and checked out the massive index *The French Canadians 1600-1900*, published by the Genealogical Research Library in Toronto. I found references to a William Sims in Argenteuil County and a reference to a William Wilson Sims in Mille Isles. Since Andrew and Elizabeth's oldest son was named William Wilson, I decided that these two were worth checking. I checked a map website to find out that Mille Isles was part of Argenteuil County and the county was definitely close to Montreal.

At this point in time, I decided to bring in the census microfilms for

Argenteuil County and check systematically for Sims families to see if more given names surfaced that were similar from the one family to the other. I was able to track William's family through a number of censuses and even found one that suggested that he was in Quebec as early as 1825. Some names were similar but this exercise brought me no closer to my goal of finding baptismal records for the two women. However, it did provide me with a lot more Quebec-based Sims names.

It was at this time that something reminded me of Marlene Simmons' website, Quebec and Eastern Townships Research Database, although I wasn't sure if it would be of value.

Baptismal record for Mary Jane Sims, Jerusalem Settlement, 1834.

I did a search on some of my names and hits came up. I then checked her listing of the records that she had entered into her database. Marlene had entered Presbyterian Church records for Lachute, Chatham and Grenville, all of which are in Argenteuil County. Records for these geographic areas also fit the time period in which I was interested. I decided to gamble that this was the area where Andrew and Elizabeth had lived temporarily. I sent Marlene $25, my list of hits and the names and birthdates for Mary Jane and

Elizabeth. This way she could check out my list and I wouldn't be purchasing copies of irrelevant records.

Her return letter indicated that she could provide transcriptions of the baptismal records that I was seeking as well as 17 other transcriptions of hits on William Sims' family. I decided to go for it all! The information in the baptismal records matched what I had in my records for the two women. I then sent a request to Les Archives Nationales du Québec for copies of the two baptisms. It was a thrill to receive the copies of the baptismal records, which represented the oldest "original" items that I had for this family.

Of course, breaking down one brickwall usually leads you to another. Now I have the challenge of proving or disproving a connection between William Sims' family and Andrew Sims' family! — Alan Campbell, ON, campbeal@sympatico.ca

Useful Advice For Posting On Genealogical Message Boards

Over the years, I have learned a few good genealogy research techniques for posting on Internet message boards. Stick to the following tips and you're sure to be successful:

Firstly, be detailed in the subject line. Don't just post "looking for ancestors". Give surnames, date range and locations. Next, post on surname boards and location boards. Post on boards for the country of origin and then try to see if there is a board for the province, state or county of origin. Also, be sure to update the information when you find more. It's better to add a reply to your own post with the new information as that bumps the thread back up to the front of the board.

Remember to keep track of the URLs of where you post and check back. Some boards will send an e-mail when someone responds to your post. But e-mails change and you can't always remember to change the information on every board. If you haven't made a note of the posting, you could forget it or have trouble finding it and updating the notification address.

Lastly, keep going back to the boards and using their search function. Many posters do not read previous posts or search through them so someone may be posting the exact information you need without ever knowing you were looking for it.

I wish I had kept track of the URLs of my postings at the beginning of my Internet research because my original e-mail service stopped providing them. My address disappeared and no more notifications came. I finally went back looking for all the posts I had done on a specific site, and was amazed to find that someone had replied almost 18 months before, and they had information that went back several more generations!

I had been successful in tracing my surname back into Hungary, and by connecting with a site for a town near mine, I had found the German origin of the family. But there it stopped as my ancestor was the only one of that surname. That response which languished for 18 months has led me to a neighboring town in Germany and some German genealogists who are very interested in knowing what happened to the people from Hessen who went to Hungary in the 1700s. They have lists of who went and where they were from. We are now in touch by e-mail and working together to expand our knowledge. — L. Blaser, ON

Curiosity Rewarded Me Nicely

Once I learned my grandmother's paternal grandfather, William C. Gray, was buried in Union Dale Cemetery in Pittsburgh, PA, I wrote to the secretary and requested records of any other Grays who might be buried there.

The secretary wrote back with a list of those buried in the same lot, which was owned by Fletcher Gray.

He had purchased five graves on 13 October 1847, for $12. Oddly enough, though, Fletcher was not there. The secretary said only direct heirs are permitted to be buried in a lot owner's lot, so the five occupants there must have been related to Fletcher.

This record from Union Dale Cemetery shows who is buried in Fletcher Gray's lot, and who isn't.

Who was Fletcher Gray? William's death certificate stated his father's name was James and since I couldn't find a burial site for James, I began to check other resources. However, there were several James Grays in Pittsburgh and it seemed impossible to determine who was William's father.

I then turned to a will index and found two James Grays for the appropriate time frame. One had "Rev." in front of his name and I quickly ruled him out as there have never been any clergymen in our family. I sent away for the other James Gray's will.

I was disappointed when William was not named as an heir, nor was there any mention of Fletcher. Reluctantly, I turned to the will of Rev. James Gray just out of curiosity.

Curiosity may have killed the cat but it rewarded me nicely. Rev. Gray was my direct ancestor and the father of William C. Gray. In his will, he listed six children: Fletcher, William C., Matilda Kinnear, Mary Knox, Jane Andrews and an adopted daughter, Eliza Kramer.

Not only had I found William's father and siblings, as well as learning we did indeed have a clergyman in the family, but I had also solved the mystery of Fletcher Gray. Or had I? He still wasn't where he was supposed to be in Union Dale Cemetery.

In 1860, Fletcher was living in the Pittsburgh area with his wife Charlotte and children. He was a riverboat pilot. Unable to find him in 1870, I headed west to Ohio, where I knew from the will that his siblings William and Matilda were living in Columbiana County. Fletcher wasn't there but Charlotte was, along with their children.

Then in 1880, Fletcher appeared again, this time living with his sister Mary Knox in Stark County, OH. He said he was a widower. This is interesting because Charlotte, still in Columbiana County in 1880, claimed to be a widow. Five years later, she and the children returned to Pittsburgh where she was listed annually in the city directories as "widow of Fletcher."

Fletcher, though, was still very much alive. He died in 1888 at the age of 75 in Stark County and is buried in Columbiana Cemetery in Fairfield Township, Columbiana County, OH.

The five graves he owned at Union Dale were taken up by William C. Gray (his brother), and wife Catherine; William's son, Harry Gray; William's daughter, Emma Nease (and baby), and William's son, James W. Gray. I still have no idea why Fletcher purchased the lot way back in 1847, when he was 34 years old. — Kathy Borne, OH, Kathyborne@aol.com

Old Pen Pals Break Modern Brickwall

My family history goes back to Catherine the Great, Czarina of Russia in the late 1700s. She enticed families from Germany, Sweden and other neighboring countries to colonize the vast steppe lands of western Russia. My ancestors qualified as pioneers, left Germany and remained in Russia until 1912, when they immigrated to America.

Through the generations, records of those families remaining in Germany were either lost or not kept up to date. This presented a brickwall to our research as all relatives with any knowledge had passed away.

I am a member of the Germans from Russia Heritage Society. This genealogy society established coordinators for the various villages in western Russia where the German pioneers settled. Our particular village was Alt Posttal, Bessarabia. The village coordinator is Dr. Horst Fode, a pharmacist in Germany. The coordinator helps members doing research.

I inherited a box of old family photographs from my mother many years ago. I went through them (after many years in storage) to see if I could dig up any clues. I came across two

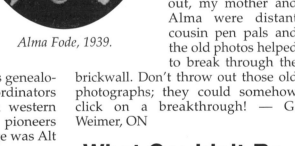

Alma Fode, 1939.

photos, one of a teenage girl and another of a young, smartly dressed lady on a city street in France. The captions on the back were addressed to my mother (Emma), from Alma Fode. My mother had never set foot off North American soil so I assumed this was a pen pal relationship. But the surname Fode rang a bell. Perhaps it was a long shot, but could this Alma Fode be related to our village coordinator Horst?

I packaged up the photos with an explanation and mailed them to Horst. Bingo! When Horst received the material he e-mailed me explaining that Alma was his aunt (long since passed away). All pictures of her were destroyed in the war; they were most grateful for them and pointed out that we were distantly related. Horst then mailed me a copy of his family history book (written in English and German) that listed branches of the family and some that had settled in western Canada. As it turned out, my mother and Alma were distant cousin pen pals and the old photos helped to break through the brickwall. Don't throw out those old photographs; they could somehow click on a breakthrough! — G. Weimer, ON

What Couldn't Be, Will

By believing what I was told, I created my own solidly built brickwall. I started my father's genealogy with very little information. My dad, Jack Neely, knew his father's name was

William Neely and that his mother's name was Eva Mae Green. He knew that most of his kin was from Hayden, Blount County, AL. My dad also told me that the Hays-Hayes, Blizzard, Reid, Graves, Yarborough and Thomas families had all married into the Neely clan somehow.

The first thing I did was to post queries on the Internet on all the Blount County, AL sites. I stated who I was and that I was seeking information on the Neelys from this area. I received many answers and found a lot of relatives that I did not even know existed. They were all happy to share their family histories with me.

This is also where my brickwall started. The Thomas kin who contacted me had done extensive work on the Thomas line; she had it well documented with all of her source information. But she had gone no further back than Benjamin Thomas, my sixth-great-grandfather who was born in Anston County, NC. She had a side note that the Thomas clan was originally from Ireland.

I searched and searched Anston County and even its surrounding counties with no luck. The next thing I tried was locating a ship from Ireland bound for the Carolinas. Once again, I hit a brickwall. I contacted my cousin to verify where she had obtained the information on Benjamin. She said her source was an old family Bible that was in very bad condition.

Who was I to argue with a source like that? For the next few years, I worked intermittently on the Thomas genealogy line but with no luck — I think I covered every county in North and South Carolina.

A couple of months ago, I was for information on one of Benjamin's sons, David Thomas. I logged onto FamilySearch.org. And there my brickwall did not just crumble; it fell over with a resounding bang!

It turned out that Benjamin Thomas was born not in North Carolina but in Talbot County, MD. I also found out that while his father, Simon Thomas, was also born in Maryland, Simon's father, Tristan Thomas, was born in England, no mention whatsoever of Ireland.

Knowing what I know about the family and their migration habits, Maryland would be one of the last places I would look for their records. Which just goes to prove the old adage: What couldn't be, will. I am currently working on this new information, doing further research just to see how far back I can go.

Just because you have been told something, don't believe it. Keep pushing and trying new angles and one day your brickwall will topple. — Laura Neely Bryant, AL, buclau@gulftel.com

A Subscription To Success

I subscribe to several genealogy magazines. I read each article, editorial, etc., thoroughly. I came across a letter to the editor from someone with my father's surname, Quitman. I had made no progress at all on that line. I knew that my great-grandfather came to the United States in 1860 from Germany, as a child of 12, with an older and a younger brother. But there was no one else on the ship by that name.

I was lucky there was only one person in the Internet phone directory by that name. I mailed a letter Thursday and received a phone call on Friday evening. His Quitmans were Hungarian and he was certain we were not related. However, he was pretty sure I was related to a person doing Quitman research that he had talked to on the phone. He gave me this other person's name and phone number. And he was right. Richard and I are third-cousins.

My second-great-grandfather's

first wife died in Germany, probably about the time of the birth of the youngest boy. My second-great-grandfather left the children and emigrated to the United States. He remarried and started a new family. He then sent for his children in Germany. (The second family knew about the first, but the descendants of the first family knew nothing about the second family!)

So I found a new cousin, got a generation further back on the Quitmans, and found a whole new branch on the family tree. — Judy Gehman, CA, jgehman@earthlink.net

Who Was Uncle Gus?

Persistence and determination has helped me to climb over or around brickwalls. But, as in the past, questions still exist. My father, Jackson Williams Mathewson, seldom talked about the past history of his relatives, both Williamses and Mathewsons. Born in 1903 in West Bay City, MI, he died in Saginaw, MI in 1965 at the age of 62 with a great number of family questions unanswered. Through the following years his old records, photographs and other items remained in the family.

In 1993, my mother's estate was passed on to me, the surviving child. One of the most prized items was a silver pewter milk drinking cup given to my dad as a baby. Inscribed on the cup was "Jackson from Uncle Gus". Who was Uncle Gus?

Meeting with other family members, more old photos, Bible listings and other letters were exchanged. New paths to follow! Checking the 1880 census and the birth page in the Bible, the Williams children were listed by name and date of birth. The children of Aaron and Martha Williams were George Elijah, Warren Aaron, Annie Marie (my paternal grandmother), Charles Oscar, and Milfred Egbert. But no Gus, or a name to shortened to Gus.

One of the documents exchanged was from the Glendale City, CA newspaper and the obituary of the oldest Williams son, George Elijah, who died in 1932. Was this man my dad's oldest uncle? Checking census and Bible records, he was born in Canada, raised in Michigan, and in 1891, married Bernice Colburn in Bay City, MI. Their first son died at an early age, but from the 1900 census there was a daughter. From the 1910, 1920, and 1930 census data and the newspaper article, he and his family lived in Glendale City, Burbank Township, CA. But, he and his family had moved from Bay City, MI to Youngstown, OH for a brief time where he worked in the interior decorating business. In the census reports and the newspaper article, he was always listed as George Elijah or simply George.

In 2002, using the Random Acts of Genealogical Kindness website, I contacted a genealogist in Bay City, MI and received extensive information about the Williams family. This included the obituaries of both Aaron and Martha Williams. In Aaron Williams' 1902 obituary: "Mr. Williams was 64 years old and resided

This silver pewter drinking cup was given to Richard Mathewson's father, Jackson, when he was a baby and is engraved "Jackson from Uncle Gus."

here about 14 years. He is survived by his widow, four sons, and one daughter. Gus Williams, his eldest son, who has been located at Youngstown, Ohio for some time arrived here last evening." My grandmother, "Mrs. J. Mathewson", is also listed.

SUDDEN SEIZURE CLAIMS VETERAN MERCHANT'S LIFE

George E. Williams Dies Of Heart Attack While Visiting Store

Stricken with a heart attack in front of his store at 103 North Brand last night, George Elijah Williams, 65, pioneer Glendale merchant, died within a few minutes. His death came as a surprise to his relatives and friends, as he had been in splendid health apparently, and had been active daily in the conduct of his business affairs.

Part of the obituary for George Elijah Williams, as it appeared in the Glendale News-Press *on 20 February 1932.*

This brickwall mystery is now solved. George Elijah Williams was known to the Williams family as Gus and to his nephew as Uncle Gus.

However, several more brickwalls are on the horizon. How did George Elijah Williams get the nickname of Gus? Plus, I have numerous pictures of my dad when he traveled to the Los Angeles area of California in the 1920s. Did he visit his Uncle Gus? More brickwalls to hurdle! — Richard Mathewson, OK, rjmadm@cox.ne

Searching For John

For several years, I tried to locate my great-grandmother's brother, John Harris. Family tradition said that he had moved to Texas in the 1890s. I had also been unable to locate his family in the 1880 census for the area in which he lived. Various attempts had been made by many researchers to identify his wife. The 1870 census indicated that she was named Jane. The marriage prospect most researchers eventually had settled on was a Mary Jane Witham; however, I was not satisfied with this marriage being his because it seemed unlikely the two of them would have encountered each other.

I located a possible marriage of J.J. Harris to Eliza J. Kennedy using a marriage index published in the Itawamba Historical Society's *Itawamba Settlers* magazine. I made a photocopy of the marriage record on a trip to the Itawamba County Courthouse. I noticed that she had been a neighbor of the Harris family in one of the censuses and felt that my research was headed in the right direction. However, the inability to locate them in later censuses kept me from being able to confirm this marriage as his.

I joined a library which provides remote access to the Heritage Quest databases, and the availability of indexes to later censuses (for which Soundex and Miracode had been available) finally proved to be the key to locating John. One day, I decided to try to locate him in the 1900 census in Texas. Using the advanced search features, I put in the surname Harris, first name of John, and state of Texas for the year 1900. I got a rather long list of hits and began to browse for one that was approximately the right age.

When I found the John in Lee

County, TX, I still was not 100 percent sure I had found my match because the birth location of his father was incorrect. However, it was a John with a wife Eliza J. and all the children at home were born in Mississippi. It seemed promising. I also noted there was a grown son in the adjacent household who was born in Mississippi. I went back and did a search on the surname Harris for the year 1900, limiting it to Lee County, TX, to make sure I had included all the grown children who might be in the area.

I moved on to the 1910 census, discovering that John was a widower at that time with one son still living at home. This time, the birth locations for both of his parents were correct. I was pretty sure that I had found my John. I found several of the sons with households of their own. I continued my search for Harrises in Lee County, TX in the 1920 census, discovering that John Sr. had probably passed away. I continued to follow his children through the 1930 census.

I then went to the USGenWeb archives where I found birth records for some of his grandchildren, listing the full names of the parents. I discovered that the middle name of John Jr. was Jasper, and I already knew that John's middle name began with a J. I also located a listing of Confederate pension applications for Lee County, TX, discovering that John Sr.'s had been turned down.

Armed with all my new information and the knowledge that John's move to Texas occurred after about 1891, I decided to see what I could come up with in the 1880 census for the state of Mississippi. Using FamilySearch.org's index with connections to Ancestry.com's images of the 1880 census, I was able to locate him as Jasper J. Harris in Lee County, MS. He'd been hiding under his middle name all that time! While there is still much work to be done on this line, the discovery of his whereabouts has made the search very fruitful! — Lori Thornton, TN

You Just Might Get Lucky

Several years ago, I wrote to the Oakland County Clerks Office in California requesting a search for a marriage record for my great-grandmother, Mary Jane Hart to John William Mcneil. I listed the various common spellings such as Mcneal, Mcneil and Mcneill and suggested a time period between 1883 and 1887. I received a response that no such record was located.

A few months ago, I again sent a request for this information having forgotten that I had already requested the information three years earlier. This time, however; the searcher found the information and was able to supply me with a marriage record dated 26 February 1884.

When I discovered the letter from three years earlier, I realized that when someone tells you that they were unable to locate requested information it doesn't mean that the information is not there. As is the case with old records, they are often difficult to read and can be easily overlooked. If you feel a record exists, then try another request.

You just might get lucky. — Linda Hahn, CA

Researching Gilbert Darling

My husband's great-grandfather, Gilbert H. Darling, lived from 1832 until after 1870. Filling in the details of his life was a challenge and finding his ancestors an even bigger challenge. The search started with information provided by Gilbert's youngest son, Frank Burt Darling, my husband's grandfather. Frank stated that his father lived in Michigan, was born in 1832, had married Mariah Abbey Glazier, and had served in the 4th Michigan Cavalry in the Civil War. This was enough information to give me a good start.

My first search was the 1850 census for Michigan. I found Gilbert as the oldest child in a family of five children with mother, Marilda, but no father. This Gilbert was born in 1832 in New York. It seemed like it could be a match. I then sent for his Civil War records from the NARA. The records confirmed that he was born in 1832 in Cattaraugus County, NY, and that he was in the 4th Cavalry. From that point on, it was easy to trace Gilbert around Michigan in the census records, find his three marriages and one divorce, and his death. Now I had to find his parents.

Knowing that Gilbert was born in Cattaraugus County gave me a place to search for his father. I had found in a marriage record that Gilbert's father was David, and I spent many years searching for a David Darling in Cattaraugus County. They were many wasted years.

Unfortunately, the Gilbert Darling I had found in the 1850 census was not the right person. When I located another Gilbert in the 1850 census of Lucas County, OH, I knew I was in trouble. This Gilbert was listed correctly as Gilbert H. Darling. He also was born in 1832 in New York and was the oldest of four children, with only a mother in the household. He lived only 40 miles from the first Gilbert, which helped to confuse the issue. His three siblings were Oliver P., William B., and Cynthia W. The mother was Concurrence, a name I had never come across before. I did a search on the Internet for the name Concurrence and discovered it was a name found almost exclusively in a certain area of Connecticut. It turned out that this was the exact area Gilbert's mother was from, and the name had been passed down for generations. Her father was William Bradford, who could be easily traced back to William Bradford of the *Mayflower*.

When I originally found this Gilbert, I thought he could be the same person as the one in Michigan, and that he was working in Ohio as a boatman in the summer of 1850, living with relatives. Eventually, I realized it was two different men. Now I had to find proof of which family was the correct one.

A record found in the Chancery Court of Lucas County, OH, gave me

US Civil War Volunteer Enlistment record for Gilbert H. Darling.

much needed information. One John Darling, of Lucas County, OH, had died in 1848 while in the process of buying a house and property in the county. He left behind a wife, Concurrence, and children Gilbert H., Oliver P., William B. and Cynthia W. Since only two payments had been made on the lot, it went to court to resolve the issue. This was a bonus for me.

I now knew the name of Gilbert's father, and knew that the children listed in the census were indeed his siblings. Tracing these siblings should lead me to more information on the family. I have not yet discovered anything about Cynthia, and William being such a common name, I have not definitely pinned down which of the many Williams is the right one. But Oliver has been easy to trace, even though he moved around frequently and married twice. His 1900 death certificate listed the names and birth states of his parents. His father was John Darling, born in Vermont, and his mother was Concurrence Bradford, born in Connecticut. I now had confirmation of his father's name and hopefully a correct place to search.

I have a 14,000-name Darling database on my computer, the result of 30 years of searching. I searched the database for all the John Darlings from Vermont and found only one that could be the father of Gilbert. He was born the same year as Concurrence, had no wife or death date listed, and was the only one in the family that didn't stay in the area. I am now in the process of searching for data on this John Darling. Had I not wasted 30 years searching for David, I may have located John by now. We have to be careful of making assumptions that we are unable to prove. — Pat Darling, MT, pdarling@bmt.net

Waste Not, Want Not

When my grandmother Sophie Roberts passed away in a small town called Lehigh in Oklahoma, my father inherited her household items and furniture. Tucked away in an old desk he found some old correspondence that his mother wrote to her family in France.

Clement Valtille in March 1919, a newly discovered French ancestor of Paul Dale Roberts.

By doing a thorough search of the letters and finding out the relatives she was writing to, he discovered over 200 relatives in France he had no idea he was related to. My father traveled to France several times, discovering his roots. While becoming friends with his newly discovered relatives, he was also given photographs of family members who are no longer with us.

It is very important to hold onto old correspondence, photographs, journals and anything else of significance when investigating family genealogies. If my grandmother hadn't kept her letters, my father would have never have discovered the French side of our family. Our family has just grown bigger, thanks to my grandmother who is no longer with us. — Paul Dale Roberts, CA

In Search Of Sister

Many times interest in genealogy comes about after the "natural resource" is no longer available to us — that is to say, our ancestors, who could have provided information, are no longer living. External help is then the only available resource, but how do you get there?

As I broadened my search for my grandmother's family, one sister kept eluding me. I could find her in the 1900 census, but she just dropped out from that point. To me, that meant marriage or death, but it was too early for the SSDI to be of any help, and in 1900 she was only 25 years of age. I never met her, and little was ever said about her, but the 1900 census had her living in upstate New York, with my grandmother, and both were teaching school. It would have been pretty easy to say that she was my grandmother's sister, and not in my direct line of ancestry, but I couldn't get to that point. If she had married, how would I ever find her, not knowing her married name, where she lived or where she died?

In this case, I got very lucky. I had used a resource, *Index of A. Cady's St. Lawrence County Cemetery Trans-*criptions, to expand some other information, and thought I would try that one again. Anne Cady has done some excellent work in cataloging cemeteries in St. Lawrence County, NY, with gravestone photographs in many cases. Since much of my paternal side of the family is from that area, I decided to really dig into that data, and see what I could find. Lo and behold, my grandmother's sister, and her husband were listed, and she was listed as his wife, by her maiden name.

I stumbled onto the Cady website while searching St. Lawrence County websites for anything that might help me, on another search. Since then I have used it several times, always with good results. While maybe not as good as the Cady site, there are certainly others out there that would be of assistance to the frustrated researcher, and I suspect that typically they would be localized to a very high degree, so get creative, and hunt them up, and use them well.

Armed with this information, I am now trying to determine if they had any children — who knows, I may find a long-lost cousin out there. — N. Roach, KS, Blair4th@sbcglobal.net

Two Heads Are Better Than One

From his obituary, I discovered that my great-grandfather, Christoph Friedrich Rosenthal, who went by the name Friedrich, was born in Wintzingerode, Prussia.

I wrote a letter to the church in Wintzingerode (then in East Germany) and received a very informative letter back from the pastor, which included Friedrich's birth information, marriage information, parents' names, wife's parents' names (including maiden names of both sets of parents), occupations, and a list of Friedrich's siblings. The youngest was a sister named Christiane

Melesina Rosenthal, born on 11 August 1832.

I had no other information on this family except for that letter from Germany and information about a few of the descendants of Friedrich. Then I came in contact with a relative who lived in the area where the Rosenthals settled, and she was also researching the family. We shared information and found that the whole family immigrated to Washington County, WI in the mid-1800s. The adult children were married except for the two youngest siblings of Friedrich. The brickwall occurred when trying to locate Christiane Melesina and her descendants in this country without knowing her married name.

After about a year of research and collaboration with my contact, there was no evidence of Christiane Melesina in the census or elsewhere. In a letter, my contact speculated that Christiane Melesina had died on the boat. In addition to me, she was working with other contacts in the area to research her other family lines. She found a Rilling contact in West Bend, WI, whose uncle had married a Rosenthal. In discussions with this Rilling contact and her 95-year-old mother who lived with her, my contact asked her if she knew of a Jacob Rilling and she said, "Yes, he was my great-grandfather" and then when asked who he was married to, she replied, "Christina Rosenthal." And she was able to provide all the dates and a complete family genealogy!

It just goes to show how important collaboration can be, and that two heads (or many heads) are better than one.

One other note: without that letter from the church pastor in Germany, we never would have known that Christiane Melesina existed or that there was another branch on the family tree to research. — Sharon Rosenthal Lemley, WI

Keep Talking To Relatives!

I became interested in my family tree in junior high school, when I had to do one of those "write down your family back to your great-grandparents" handouts. I prodded everyone on both sides of my family with questions about ancestors and diligently wrote down all the information I gathered.

Katherine Fox Owen Sellers Moore.

Some of what I learned had to do with my second-great-grandmother on my father's side. Everyone told me her name was Kate Moore. I knew she had married my second-great-grandfather Sellers, and that was about it. When I started trying to do more research on her, I hit a brickwall immediately. I simply couldn't find a Kate or Katherine Moore who had married Cornelius Sellers.

Then, only a few years ago, I learned my grandfather's sister was still alive. I called her on the phone and introduced myself. She sounded somewhat suspicious of me, and she definitely didn't sound interested in family history research, but she was willing to listen to my questions.

Imagine my surprise when I asked her about Kate Moore (her grandmother) and she told me that Moore wasn't her maiden name; it was from her second marriage! My second-great-grandfather had died young, and, with a young son (my great-grandfather) to raise, Kate had remarried soon after.

What was even more amazing was that I had purchased a family history of the Moore family of Burlington County, NJ about a month prior to that phone conversation, in the belief that Moore was Kate's maiden name. Of course, I hadn't found her in the book. After speaking with my great-aunt, I went back to the book and did find her — with her second husband, George W. Moore. I discovered her maiden name, Katherine Fox Owen, and a whole new branch of my family descending from my great-grandfather's half-brother.

Make the effort to talk to as many of your relatives as possible. You never know what you may discover! — Janice Sellers, CA, janice@seismosoc.org

What A Difference One Handwritten Alphabet Letter Can Make

According to the Ross family Bible kept in Ashfield Township, Huron County, ON, my great-grandfather Donald Ross was born on 5 May 1824 in Cawdeary, Strathcarron, Kincardine, Ross-shire, Scotland.

On our first trip to Scotland in 1974, we set off in our rental car from Prestwick to the Northern Highlands looking for Cawdeary. Our Strathcarron location was about an hour north of Inverness on the northern border of Ross-shire.

When we arrived, we went to a Tourist Information lady in Ardgay, a Mrs. Urquhart, and asked where we might find Cawdeary — not really sure if it was the name of a house or a small community. She did not know where it was. So we checked into a bed and breakfast in Bonar Bridge, just across the water from Ardgay, we had told her where we were staying that night — and she was going to rethink.

Early the next morning, before the Scottish porridge was ready at the bed and breakfast, the Tourist Lady phoned to say she made an appointment for us to meet Maggie at Cawdearg — with a G — but we had to be early since Maggie was an elderly lady who rode her bike to a fishing lodge to make the beds each day.

Cawdearg croft in Strathcarron, Kincardine Parish, Ross-shire, Scotland.

When we arrived, Maggie gave me a big hug and said "You are a Ross because I can tell by your dark brown eyes". She made me feel like I was home. We enjoyed a short visit and were shown letters from my grandfather in Canada to Maggie's mother — I recognized the writing. We were shown through the croft and saw the weaver's shed where Donald Ross' father, William Ross, supported his family as a weaver.

We have learned from the current owner that Ca'dearg dates back to 1650 when the Marquis of Montrose was fighting battles in the area and he laid his wounded on a small brae at the front of property. It was named "Ca" meaning "soldier" in Gaelic and "dearg" meaning "red" in Gaelic from the blood of the soldiers. It is not known when the W was added since there is no W in the Gaelic language.

According to the owner, the property came into the family in around 1746 when the Scottish Chief Ross of Pitcalnie allocated it.

The Cawdearg croft is owned by a descendant from the original family — who is a fourth-cousin of mine. It has been nicely enhanced over the years — and has always had someone living there. The current owner has kept it in good repair as you can see from the photograph.

Thanks to a conscientious Tourist Information lady we found Cawdearg and not the Cawdeary that we thought that was written in the family Bible. All the difference of how one letter was formed. We also learned to pronounce Cawdearg as Ca-jer-ic. — Earl Ross, MI, earlross@prodigy.net

Information Is Out There Somewhere

When I first started researching my family tree, I concentrated on finding out where and when my great-grandfather Thomas Robinson, was born and where and when he died.

I started on the where and when Thomas was born. I tackled the Bedford Township censuses for 1861, 1871, 1881 and 1891. Thomas was listed with his wife Johanna and his children up until 1881. Johanna was listed as a widow in 1891, there were four children still living at home at that time. Thomas and Johanna's youngest child Daniel was my grandfather. Taking Thomas' age and place of birth from the censuses, he was born in approximately 1808 in England. That is when my brickwall came up.

The Robinson surname is very common in England; I had no idea where to search for my ancestors in England. According to the censuses, Thomas had died sometime between 1881 and 1891. Then my father Allen remembered something that his father Daniel had told him about Thomas. Thomas had died when Daniel was 13 years old; Daniel was born in 1873, so Thomas had died sometime in 1886. I ordered the 1886 death indexes from the Archives of Ontario located in Toronto. I found Thomas' date of death in the indexes; he died on 26 September 1886. I then ordered the registration reel that contained Thomas' death registration from the Archives of Ontario as well.

Rather than travel to Toronto, I used the local library's inter-library loans department, to order in the reels I needed. Thomas' death registration mentioned what I already knew, his age and he was born in England. Thomas' religion was Wesleyan Methodist but a lot of people in the area were Anglican, including some of my other ancestors in the area. I decided to try the Anglican Diocese of Ontario located in Kingston, which covers the area that Thomas was in. I wrote to the diocese and told them what names I was researching from that area and was pleasantly surprised when I received their research information. Thomas Robinson was in their registers, it told when he was buried, what cemetery he was in (family rumor had him buried in the field next to his home) and where he was born in England — Liverpool.

Finally, I thought, a mention where Thomas had come from in England. There was a fee for the research the diocese did for me, but it was well worth it, besides knocking down my brickwall they had lots of other useful information about other branches of my family tree.

I haven't found Thomas' exact date of birth yet, but now I know where to start looking for it.

I think the moral of the story is to

find as many sources or documents on the person you are researching that you can. Listen to the odd tidbits from the memories from the older relatives. One of them is bound to have that bit of information to get you further back or least point you in the right direction to keep going in your research. Sometimes it can be frustrating but don't give up; the information is out there somewhere. — Roberta Robinson, ON

A Tricky Technique

When a mathematician finds a new approach to solve one problem or to complete one proof, it is often considered a mere trick. However, once that approach has been used to solve additional problems or finds other uses, it is considered a technique. Whether trick or technique, here's how I found my great-grandfather John Lenz's ancestors in Austria.

John first appeared in the US in 1888 when he married Katherine Stoll in La Crosse, WI. From that point forward, we have lots of information about John and Katherine but my every attempt to discover where he came from in Austria failed.

However, it was well-documented that Katherine Stoll had been born in Castle Berneck near Kauns in Tirol, Austria.

After many fruitless searches for

John Lenz's roots, I followed a hunch. John and Katherine seemed to marry a short time after John arrived in the US. Could they have known each other in the "old country"? I decided to write to several parishes and government officials in Kauns and other small towns in that area of Tirol.

I heard nothing for a long time until one exciting day, a thick registered letter arrived from a priest in Tirol. His housekeeper had searched their records and found John Lenz! My great-grandfather was the youngest of six children born to Alois and Cordula (née Spaiser) Lenz who were married in 1841. The housekeeper had found several more generations, ending with Mathias Lenz (who died in 1762) and his wife Catharina Trencher. In addition to a three-page summary of her findings, the housekeeper sent copies of the actual church record for the relevant entries. This was indeed a thrilling breakthrough.

John Lenz, great-grandfather of Jerry Lenz.

My hunch had paid off, albeit only because of the generous help of two wonderful Tirolians, whom I hope to meet some day so I can thank them. Was my solution to finding my great-grandfather a trick? Perhaps so, or maybe it is already a well-known technique.

If not, maybe it will become a technique useful to other genealogists and family historians. — Jerry Lenz, MN, jlenz@cloudnet.com

Home Court Advantage

My ancestor, Philip Lockwood, born in 1787 in New Jersey, was, according to my grandmother, the first Baptist minister in the Western Reserve. He died in 1864 in Lake County, OH, and early in my research I was elated to find his obituary. Much to my distress, however, it didn't list the names of his children. It merely said that he and his wife had been the parents of 13 children, "nine of whom grew to maturity." He did not leave a will, and I have never located the Bible mentioned in his estate settlement.

Over some 40 years I researched many records: censuses, marriage records, land and probate records, other court records, etc. Finally, I had located eight children of Philip's who married and had families. Then, in an effort to look at every possible film available for the area, I found a school census for 1842 that showed Philip's household had a student named Phebe, who was probably a teenager. Phebe Lockwood was new to me, as I had never seen her name on any other record. I added her to the family group sheet, and for some time assumed she must have died without marrying, since the marriage records

Court document dated 1914 listing all living relatives of Philip Lockwood's daughter, Anna Maria.

for the area didn't yield a record for her. She was not in Philip's household in 1850.

Not knowing her given name, until I found it in the school census, made it difficult for me to recognize the fact that in the 1850 census she was a married woman living in a household surrounded by Lockwood families. (Had I known I was looking for a Phebe, I might have investigated this household earlier than I did.)

For quite a few years I had been attempting to find a court document, a deposition that would clarify some questions which were raised in the typed copy of the deposition, which I had received from a distant relative. This deposition was made regarding some property which had belonged to Philip's daughter Anna Maria. The niece giving the deposition listed her genealogy as partial evidence that she was entitled to the property. I had tried numerous times to locate the original record. Finally, in 1999, I communicated via e-mail with a kind researcher in Perry, OH, who agreed to look once more for this document.

As it turned out, the deposition I sought was not actually a court record, but a statement made to a notary. Therefore, there was not an original at the courthouse. However, in her search for it, the researcher found another court document dated 1914 relating to this same property. And in it, the niece had been asked to list all living relatives of Anna Maria's.

By this time, I was well acquainted with most of the names in the 1914 record. However, listed there amongst them was Philip's daughter Phebe "Edwin", listed as a "sister of the deceased," and also the names of two of her children! Knowing her married name, I was then able to easily locate her in two censuses. She had married a Thomas Edwin in about 1845, and they had four children. Philip's obituary said he had 53 grandchildren. Adding them up, that was the total I now had!

When the family you seek lived in the same county for several generations, look at every film and record available. — Marcia Green, CA, mwverde.mwg@verizon.net

Keep On Digging

For many years, I have wanted to research my great-grandfather. My mother knew a female cousin had done research more than 20 years earlier. The cousin did not have children but my mother thought she had nephews living in a little town in Wisconsin. I sent letters to the three people in town with that name. I received one reply and as luck would have it, this nephew had all of the research information!

I sent him a picture of my great-grandfather. He had a different photo of the same man with a woman and child (my great-grandmother and their first son). He didn't know who they were until our correspondence. He transcribed her information, which has checked out for the most part. I have made a few modifications. Thanks to my mother's cousin's research, I have been able to find many relatives — some still living. With a little perseverance, I was able to obtain information from people who are no longer around. Remember, just because the person is gone, it doesn't mean the information is. Keep digging! — Carolyn Harmon, IL

Kissing Cousins

Two years ago I traced my line to Penelope Van Princis and Richard Stout. These two people have a multitude of descendants starting with their 15 children. There are many genealogists working on this family tree so it was easy to find them.

I went to the family trees at WorldConnect and while I was entering in some of the names that connected to my tree, I found a tree that actually led to my second-great-grandmother, Elizabeth Alice Stout. I decided to use this tree and traced backwards from Elizabeth Alice, who at one time had been a brickwall for me.

A distant cousin had sent me her name in an e-mail. She had found a posting on the Cooney/Stout message board at Ancestry.com. I had known her name was Elizabeth Alice from censuses and from the message board I found that she was the daughter of Richard Stout and Harriett Ann Cooney. I began to work backwards from Elizabeth Alice in the family tree that I got at WorldConnect. I traced her back to Samuel Stout, born on 10 April 1740 and then began to work on Samuel's sisters and brothers.

One of his sisters, Margaret Stout, born on 26 July 1744, had married a Daniel Osborne. The name seemed familiar and as I worked down the line, more and more of the names seemed familiar so I checked them on my index and sure enough, I had already listed them.

Margaret Stout was my husband's fifth-great-grandmother as well as my fifth-great-aunt. Working through the line, I found that my husband is my sixth-cousin. I could hardly wait until he got home to tell him!

When he came in the door, I said "Hi cousin". He looked at me quizzically and I told him the story. He thought it was quite funny and when our 11-year-old grandson came in to see why he was laughing, he told him why. Krystopher looked at me in horror. "You mean to say, that of all the people in the world you chose to marry your cousin?" he asked.

We have had a lot of fun sharing the information that we are cousins with both my family and his.

Doing genealogy research, you never know who you may end up related to! — Judith Henderson, CO, BlkUni42@aol.com

Intestate Investigation

My great-grandmother was Margaret Mulgrew. I knew that she was born in Shantavny Townland (an area generally known as Ballygawley) in County Tyrone, Ireland in 1839, and that she had immigrated to the United States in 1855. Later, in about 1860, she joined her brothers (among them, Peter) and sisters (among them, Catherine) in Pawtucket, Providence County, RI, where she married Matthew Goodwin.

Having been in touch via e-mail with some Mulgrew families in Australia, I knew that their ancestors (brother Francis and sister Sarah) had immigrated there from Ballygawley, County Tyrone, in the late 1840s to early 1850s. There was a story handed down that some letters had been written from those immigrant Mulgrews to a Peter Mulgrew in Rhode Island, perhaps the Peter Mulgrew of my family. Later, a baptismal record was found for Francis Mulgrew — he was born in Shantavny Townland, of the same parents as my great-grandmother Margaret.

So there were cousins in America and in Australia, finally connected

after brothers and sisters had parted 150 years ago! It would be great to find more cousins still living in County Tyrone, but what were the chances, given the time lapse and the fairly poor Irish records?

The gravestone of Isabella Mulgrew in Ballygawley, Co. Tyrone.

However, Margaret's older sister Catherine died in Pawtucket in 1906. She died intestate, but there were some probate records. Among the papers was one very crucial piece of evidence. The Petition for Appointment of Administrator for the Estate listed the heirs-at-law of Catherine Mulgrew: Peter Mulgrew, Providence, Brother; Terrence Mulgrew, Pawtucket, Brother; Margaret Goodwin, Providence, Sister; Sarah Geis, Australia, Sister and Isabelle Mulgrew, Ireland, Niece.

A niece, Isabelle Mulgrew, in Ireland! I thought I knew who that might be, based on research and other correspondence. But to be sure, I checked the 1901 census for County Tyrone. There were three Isabelle Mulgrews. Two were ruled out because each had siblings, who would have been named as heirs-at-law also. The third Isabelle was a resident of Shantavny. She was a married woman — married to a John Mulgrew — the same as her maiden name. She was the daughter of Bernard Mulgrew of Shantavny. Bernard, then, was a brother of the Rhode Islanders and Australians, who had remained in Ireland.

John and Isabelle Mulgrew had a daughter who married into the O'Hanlon family, and the O'Hanlon descendants live in Ballygawley today. I have not yet met these cousins, but look forward to that happening soon! — Loree Muldowney, CA, Loree@dc.rr.com

New York Odyssey

Genealogy sometimes takes on the aspects of a mystery story. Take for example, the series of events that occurred on an ancestor search in upstate New York.

Jonnie, my travel buddy and friend of 40 years, is a crack researcher, with an eye out not only for her own ancestors, but for mine, too. In the New York State Archives in Albany she found an item that said "Benjamin Sweet, from Brutus, New York, settled on Lot 76, Marcellus, in 1804." That being my Benjamin, I copied the reference, not knowing how meaningful it would become.

On a later April day, Jonnie and I set out to do some serious research in historical society libraries in Onondaga County. First stop, Tully, about 20 miles south of Syracuse, Onondaga's county seat. Jonnie's ancestor had lived there and one of mine was reported to have died there.

The Tully Area Historical Society historian told us that boundary lines changed as counties became more populated and that boundaries of three adjacent towns — Tully, Marcellus and Spafford — had been redrawn so that parts of "old Tully" were not necessarily Tully now, but

may be part of Spafford or Marcellus. She suggested we check with the Spafford historian. Spafford wasn't one of "my" towns but maybe Jonnie would find something useful there.

A phone call assured us the Spafford historian was home. Jonnie asked her to check for records while we drove to her house. If it hadn't been for the complicated directions Jonnie had jotted down, we'd still be wandering country roads, looking for "the house across from the fire station."

Part of the gravestone for Winthrup Graham.

The Spafford historian had a record, alright, but not Jonnie's. She held out a photo of the gravestone of Winthrup Graham, father-in-law of my Benjamin Sweet who'd bought lot 76 in Marcellus. Winthrup was my ancestor who was supposed to have died in Tully.

"Where is the grave?" I asked.

"We don't know where it is now. The tombstone *was* stored in a woman's barn."

"A barn?"

"Yes, Helen's barn out on Willow-dale Road."

I squinted at the somewhat blurry photo and tried to copy the inscription on the stone. "Do you have an extra photo of the tombstone?"

She shook her head and my heart plummeted.

"I could call Helen, if you like, and ask if she still has the stone."

The patron saint of genealogists, if there is one, was smiling on us that day, for not only did the stone still rest in the barn, we were invited to come over and see it.

Helen lived on a rutty country lane that looked like something out of the *Beverly Hillbillies* before they "moved to Beverleee." Twists and turns and uphill and down, we drove. Ruts finally gave way to good road again and there stood the sign in front of a vintage house.

Helen came out to greet us, hands holding two flashlights she said we'd need to see the gravestone well. As we walked across the road and down the hill a bit, Helen told us the story of how she became the keeper of the stone.

She had hired a young man to come with his backhoe to do some work on her property. He noticed that her house and barn were old and the conversation turned to the history of the area. When he learned she was a member of the local historical society, he told her that he'd been digging a ditch alongside another road and had unearthed a broken gravestone, and would she like to have it?

She opened the barn door for us to enter, shined the flashlight beam toward the far wall, and there stood the grave marker of Deacon Winthrup Graham, who died on 20 March 1803. Helen told us the ditch where the stone was found is near lot 76, the property purchased by his son-in-law, Benjamin Sweet! Boundary line changes had designated that lot not in Tully but in Spafford.

Now that I had the answer to one genealogical question, I had dredged up still another: where was Winthrup Graham's body in that year from 1803 when he died until 1804 when Benjamin bought lot 76? I was to learn later from a deed in the Onondaga Courthouse, that in February 1803 Winthrup Graham had purchased part of lot 77, adjacent and just east of lot 76, the very lot that his son-in-law would buy a year later!

We parted with many a thank-you, my camera holding precious film records of the strangest genealogical find of all the years of our ancestral quests. Maybe patience, persistence and passion paid off, but I suspect that a touch of insanity is what did the trick. Why else would two grown women go chasing a gravestone down a strange country road? — G. Diane Altona, CA

Go With Your Gut

I slammed into my brickwall full force! I had been looking for my ancestor Levi Trask's burial spot for eight years. After attending a genealogical conference, I learned some things to try to break through the brickwall. Someone had said sometimes messages were written in the margins of the death books. I had already sent for the death record with no results, so I was willing to try anything to find his grave. So I went to the townhall in Peabody, MA, to check the death register with my own eyes.

The clerk was very nice in assisting me; again I had no results. I left disappointed and was walking across the street to where I parked my car when I noticed a funeral home sign. I thought to myself; you've tried everything else why not go and ask, it can't hurt. I spoke to a nice gentleman who told me he did not know where Levi was buried, but he knew of someone who was about to retire that might. He called him up and asked him if he knew where Levi was buried. Yep, he sure did! The gentleman then gave me directions to the cemetery where I was to meet this other man who would take me to the right plot.

Lo and behold, he directed me right to Levi's stone and the rest of the family was altogether. I was so thrilled to have finally found him that I started to talk to Levi's stone saying, "Do you realize how long I've been looking for you?" I think the man wondered if he had a crackpot on his hands because he asked me, "Where are you from again?" My suggestion to break through your brickwall is ask those questions and go with your gut feeling! Good luck in your search. — Diane M. Gusciora, PA

Going Back To My Roots

I felt very lucky to know that my English ancestor, James Shepherd, had immigrated with his family from Wiltshire, UK, to Canada, in 1832, when he was only two-years old. A great-aunt had written to me saying that oral tradition had also held that he was from Gleason, but try as I might I could not find Gleason on a map. So I looked up all names that started with G that might sound like Gleason, especially if heard with an English accent. No luck there. I tried the same thing with all place names that started with C. Nothing really fit; the closest names were Cleyhill, Colerne, Ceawlin and Corsham. In the IGI, there were a lot of Shepherds in Colerne Parish so I started looking through Colerne parish records and I was surprised to find that there was a James Shepherd of the correct age! My cousin was convinced it was the correct family. However, I didn't see all of the other family members I expected to find, so I kept looking through the other parish records that I had on my list to

view. When at last I got to the Corsham Parish film I was amazed to see all of the family right there in the records, patiently waiting for me to find them.

Once I had located them, I saw that James Shepherd was baptized in the Corsham Parish, but he and his siblings were born in a place called Green Hills. Now I had a second challenge in front of me. Green Hills could not be located on any map that I had or could locate.

James Shepherd, who immigrated to Canada, from Wiltshire, UK, in 1832.

Finally, a few years ago, I was fortunate enough to make a trip to Corsham and, of course, as you might imagine, I went directly to the local library and inquired about Green Hills. I was really disappointed when the librarian said she had never heard of it! However, she said she did know of an old-timer who might know more about the area. When contacted, this individual cheerfully told us that Green Hills was a mile outside of Corsham in the countryside at a place now called Neston. Green Hills is a place name that is no longer used, so it was no wonder that I couldn't find it on a map. Since I was visiting the Corsham library, I had an opportunity to view a map of the area from the 1820s; no surprise, there was Greenhill, just a short distance from Corsham!

A section of the 1820s map found in the Corsham library, that helped Judy McAuliffe locate the Shepherd family.

Finding places that have changed names can be very challenging unless you search a time-appropriate map; and they can be even more challenging when oral history has distorted them. It takes a certain amount of persistence, but the ancestors will still be there waiting for you when you find that location. — Judy McAuliffe, CA

From Friends To Family

Over 30 years ago, I was introduced to a young woman by the name of Peggy. At the time, our husbands were playing in the same band and she and I became good friends. Peggy and I remained friends throughout the years, through the good times and the times that were not so good. Neither of us had sisters, so I suppose we substituted with each other. We live about 45 minutes apart, in the northeastern corner of Mississippi.

Around eight years ago, I became interested in genealogy and started researching my family tree. I found a great-grandmother by the name of Margaret Goodwin in Jefferson County AL, and began working on my Goodwin line. Using the Internet to find other Goodwin researchers helped me find Ron Goodwin, who had written a book titled *Theophilus*. This book follows the family of Theophilus Goodwin from Virginia to South Carolina to Jefferson County, AL and other locations. I promptly ordered the book and found it was a treasure trove of genealogy information, totally filled with my line of Goodwins, which were in Jefferson County in the mid-to-late 1800s.

Imagine my amazement when I found my best friend Peggy's mother listed in the book as a descendant of Theophilus Goodwin! Peggy's mother, Lois, is 90 years old now and is one of the most precious people in the world, I love her dearly. How wonderful to be related to her! My mother passed away several years ago but she was very much like Peggy's mother, she was also kind and caring but full of fun. Now I wonder if it was that Goodwin gene pool that gave them their personalities.

Peggy's grandmother and my great-grandmother shared a common great-grandfather. Oddly enough, Peggy's ancestors had moved from Jefferson County, AL, to Prentiss County, MS, in the late 1800s. My mother's family moved from Jefferson County, AL to Tishomingo County, MS, about 1925. Prentiss and Tishomingo Counties are adjoining. I am sure that neither family knew of the relationship to the other.

In the case of my Goodwin line, a publication by another researcher certainly knocked down a brickwall for me, not only did it help me find ancestors, it enlightened me to the fact that my friends were also actually family. — Judith Walker, MS, jwalker3@pngusa.net

The Power Of Pork

When I retired, I was determined to learn about my roots. On my father's side, I knew that my great-grand-parents, Matthew and Elizabeth (Horrobin) Ward, lived in Skegby, Nottinghamshire, in the second half of the 19th century. They ran a small butcher shop and raised eight children. Four of these children came to Canada and four remained in England. Six had children, and using the genealogist's and family histori-an's usual bag of tricks, (parish records, censuses and interviews with old timers) I successfully contacted living descendants of five of them.

This left me searching for my great-grandparents' eldest child, Thomas Watson Ward. His birth was recorded in the family Bible, and I found out that he married and had a daughter and at least four sons. I also learned that Thomas had moved to nearby Kirkby-in-Ashfield at the turn of the century, and had become a butcher, like his father. There were scraps of information about his daughter and sons, but the trail swift-ly ran out. Marriages and baptisms were not recorded in the local parish register, and none of the elderly rela-tives had further information. How could I break through this brickwall?

In desperation, I turned to a less formal tactic. I wrote the local news-papers. And here is where I made a conscious decision. Rather than writ-ing a bland letter focused on my needs, I wrote a story focused on their readers. Here, in part, is what I wrote:

I am writing to ask the help of your readers, and I am prepared to pay — in pork!

Last year, I came to Sutton-in-Ashfield in search of my ancestors, and found a fascinating photograph of a man in a top hat standing in front of his new pork butcher shop in Victoria Road, Kirkby-in-Ashfield.

The man is Thomas Watson Ward, *and he was a butcher in Kirkby-in-Ashfield from 1895 until he retired to Skegby in the 1930s.*

Thomas Watson Ward had a brother, William Oscroft Ward, who left for Canada in 1885. That brother, William, was my grandfather. He too became a pork butcher, but in Toronto, Canada!

Much of William's success in the new world was attributed to his excellent sausages concocted from a recipe William brought from Skegby, where his father, Matthew Ward, had also been a pork butcher.

Here is the challenge: I want to find Thomas Watson Ward's family, and I am offering ten pounds of the best pure pork sausage in your region to the first person who leads me to a living descendant of Thomas Watson Ward.

Please ask your readers to get in touch if they can help. And since I assume that the winner will also be a pork sausage lover, I will let them choose the butcher for the prize, but I will pay the bill! Thank you for your cooperation.

I sent the letters in early June and crossed my fingers, but I didn't crank up my expectations. English newspa-pers must get inundated with requests from North Americans who expect their letters will unleash the key to their whole family story. I could see my letter being crumpled and pitched into the editor's dustbin. I shouldn't have been so pessimistic.

On 21 June, *The Mansfield and Ashfield Observer* published my whole letter, and the photograph, with the headline "Tasty challenge to readers to pick up a porky prize — Calling all pork sausage lovers — I will pick up the bill!"

About the same date, the *Ashfield Chad* newspaper also published the story, slightly rewritten, with the pho-tograph, and gave it the headline "A pork prize for tree help".

I was delighted that the papers picked up the story and even ran the photograph, but a new layer of doubt emerged: Were any of Thomas' descendants still alive? Would they see the story? I didn't have long to worry. Here is what followed:

On June 21: Linda Brooks of Kirkby, a granddaughter of Thomas Watson Ward, heard of the article and had her son contact me. Soon I was on the phone with Linda herself, who regaled me with stories about her grandfather and of our great-grandfather. As coincidence would have it, Linda turned 90 that week. She said she couldn't think of a better present than getting back in touch with the rest of the Ward side of the family.

On June 22: I had a telephone call from Roger Bale, also of Kirkby, and a

Thomas Watson Ward and son outside Thomas' butcher shop in Victoria Road, Kirby-in-Ashfield, Notts, England, around 1900. The building was still standing in 2003.

great-grandson of Thomas Watson Ward. He had papers and photos of the family and we planned to share his and my material.

Also on that day, David Connah called to say that his wife, Wendy, might be a relative. I called Wendy (Ward) Connah and found that while she was not descended from Thomas and Elizabeth, she is a granddaughter of Sam Horrobin Ward, one of Thomas' brothers. And she had researched the Ward lineage back five generations before Sam and Thomas!

We agreed to share what we have.

Then on June 26: An e-mail arrived from Richard Ward in Sheffield, a second-great-grandson of Thomas Watson Ward. He also put me in touch with his grandfather, Clifford Ward, another unknown relative!

On June 28: The mail brought a letter from Ernest Ward, grandson of Thomas Watson Ward through his son Sewel. I called Ernest and got more information about Sewel and Thomas.

Next, on July 5: *The Nottingham Evening Post* rewrote the story and added the headline "We'll meat again... pork sausages reward beefs up search for relatives", and ran it with the photograph.

Then on July 16: Two letters arrived. The first was from Brian Marshall of Aslockton, who has seen the article in the Nottingham paper. His mother was the sister of Sewel Ward's wife. The second letter was from Rose Arbon of Kirkby — not even a relative! Rose knew Thomas Watson Ward's son, Noel, and she felt compelled to write since Noel and his wife May had no descendants. Talk about the generosity of strangers! Rose also sent me a photo of Noel and May in their later years.

Finally, on July 16: I fired up my e-mail and found a message from Alan Doxey, another great-grandson of Thomas Watson Ward. His mother was Irene (Ward) Doxey and her father was Bill Ward. I called Alan. He remembers his Aunt Lizzie, and uncles Noel and Sewel, and has stories and photos of his grandfather Bill, who was active in the general strike in 1926.

Who won the 10 pounds of

sausage? Linda Brooks, of course, the birthday lady. The next year, I had the honor of visiting her in her retirement flat in Kirkby and we chatted like old friends. I asked her how she wanted to receive her prize, and she decided to throw a dinner for the two dozen ladies and gentlemen in her building. And she did just that, with the help of the staff: bangers and mash, peas, pudding — and a spot of sherry. One of the local newspapers even did a follow-up story on the party!

Linda won the sausage, but I was the big winner. For the effort of writing one letter, I was reunited with a whole branch of my Ward family, and learned many stories about our common ancestors.

The day my letter went out, I only knew of Thomas, his wife and his five children. Two months later I had 75 names in the Thomas Watson Ward descendant tree, and had made friends with a good dozen of the living ones!

Writing a letter to a local English paper can be a long shot, but it is well worth considering if other forms of research have failed. And you might improve your chance of getting your letter published, prominently, if you turn your request into a somewhat quirky story that the editor suspects will grab the attention of a wider readership. — Doug Ward, ON, dougward@magma.ca

Tax Rolls Provided Critical Clues

My mother's ancestor, Keziah, was an herb and root doctor who died in 1886 in Hamilton Co., TX, as the wife of Nathan W. Laird. The 1860 census showed Nathan with several children and no wife. She was the widow Keziah Hardin with several sons, some of whom were grown. Deed records showed Nathan and Keziah as close neighbors. I tracked them to

northwest Arkansas where they married in 1861 in Washington Co.

The first big roadblock was finding no evidence of Keziah's first husband in that county. The son, John Smith Hardin, was of an age by the mid-1850s to be on tax rolls himself, especially the poll tax list. It seemed likely to be laborious and unrewarding, but I decided to check tax rolls in Little Rock for some counties across northern Arkansas. I found a John Hardin, Jr., who first appeared in 1854 on the rolls of Lawrence County in northeast Arkansas.

A visit there rewarded me with a probate record from October 1856, showing Keziah as the widow of Anderson W. Hardin, also the name of John S. Hardin's first son. Anderson first appeared on tax rolls in 1851. Deed records showed two other Hardins living in the same neighborhood — Joseph G. Hardin and John S. Hardin, both born in Kentucky. This was interesting since their ages suggested that Anderson might be a brother.

Census records showed Anderson and Keziah's sons were born in Kentucky before 1849 and in Illinois in 1849. They were listed out of place on the 1850 census index for Illinois in Franklin County as "A.W. and Cerzia Hardin." Just south, in Williamson County, was Joseph G. Hardin, who also had children born in Kentucky

Gravestones for Keziah Hardin and Nancy Eliza in Ward Cemetery, Hamilton Co., TX.

and Illinois. Listed with him was "Emma" later found to be Amy Hardin, age 69, born in Tennessee, evidently Joseph's mother.

The big hurdle now was locating them in Kentucky. An Anderson Hardin that fit the previous data was listed on the 1840 census for Jackson County, TN, then adjoining Monroe County, KY. Also in Jackson County, TN, on the 1820 census, was Enoch Hensley, whose daughter there evidently married John S. Hardin in the mid-1820s. John S. arrived in Lawrence County, AR., before 1840, had children born in Tennessee and was listed next to Enoch Hensley on both the 1840 census for Lawrence County, AR and the 1830 census for Warren County, TN.

Records for both Jackson and Monroe Counties did not survive, so I checked the tax rolls in Frankfort. Anderson was on the Monroe County list for 1839 and 1842-49. Joseph G. was found from 1841 to 1849, and Amy from 1821 to 1825. The FHL film Marriages of Barren County (parent of Monroe County) show John Hardin marrying Amy Gist in January 1800. John Hardin was on the 1820 census for Monroe County and had a boy aged 10-14 and three boys under 10. John gave consent in 1816 for their first child, Talitha, to marry Jonathan Mulkey.

A Mulkey book showed he was the son of Rev. John Mulkey of the old Mulkey Meeting House near Tompkinsville, now a state shrine, and they also moved to Franklin County, IL in 1849. Circumstantial evidence was now strong.

Monroe County tax rolls listed Madison H. Hardin, starting in 1837. I now suspected John S., Joseph G., Anderson W. and Madison H. were the four boys in John's household in 1820 as the age range fit. Listed with Madison H. and family on the 1850 and 1860 censuses for Monroe County was Dorcas Page, mother-in-law. A

son of Anderson and Keziah bore the Page name.

I was convinced they were four brothers, yet had no firm proof. Turning my attention to the Page family, I found a small book about John and Dorcas Smith Page of Monroe County giving a daughter Malinda, as wife of Madison Harrison Hardin. I contacted the book's author, who referred me to a Page researcher, who knew of a descendant of Madison H. This descendant had an original letter from Anderson to Madison dated 1850.

I obtained a copy in the original handwriting. It was from A.W. and "Kisire" Hardin of Franklin County, IL, to brother M.H. and Malinda Hardin. It mentioned that "our brother John S. Hardin" (called Smith farther on) had come with a wagon to take their mother home with him to Arkansas and A.W. and Keziah had decided to move there also. It mentioned that Joseph (brother in the county just south) was also coming later that year. Other names given fit into their wider family, compliments were given to Grandmother Page.

This letter provided the final evidence to confirm my previous theories and some difficult roadblocks had been bypassed. — Don R. Jackson, MO

Gabriel Came Three Times From Norway

After my father's stroke in 1992, I took over the family tree research. All that was passed down to me was that Gabriel emigrated from Norway three times until finally settling in Perley, Norman County, MN. I verified with my father's sister that Gabriel did indeed immigrate three times as she wrote a story about him for school when she was an adolescent.

My father's research placed the

dates for the first immigration about 1890 and the last immigration in about 1911 but had no guess for the other date. I knew Gabriel was born in 1873 in Rogaland, Norway, so the vessels would come from that area. I inspected the naturalization record for Gabriel and found that he immigrated through New York in June of 1890. Next, I checked the microfilm for all vessels arriving in New York at that time and located a Gabriel Johansen, age 18, on the vessel *Britanic* arriving on 27 June 1890. Since Gabriel's father was Johannes Line, I could apply Norwegian naming patterns to assume this was the first voyage of Gabriel.

Looking for his final voyage, research indicated a marriage in Norway in 1909 to Inger, a child named Elizabeth born in Norway in 1910 and a child named

Gabriel Line, c.1909.

Norval born in Minnesota in 1911. No New York immigration was located so the next logical place would be Quebec. Checking the St. Albans Border Crossing records for immigrants traveling to the US from Canada produced a Gabriel Line, age 38; Inger, age 35; and Elizabeth, age one, arriving on 13 May 1911 on the *Empress of Britain*. Reading the microfilm records for the above ship confirmed the dates of birth and destination as Perley, MN. Also on the ship manifest was a Karl Line, age 22, who was determined to be Gabriel's brother.

Now the brickwall. Somewhere between 1890 and 1911 was the miss-

ing voyage of Gabriel. Since no records were kept of people leaving America to Norway, it would be like looking for a needle in a haystack, checking all the ship manifests entering America between 1890 and 1911. What to do? I rechecked the Quebec and New York passenger ship indexes using various spellings with no luck. To narrow the scope, I found Gabriel in the 1895 state census for Minnesota and 1900 census in Norman County and found his homestead in Canada from October 1902 until October 1906.

Since Norman County in Minnesota borders North Dakota, I inquired about naturalization records for the surname Line and came up with two possible matches; a Johan Line and a Helge Line who were Gabriel's brothers' names in Norway. I sent for the records and when they arrived, both had immigration ports and dates. Johan's date conflicted the homestead dates in Canada in 1906, but Helge's date of May 1902 through Boston seemed plausible. I reasoned that since Gabriel traveled with his brother Karl in 1911, maybe he came with his brother Helge in 1902.

Reading through the ship manifest in Boston for 1902, I located Helge on the ship *Ivernia* and, lo and behold, there was Gabriel! Gabriel was listed as paying for Helge with the final destination being Moorhead, MN. Brickwall solved. — Richard Line, CA, olmanrhl@aol.com

Be Sure You Get The Spelling Correct

I had tried for 25 years to find the maiden name of my second-great-grandmother, Martha Clark, who was born in New Jersey and lived most of her life in Illinois. We knew nothing about her family.

I tried for many years to find her name through her son, my great-grandfather, Albert Clark, and also ordered many records on her and her husband, Hezekiah Clark, and several of their other children. I ordered obituaries, death records, land records and other items. I found them on census records, cemetery records and in books, but Martha's maiden name was never listed. I could not find a marriage record.

Then I found out, that in Illinois, marriages after 1878 recorded the maiden name of the mothers of the bride and groom. I would have never thought of looking up the fourth marriage of a brother to my great-grandfather, who was Martha's oldest son. Her son, Hezekiah Jr., had been married three times before this date but no maiden name of the mother was listed. I ordered a copy of the fourth marriage license in Christian County, IL and it gave his mother's maiden name as Martha Kesley. I was overjoyed and spent the next two years looking for Kesleys in both Illinois and New Jersey and finding very little. Then one day a relative looked Martha up on Ancestry.com and put in her name as Martha Kesley and her husband as Hezekiah Clark with all appropriate dates. Lo and behold, it came back with a Martha Risley married to Hezekiah Clark with all the same dates! I then went back to the original marriage record, and analyzed the recorder's script and realized that what I thought was Kesley

was indeed Risley which can be seen in the way he made his Rs.

Martha's line goes way back in New Jersey and Connecticut to the early 1600s. Since she moved to Illinois as a child, I now know she and my second-great-grandfather were married there and her parents lived and died there. My longest brickwall had now become a long addition to my family tree.

ILLINOIS STATE BOARD OF HEALTH.

Return of a Marriage to County Clerk.

1. Full name of GROOM, *Hezekiah Clark*
2. Place of residence, *Noble Illinois*
3. Occupation, *Merchant*
4. Age next birthday, *58* years, Color *White* Race *none*
5. Place of birth, *Harvel Ill Illinois*
6. Father's name, *Hezekiah Clark*
7. Mother's maiden name, *Martha Kesley*
8. Number of Groom's marriage, *Four*
9. Full name of BRIDE, *L. J. Duvall*
    Maiden name, if a widow
10. Place of residence, *Noble Illinois*
11. Age next birthday, *31* years, Color *White* Race *W...*
12. Place of birth, *Michigan Co Ill*
13. Father's name, *Joseph Truman*
14. Mother's maiden name, *Margaret Mamis*
15. Number of Bride's marriage, *Three*
16. Married at *Taylorville* in the County of Christian, and State of Illinois, the *7* day of *April* ... 189 *1*.
17. Witnesses to marriage *Nancy Brooks*
    Julia F. Boxter

2ⁿᵈ. 2ᵈ.—At Nos. 8 and 15 state whether 1st, 2d, 3d, 4th, &c., marriage of each. At 17 give names of subscribing witnesses to the Marriage Certificate.; If no subscribing witnesses, give names of two persons who witnessed the ceremony.

April 7 ... 189 *1*.
We hereby certify that the information above given is correct, to the best of our knowledge and belief.

Hezekiah Clark [Groom.]

Bev Nelson spent 25 years looking for the maiden name of her second-great-grandmother, Martha Clark. She finally found it on the marriage license shown above (entry # 7). Or had she?

Through this, I have learned to never give up, follow every lead, even a fourth-marriage certificate, and also be sure a name is spelled correctly, and it pays to look at other letters when written by hand. — Bev Nelson, WA

Don't Be Afraid To Ask

How can you contact living relatives in the old country? I looked on the Internet and found a business near the old farm. I sent an e-mail and asked them to check their phone book for McGinn and McGuigan families living in Clogher. The owner sent me a list of three McGinns in the phone book. I wrote each of them and did not hear back.

One day I got a letter from the town pharmacist. He mentioned that one of the McGinns had given him my letter since he was from Newtown Saville and his mother was from Tullanafoile Townland. He mentioned that he spoke with old Bridget McMaugh there who knew everything and she remembered my grandmother's brother and their cousin. He said he would get back to me with more details. After a year I was nervous that if Miss McMaugh died I would never get the information. I decided to write to her myself and within a month she wrote back with the name and addresses of both my second-cousins. I wrote them and they both wrote back and shared stories and photos. They were unaware that they had "friends" in the USA.

Apparently, in Ireland, first-cousins and closer relations are family, second-cousins and more distant relations are "friends". — Kevin Cassidy, NE, kmct@earthlink.net

A Cavender By Any Other Name?

My husband's second-great-grandfather, Henry East, was born in September 1832 in Chatham County, GA. According to Chatham County marriage records, he married "Miss Jane Cavender of Tattnall County" on 11 March 1852. We tried for years to find Jane's parents. It should have been simple to find a Cavender living in Tattnall County on the 1850 census. Not so! We could not find any Cavenders in Tattnall or any surrounding counties.

We researched deeds, wills, census records, etc., and found nothing. Thinking that perhaps Henry had served in the US Civil War, I looked for a pension or service record hoping to get some clue there about my mysterious Jane Cavender. No luck.

Since I knew that Henry had probably not served, I went next to the Southern Claims Commission records (records of those who did not side with the South and were seeking reparations from the US Government for damages to their property). I found that Henry had made a claim.

When I got the copy of his claim, I discovered that he had not served due to a crippled arm. Then I noticed that one of his witnesses was his sister-in-law, Mrs. Osteen. Henry only had brothers, so their wives would be "Mrs. East." Mrs. Osteen had to be his wife's sister. I then went to the Chatham County census for 1860 and found the Osteens living very close to the Easts. Mr. Osteen's name was Solomon and a check of the marriage records showed that he had married Miss Mary Carpenter of Tattnall County on 31 December 1854. Another Carpenter sister, Georgia, had married Henry's brother, Valson East, on 10 May 1851. (I already knew who Valson's wife was, but did not connect the Carpenter/Cavender similarity). It was then a simple matter to go to Tattnall County and find Jane's parents, siblings, etc.

A simple thing like a misspelled surname on a marriage license had caused years of fruitless searching. But, in the end, I discovered many other things: an ancestor's disability, his brother's wife and his wife's parents and siblings. — Gail East, GA, gaileast@att.net

A Search For The Missing Twins

I had been told that my grandparents had twin girls that passed away at birth but no one seemed to know much about what had happened.

The twins were my dad's sisters and would have been older than him. Dad was the oldest sibling of three brothers. I asked my uncle Charles and he told me they had died of the influenza. I asked him where they were buried and he didn't know. This was a mystery that I had to solve.

The death certificates for Joseph Salvia's father's twin sisters showed that they been born premature and died at birth. He also found out where they were buried.

I went to the genealogical center of the New York Public Library and found birth records on microfiche. I knew my grandparents had been married in 1916 and that my dad was born in 1918 so I looked in the files of 1917. Sure enough, there was a record of the twins. The last names were misspelled but the first names were the names I had been given by the family. I was then able to determine the exact day of their death.

Jotting down the certificate numbers, I was now able to send away for their death certificates held by the Municipal Archives in New York City.

When I received the certificates, I discovered where the babies had been buried.

The cemetery names were on the certificate. The babies had not died from influenza; they died because they had been premature.

I had solved the mystery of the missing babies and broken down a brickwall. — Joseph Salvia, NY, sage150@optonline.net

Networking On The 'Net

I began my genealogical quest for my maternal (Hawley) ancestors back in the late 1950s. My grandmother told me that my great-grandfather's name was Leon and my great-grandmother's name was Inez. Grandma told me that the family never spoke to each other. They had lived in Hesperia, MI and after Inez died, he moved to Lorrain, OH. She had nothing more to tell me other than Leon married a second time to a woman named Oga.

While living in Boston in the mid-1980s, to further my curiosity I visited the Waltham, MA branch of the NARA. I found Leon in the 1880 census living at home with his father, Dr. Henry Hawley and his mother, Clarissa. I later discovered there were 13 children from that marriage. My interest was rekindled. My new goal and subsequent hobby was to find as much as I could about Henry and Clarissa, Oga and the children.

I had the names of the children and I knew that Henry and Clarissa were born in New York. I contacted a cousin in Cleveland who sent me a family tree that showed some of the names, but more important, showed that Henry Charles Hawley came from Schuyerville (Shodack), Renssalaer County, NY.

I sent query letters to genealogy societies in Renssalaer and was informed that there were no records. The Hawley Society had no information. So I went to the Internet and began to search, and I hit pay dirt.

Since then, I have found cousins descended from all but three of my great-grandfather's siblings. A cousin in Lorrain, OH gave me information about my great-grandfather's second wife, Oga: Her name was Ogaretta and there were three children from that second marriage. I have been in contact with that part of the family. I now have copies of photos of my ancestors. One in particular is a photo taken in front of the Dr. Henry C. Hawley home in Hesperia, MI. Standing there, in a beard, is my second-great-grandfather. Another photograph is of nine of the 13 children of Henry and Clarissa. But my prized photo I got from a newly discovered cousin was of my great-grandparents Leon and Inez with two of their children: my grandfather and my aunt Grace.

About five years ago, I discovered, again via the Internet, that my second-great-grandfather, Dr. Henry Hawley had three siblings: Sarah, John and Koert. I also verified that his father's name was Charles Henry Hawley.

Just the other day, while searching through message boards on USGenWeb.com, I found a message

from a descendent of Koert. She lives in New Zealand. We've been in contact via e-mail and I now have a photo of Koert in his Civil War uniform.

I have many more brickwalls to hurdle in the years ahead, but they are getting to be fewer and fewer thanks to the power of the Internet. But, most of all,

Koert Hawley (above), and the H.C. Hawley home in Hesperia, MI (top left).

there are many people that volunteer their time to look up information. It is primarily because of their help that I have narrowed down my quest. — Glen Hawley Carlson, MI

Redo Your Research!

I knew my third-great-grandmother, Sarah Elizabeth Denham, the daughter of John and Jane Denham, was baptized on 25 February 1835 in Wells, Somerset. The next step was to look at the 1841 census for Wells to find the father's age and if he was born in the county of Somerset or not.

Unfortunately, I did not find the family and on a second look at the census I found my Sarah Elizabeth and her younger sister Caroline staying with the inn keeper's wife. Where were the parents of the two girls?

From the 1861 census in Cardiff, Wales that had given me the lead to Wells, I already knew that the girls' mother was a widow so I decided to look at the civil records for Great Britain to find when and where the father had died.

Sometimes you have amazing luck and I found the father in the very first fiche I looked at! He died in Wells on 11 July 1837 at the age of 39, just after civil registration began. Now, I thought, why did the mother leave her two daughters with the inn keeper's wife?

My brickwall was solved when I decided to go back and re-read the 1841 census. Knowing the father was dead, I looked at the census differently and suddenly realized the two sisters were with their mother Jane, who had remarried and her second husband was the inn keeper!

I should have realized this before as the two girls' names are mentioned, then the name of their half-brother. The order of the siblings should have alerted me to the fact of a remarriage. What had also confused me is that in the 1861 census the mother had gone back to her first married name.

Once I knew about the second marriage and birth of the half-brother, I quickly found those dates in the parish records for Wells and sent for the civil records to hopefully gain the mother's maiden name. Both documents showed Jane Oldery/Olderly married to John Denham and then to James Sames.

Now I know to keep my eyes open to all kinds of possibilities, and how it is wise to go back and redo your research. — Pamela Voss, BC

Looking For Ward

While my husband and I were researching land records for the 1840s in a Missouri county we hit a brick-wall in trying to identify a name for a husband who had married and died within the 1830-1840 census years.

My ancestor, Sarah Ellis, had first married a John Carver who died around 1829-30. She then married a Ward sometime after 1830, then this husband died sometime around 1840, before the census was taken. Since this second husband was my ancestor, I needed his first name.

We knew that Sarah had been left some land after her first husband's death, and we also knew that she also sold the land after her second husband died, so his first name did not appear on the sale. Nowhere could we find his given name listed. We were at a dead-end.

As we were leaving the courthouse my husband notice the abstract company across the street. He suggested that we try to see if they might be able to shed any light on the problem. Indeed they did! We explained to the owner of the company our dilemma and asked if there was a way to find who Sarah was married to when the land was sold. Since we had a land description, she was able to go to her tract books and came back with the name of Sarah's second husband, Matthew Ward. — Gloria Durbin, IL

Look Forward And Be Persistent

My maternal grandfather, Samuel Sharpe, came to Canada as a home child in 1911. I grew up knowing virtually nothing about him other than he had come from England as a young boy. In fact, I didn't even know he had been a home child until several years after his death. Once I developed an interest in genealogy, I discovered that three of my four grandparents had been home children. Imagine the number of brickwalls I've come up against with those kinds of odds!

My grandfather was born in Liverpool in 1896. His Canadian military record showed his parents' names to be William and Kate and his 1964 death certificate identified his parents as William and Catherine (née McEwan). His birth certificate named his parents as William and Catherine (née McKeowan). I eventually found their 1887 marriage and it seemed that there probably would have been other children born to the couple. The surname Sharpe is quite common in Liverpool, so I didn't dare order birth certificates of every child born with that surname from 1887 on.

My search of the 1891 census eventually turned up my great-grandparents, William and Catherine Sharpe, with a two-year-old son named William T. It was easy enough then to find the birth reference and order the certificate — William Thomas Sharpe, born in 1889, was definitely my grandfather's brother. Now I was on a mission. Maybe there were living relatives in Liverpool who didn't even know about their Canadian branch of the family! Find them, and perhaps I might find out about my grandfather's past.

In 1910, a William Thomas Sharpe married Maria Whitby — and the certificate showed that it was my grandfather's brother William Thomas! Then I searched the Sharpe births, starting at 1910, and found two children born with a mother's maiden name of Whitby: William Thomas, born in 1912 and Samuel, born in 1915. Their birth certificates were quickly added to my growing file. Then I turned my attention to marriage entries to see if either of those boys had married. I didn't find another entry for a William Thomas but a Samuel Sharpe married Esther Rawley in Liverpool in 1938. Going

back to the birth indexes, I recorded five Sharpe references with a mother's maiden name of Rawley — the last being in 1951. Now surely I would find living relatives in Liverpool. But I still had to prove it.

I ordered the 1938 marriage certificate for Samuel Sharpe, stipulating the condition of the groom's father's name being William. It was rejected, with the explanation that the father's name was Samuel Thomas. But what if that was an error and the registry clerk had entered the groom's first name rather than the father's? My Samuel's father's name was William Thomas, a rice mill worker.

Birth certificate of Samuel Sharpe, born in 1915.

Some months later, a routine visit to the Ancestry.com website turned up references to the UK death registers beyond 1983. I plugged in the surname Sharpe and up came several deaths in Liverpool — but the one that intrigued me was the death of Samuel Sharpe in 1989, showing a birth date of 8 February 1915, the very date of birth for my Samuel. That death certificate was ordered and when it arrived, it proved that the 1938 marriage was probably mine. The informant was Samuel's son — with the same name as one of the children my notes showed had been born to Samuel and Esther Rawley.

The previously rejected 1938 marriage certificate was quickly ordered and it convinced me that I had the right couple. Although the groom's father's name was shown as Samuel Thomas, the occupation was rice mill worker — the first given name had to be a mistake!

Back to the Internet search engines

to pull Sharpe references in Liverpool from the UK telephone directory. Letters were sent to several Sharpe listings but the one I expected would be most promising was the letter addressed to a Sharpe family at the very address shown as the residence of the son who registered Samuel's death. What a coup!

It didn't take long for me to start receiving e-mails from various Sharpe families living in Liverpool. Their parents were Samuel and Esther and their grandfather was William Thomas Sharpe, the son of William and Catherine! The letters from Canada had started a flurry of telephone calls in England amongst the five siblings — they had no idea that they had family in Canada! Their grandfather William Thomas had served in WWI in Germany. On 1 January 1919, as he boarded the ship to bring him home to England, the plank collapsed and he drowned. He is buried in Germany. His widow Maria subsequently remarried and had several more children.

Marriage certificate for Samuel Sharpe, who was married in Liverpool in 1938.

William Thomas did not live long enough to share his family's stories with his only surviving son. Samuel was just shy of four years old when he lost his father. His children and grandchildren are just as delighted as I am that I found them.

I still have not found any death records for my great-grandparents, William and Catherine. But by looking forward, I finally found out a little about my grandfather's family and have expanded my Christmas card list with names of several very welcome newfound cousins! — Bonnie (Cherryholme) Fowler, ON

Check Those Records

An important line for me to research is my maiden name. Imagine my dismay when I hit a brickwall and he was also my immigrant ancestor!

Along with other genealogists in the family, I knew that Charles Robinson, my fifth-great-grandfather, had embarked on the *Active* as a private in the New South Wales Corps. The *Active* was part of the Third Fleet that arrived in Sydney, Australia on 26 September 1791.

Charles Robinson's enlistment papers gave his place of birth as Birmingham, Norfolk, but Birmingham is not in Norfolk.

My hunch was that the county was correct and the place name was where the error occurred. I wrote to the Norfolk Family History Society and asked them, allowing for a Norfolk accent and a local enlisting in the army in London on 20 August 1787, what place name in Norfolk would sound like Birmingham? They suggested Briningham. At this point, I did not know other genealogists in the family had tried Briningham with no luck.

My luck came when I ordered the film from the local FHC for the parish records of Briningham. There he was, Charles Robertson baptized in 1756 and the son of William and Mary Robertson.

Passing this good news onto others, I discovered that they had asked the Norfolk Family History Society to do the research for them and a blank had been the result. This was because the Society always looked at the Bishops transcripts. On the Bishops Transcripts, Charles had been left off, probably because it was such a small parish and the minister had done the year's events by memory!

A good rule is to always check both parish records and Bishops transcripts. — Pamela Voss, BC

Do You Want Fries With That Ancestor?

The Piedmont, SC *Messenger* newspaper for 17 June 1902 (or '03) carried the following item:

Mr. Z. T. McKinney, of Fry, Pa. was in Piedmont Tuesday. Mr. McKinney was connected with the Piedmont Mfg. Co. in its early days and is regarded as one of the best mill men in the United States. His old friends note with pleasure...

Thus, in 1996 I began research from my home in Georgia seeking a Fry, PA where my grandfather, Z.T. McKinney, may have been involved in a cotton/textile mill operation. This effort led to a three-day trip traversing Pennsylvania, during which I visited the communities of Frye and Frey, to no avail. Subsequent efforts relative to Frytown and Frysville held no promise. At this point I considered Fry, PA a brickwall and gave up on it.

It continued to bother me that I couldn't connect my grandfather with a move to Pennsylvania, since all previous evidence had found him confined to the South. In July 2000, it occurred to me that PA might have been a misprint — that perhaps it should have been Fry, GA. I looked for a Fry, GA., without success. But, the idea of a mistaken state abbreviation inspired me to consider the other states with abbreviations ending in A, i.e., CA, IA, LA, MA, VA and WA.

I discovered a Fries, VA. It is a tiny town off the beaten track, but my wife and I would soon be in the vicinity as we traveled to visit our daughter in Northern Virginia, so a detour was planned.

Upon arriving at Fries, VA the first thing one encounters is a sign stating: *Welcome to Fries — Where the Trail Begins.* Wrong! For me it was where the trail — and the brickwall — ended. I foresaw this conclusion as soon as I glimpsed the early 20th-century mill behind the sign. This was confirmed when I learned that my grandfather had been the first superintendent of the mill, responsible for getting construction completed and production begun.

The mill site was carved from virgin forest solely because of its riverside location. The mill's owner was a man named Fries (pronounced Freeze). Thus, it was natural that the subsequent mill village and town bore his name. The local residents jokingly say that they pronounce it 'freeze' in the winter and 'fries' in the summer. — Jack McKinney, GA

How I Found My Grandfather Using A Newspaper Ad

I never knew my grandfather and in January of 1996 it hit me like a ton of bricks: I never knew any of my grandparents.

Bit by bit, I pieced snippets of information together. I knew my father was born in Haliburton, ON, so why not start there? I learned that in 1885 he married a Kellett girl from Minden; they had a family of four children and decided to leave Haliburton Village. I traced them through Huntsville to Powasson, ON, where two more children were added, and then on to Cache Bay, where three more children were joined the family. The family, now with some children married and away on their own, moved to South Porcupine, ON. From there, the remaining children married and spread out over the province. In 1927, the parents moved to Kirkland Lake and operated a restaurant for a few years before returning to South Porcupine. In 1930, grandmother died and was laid to rest in the Tisdale cemetery. Grandfather, alone now, sold his home and moved back to

Kirkland Lake and then, in 1937, back to Haliburton. Then, the trail goes cold. What became of grandfather?

Nobody seemed to be sure. Not surprisingly, it became an obsession for me to find him. Through my initial research, I learned that he died in Haliburton in 1943 but beyond that, there seemed to be no record of him. A local funeral home told me all about his casket and cost of the funeral but no one actually knew where he was laid to rest. The town cemetery records held no record of my grandfather.

Undeterred, I placed an advertisement in a local Haliburton newspaper and what a stroke of luck! A gentleman phoned me who said he remembered my grandfather. In fact, he said he could show me a house in Haliburton that my grandfather built. Better yet, he said he would show me where grandfather was buried! What a breakthrough. It turns out that my grandfather was actually buried in somebody else's family plot. This fellow also showed me a family Bible in which they referred to my grandfather as "uncle". It was like a great weight was lifted off my shoulders. I had found my grandfather! It didn't take long for a monument to be placed in the local cemetery.

The question remains, however, why my grandfather was referred to as uncle in a seemingly unrelated family's Bible? Further still, how did he come to be buried in their family plot? One brickwall has crumbled, but it seems another has risen in its place. — Lloyd M. Miller, ON, lmmiller@sympatico.ca

Irish Marriage Indexes

Don't let spelling slow you down in your search for a marriage certificate.

I knew that Patrick Cassidy had married Ann Murphy in Ireland in about 1877 according to the 1900 US census. My local FHC has indexes for Irish marriages from 1845 to 1921. I thought it would be a simple search to find corresponding citations in the same year for both names. I also knew the Cassidy family hailed from Newry, which is in both Counties Armagh and Down.

I could find an Ann Murphy in Newry but not the corresponding Pat Cassidy. I decide to search a few years earlier since the census information is often a bit off. I did find a match between the two names in 1873 for County Armagh. I thought maybe they lived near Newry or this was Ann's home parish. I wrote to Dublin for the certificate and was shocked when I received two marriage certificates!

The St. Patrick/St. Colman RC Cathedral in Newry, County Down, Northern Ireland, where the Cassidy-Murphy wedding took place.

A Patrick Cassidy and Ann Murphy had indeed gotten married in 1873, just not to each other, so I had the wrong people. They had identical marriage index citations because they married in the same place at the same time but not each other.

I decided to go back and see what might be up with the other Ann Murphy and try to find Patrick Cassidy. I looked along all the names on the page near Cassidy until something jumped out at me. Patrick Cassiday had a matching citation to Ann Murphy and I got their marriage certificate from Dublin proving they married in Newry in 1877.

Likewise, be careful with unique spellings. The prefix O' in Irish surnames caused me a few problems finding marriages in the index. I could not find the Denis Buckley-Margaret O'Callaghan marriage from 1885 nor could I find the John O'Riordan-Honora Buckley marriage in the mid-1890s. I left the FHC flustered. Months later when I learned that the O' prefix was often dropped; I searched the indexes again and quickly found the marriages under Buckley-Callaghan in 1885 and Riordan-Buckley in 1894. — Kevin Cassidy, NE, kmct@earthlink.net

It Was In The Diary

I was fortunate while growing up to know who begat who back to my second-great-grandfather, Isaac Fleming, and his wife Kitty Ann Hilton. I also knew he came to Moultrie County, IL from Knox County, OH sometime in the second half of the 1800s. The problem was who were Isaac's parents?

Researching the Knox County, OH records, I found the marriage for Isaac and Kitty Ann in 1837, the census entries in 1850 and 1860, a few land records but not much else. There were also Flemings in Delaware County, which is the next county to the west. I checked land deeds, probate, court records, county histories, censuses,

etc., but could find no connection to my Isaac.

A query I placed in the Moultrie County (IL) Historical and Genealogical Society quarterly prompted an answer from a collateral descendant of Isaac's son Benjamin, my great-grandfather. He didn't know who Isaac's parents were but had two of Benjamin's diaries. The following are entries from the 1864 diary:

Sat Jul 30: Hot & cloudy & rain p.m. I & Cis go to Aaron Brickers got there at 6 p.m. a hot hard drive of it

Sun Jul 31: Dull cloudy & very hot I at Aaron Brickers all day rain a little at night hot & sultry at A. Brickers at all night

Mon Aug 1: Hot cloudy & rainy I went to Vandalia & Mulberry Grove from Aaron Brickers staid at E. Rosebrook hot & sultry night

Thur Aug 4: Morning hot hard rain p.m. I from Thos Davis to Polly Flemings all night rain at night dull & cloudy

Fri Aug 5: Morning dull & cloudy rainy I went from Polly Flemings to A. J. Flemings there all night & rainy rain at night

Who were these people and why would Benjamin and Sarah Ann "Cis" Bricker be visiting them. Could they related to Benjamin and therefore to Isaac?

I knew Aaron Bricker was an uncle to Sarah Ann. It seemed likely the others mentioned in the diary were probably related as well. The 1850 census for Fayette County, IL showed a William Fleming and his wife Jane with several children. Further research into

Benjamin Cecil Fleming.

Bond and Fayette County records proved all the people mentioned in the diary, other than Aaron Bricker, were the families of Isaac's brothers and sisters and Isaac's parents were William and Jane Fleming. — Helen Robinson, CO, lhbgr1@comcast.net

Use The Conventional Methods

My brickwall was my grandfather, Melton (or Milton) Hansen. All I had to go on was his marriage license to my grandmother, Florence Frederickson. They were married in Racine, WI on 6 May 1927. It said he was 22 years old and born in Wisconsin to Hans Hansen and Mary Jacobsen.

Racine has a very large Danish population and searching for a Hans Hansen was worse than looking for a John Smith. The family story said Milton died either right before or after my mother (their only child) was born on 25 November 1927.

I spent years and a lot of money looking for a death record or even a birth record with no luck. This was before the Internet made life so much easier.

About a year ago, I was searching census records on Ancestry.com. Just for the heck of it, I entered Milton's name. In the 1920 US census, I found a Milton, age 15 (which fit) living in Montana, which really threw me. He was living, along with other siblings, with his aunt and uncle, Agnes and Anton Pedersen. I knew it was a long shot, but I went to the USGenWeb project for Montana, Sheridan Co. Very helpful website, but there were no hits for Milton or any of the other Hansens listed. There were links for volunteer look-ups — but I wasn't sure what I needed, let alone if it was my grandfather. There was also a link to the local funeral home, and since I

usually always start with an obituary, I decided to see if they had a death date or obituary for this Milton. The funeral director and owner, Mr. Fulkerson, answered my query. The local historical society had published a book in the 1970s about the history of Sheridan County.

He also located an obituary for Martha Krogedal who had a brother named Milton, and parents called Hans Hansen and Mary Jacobsen. This was the correct Milton, but I didn't know if it was my Milton. He also sent me a scan from the history book about how Hans and Mary drowned in Brush Lake in 1915, leaving six orphans in the care of Mary's sister, Agnes Pedersen.

Mr. Fulkerson also found a contact for a family member. A few letters and photographs later, I found out this was my grandfather — who died in April of 1973. Even though my mother and I didn't know him, I found a whole new rather large family.

My solution used the conventional methods, but my advice is don't give up and pursue every avenue, no matter how remote it may seem. Use every resource and ask everyone you can think of. This probably seems very simple by today's standards, but this search took me over 20 years. — Roxanne Darracott, WI, roxdarr@aol.com

A Fortunate Mistake

Family tradition says that my second-great-grandparents, John Lawlor and Sarah Long, came from "somewhere in the Northern half of Ireland".

Lawlors were uncommon in that half of Ireland. I checked the Householders Index and found only four places where Lawlors and Longs lived in the same parishes. The biggest concentration was in Drogheda, but I couldn't proceed further until I checked the 1910 US census. It said that my second-great-grandmother came from Maine. This was clearly a mistake, but why Maine?

There is a Bangor in Maine and another one in County Down. Could it be that the census taker was told that she came from Bangor and he wrote Maine? Sure enough, Bangor Parish in County Down was one of the four places where Lawlors coexisted with Longs. There was a Susannah Long on Main Street in Bangor. — John Sullivan, CA

The Christening Gown

My father, Jackson Williams Mathewson, was born on 23 May 1903 in West Bay City, MI to Anna Maria and Cecil Raymond Mathewson.

In old family boxes, there were a large number of old family photographs, many of Cecil's time spent in the U.S. Life-Saving Service. But when and where did my grandfather serve? Searching the Internet, I found the NARA website. I requested information about Cecil's service time and a microfilm of his complete service history was sent to me.

From his employee records, a historical mystery of several photographs is solved. In one photograph that came from the old family boxes, my grandmother Anna Maria is holding her son (my father) in a white gown and cap. On the back of the photograph is "Jackson Williams Mathewson on the day he was christened September 20, 1903." On this same day holding him was his father in his U.S. Life-Saving Service uniform. From the employee register of the Thunder Bay Island Life-Saving Station, he served there from April 1901 until August 1906 and his crew position was "#8", the number on his surfman's uniform. After all these years, from Cecil's records, it is now

(Above) Jackson William Mathewson on the day he was christened. (Left) The framed christening gown.

determined that my father was christened 1903 in Alpena, MI where he lived until about three years of age.

For many years, we have had the gown my father wore on that September day in 1903 and on my 70th birthday, my wife had it framed for me. A memorable birthday gift and another brickwall solved — Richard J. Mathewson, OK, rjmadm@cox.ne

Using The IGI For Ireland

One way to find the place of origin for Irish ancestors is to use the IGI and hope for good luck. The IGI has Irish births listed from the beginning of civil registration in 1864 and ending a few years later.

As all eight of my great-grandparents were born in Ireland from 1849 to 1870, I hoped a parent search would flush out my ancestors in the IGI or at least their siblings who were born after 1863.

Couple by couple, I entered my second-great-grandparents' names. Michael Cassidy and Mary Reavey lived in Newry, County Down and their son was born around 1850. If he was an older child, his youngest sibling might show up in the IGI. Unfortunately, no names came up.

Next, I tried Dominick Benson and Mary Fahey. Their daughter, Bridget, was born around 1854 and again, I was hoping that some younger siblings might appear. Only one name did, Dominick Benson. Up until this moment, all I knew was that the Bensons were from County Sligo but this birth record would give me a parish name to search further.

Then, I entered Patrick McGuigan and Catherine Mallon. Nothing came up. I moved onto Patrick McGinn and Alice McWilliams. Three children came up: Patrick, Biddy and James. This too, was exciting because it corrected my family tradition that they were from Omagh and properly identified the parish as Clogher, County Tyrone.

Encouraged, I moved onto my mother's side of the family which I hoped would bring better results since both my maternal grandparents were Irish-born. Denis Buckley and Catherine Cahill returned no hits. Likewise with Maurice O'Callaghan and Mary Mahoney.

My last two couples was successful though. Daniel Riordan and Mary Ann Desmond had daughters Julia and Catherine. It identified their birthplaces as Macroom, County Cork, which was a great help. Lastly, the search for John Buckley and Honora Curtin brought up my great-grandmother Honora and her brother Denis in Mallow, County Cork.

John Riordan, younger brother of Julia and Catherine, and Honora Buckley of Cork City, County Cork, Ireland.

These results also reinforced a genealogy rule that you always search by family and not just your ancestor. Of the four couples that had IGI matches, only one of the entries was for my direct ancestor's birth. The others were all just siblings but the geographical information gained from these collaterals was key. — Kevin Cassidy, NE, kmct@earthlink.net

Which John Rogers Was Mine?

About 20 years ago, our local genealogy group discovered the IGI and we thought it the most marvelous tool for genealogists. I quickly found my John Rogers and his wife listed.

One day, I was sharing information with a fellow genealogist who was also researching a John Rogers in Camborne, Cornwall England. We had both found the same John Rogers on the IGI and had him married to different women and each having a family!

Using church records suddenly seemed a more accurate way to do research. I found the marriage for my friend and her John Rogers, his marriage entry gave him as a temporary resident, which means he was not from Camborne. So the IGI John Rogers was not my friend's, but I didn't know if he was mine. There are too many John Rogers in the church records to choose from and I wanted the correct one this time.

I then turned to the census, the 1841 census showed a John Rogers married to Peggy and his age was given as 56, so he was born in 1785 in the county of Cornwall.

There he was again on the 1851 census and this time I knew I had the correct John Rogers as his grandson Charles Tangye (the surname I am descended from) was visiting the night of the census. This time, the census stated John was born in Camborne and 65 years old, so he was born in 1786.

Now knowing John Rogers was born in either 1785 or 1786, I returned to the church records and although there may be many John Rogers in Camborne, none was baptized in 1785 or 1786. I did, however, find a John Rogers, the son of Henry and Lucretia, baptized on 9 March 1783, and another, the son of Richard and Rebecca Rogers, baptized on 22 June 1788. How to find out which John Rogers was mine?

I researched both families of the John Rogers, looking at the siblings to see if I could spot a naming pattern. I also looked at John's own children to see if that would help. There was no decisive naming pattern to conclude which John Rogers family was mine.

Finally, after working on the brick-

wall every now and again for 20 years, I decided to give it one last shot and look at the death records even though death records in the time period I needed tend to be vague.

Surprisingly, I found a John Rogers dying on 1 July 1834 at the age of 51. Quickly I did the math and realized he was the 1783 John Rogers, the son of Henry and Lucretia. That left the 1788 John Rogers, the son of Richard and Rebecca, as mine, as he appeared on the censuses. I also noticed the death record gave the John Rogers as from "The Comb" in Camborne, meaning the village, and I realized my family had always been given as "Of Town".

What a thrill finally finding my John Rogers. Yet all along, I knew deep down that he was mine, but one must prove it first! — Pamela Voss, BC

A Christmas Story

Several years ago when I retired, I had more time to devote to my genealogy. My mother was French-Canadian and I was able to find records in Chatham, ON, where my mother was born, back to the 1800s. The many volumes of priests' extensive records made my search very easy on three of my great-grandparents' lines. The library where I was living had the many volumes of these records. I was able to follow the Dumas, Gouer and Pinsoneault branches back through Montreal and Quebec to France in the 1600s. My great-grandfather Thibodeau was another story. I hit my brickwall in the early 1800s.

One year, the day after Christmas, I was "Christmased out" and escaped to the library to do some research. I was talking to someone who was there to escape also. She said that Thibodeau was a common Acadian name and I should look in a set of books that had records of Acadian families who had returned to Canada after they had been exiled in 1755. It took me all of five minutes to find my line. I was back to France in the 1600s. I'd been living in Cajun country for 40 years and didn't know all the Thibodeaus were my cousins. It truly was a Merry Christmas! — Maggie Steele, magsteel@voyager.net

Big City Syndrome

Many genealogists encounter a brick-wall when they have to research large cities that may be partially indexed on the Internet. It goes without saying that the area you need in that big city won't be indexed. I personally deal with this problem for Detroit, MI and Brooklyn, NY for 1900 to 1930. As an example, Brooklyn boasts more than 1,600 enumeration districts in 1920 and the city gets larger every census year. You know your family is in there but the indexing project on the Internet is such a slow process that you want to pull out your hair.

For the earlier years, your FHC may have the indexes in book form and you can copy the pages. But what if you aren't sure of the surname spelling or what if it's a very common name such as my grandfather William Carpenter. If you are lucky to find an index book, either of those predicaments can mean copying a whole lot of pages. If you need the later years (1900-1930), those indexes aren't on the FHC shelves yet. There is an easier way and you can conquer this problem from home.

I subscribe to Ancestry.com's Images Online which is fairly good with the census years, except 1900 isn't indexed at all, 1910 is partially indexed but none of it is linked to images of the census pages, and a large part of 1920 has also not been indexed. I cover some of the incomplete decades by also subscribing to Genealogy.com so I can view their collection of 1900, 1910 and 1920 census pages which are nicely linked. Usually these two websites will give

me the census pages I need but, on occasion, the person I seek won't be listed in either website and based on the city I am searching, it's pretty safe to assume that it's the dreaded big city syndrome, as I call it.

Genealogy.com.

To get around this pesky brick-wall: Census pages and directories can give addresses for your family. I use the address closest to the census era I need. I then find a street map of the large city. You can use MapQuest.com because many addresses may still be in existence and MapQuest will pinpoint those exact address locations for you, or you can be a little more creative. I got lucky and found a street map of Detroit for 1898 on eBay.com for $8. This older map will correlate better with the enumeration district descriptions. Once I obtain my map, I find the street that I need. Then I go into Ancestry.com and read all the descriptions of the enumeration districts in my large city. Using my map as street coordinates, I narrow down the enumeration district(s) that I need and that is where I will spend my time searching.

Don't be discouraged by thinking that you don't have the patience to read all the enumeration district descriptions. If you find the right coordinates, you won't need to read any further. For the enumeration districts without a description, I recommend going into each one until you obtain three street names. Armed with your map, three street names are all you should need to ascertain whether it's close to where you want to be or move on to the next one. This will eliminate the need to know the spelling of the surname and common names, such as Carpenter, aren't an issue either. It takes patience but it consistently helps me climb my big city brickwalls! — Kate Sprague, CA, treetracerette@yahoo.com

Check For Connections

In obtaining death certificates for my grandparents, I immediately ran into a brickwall on my maternal grandfather's death certificate. It was one of many I would encounter in his family. He was not a communicative person and as my research progressed, my mother was shocked to learn she had 11 great-aunts and uncles — she knew of only two!

My grandfather's death certificate stated his father's name as Monroe Eikenberry and his mother's name as "unknown." Another example of how family history was not discussed by him as his own son who gave information for the death certificate did not know his grandmother's name! I had not intended to research our family beyond our grandparents but the "unknown" great-grandmother spurred me on — that just wasn't right!

I soon learned that my great-grandmother's first name was Amanda, thanks to an 1880 census taker who ignored the rule of using first names in the census. I found great-grandfather [George] Monroe Eikenberry in Butler County, IA, with wife Amanda, age 26, born in Indiana, and oldest son Fred, age six, born in Illinois, which matched my grandfather. The other clue furnished by my grandfather's death certificate was his middle name, Welch. That seemed

likely to be the surname of his mother. I then set out to research every Welch family in the state of Indiana in the 1860 census, looking for a daughter Amanda, age six.

I was about halfway through this task when I chanced upon a query from one Jill Martin, researching her grandmother Bertha Eikenbary Mayfield. The name Bertha rang a bell, as the one great-aunt who my mother knew of was named Bertha. I contacted Jill and sure enough, she was my second-cousin. Jill had in her possession a letter written on 18

Wedding photo of George Monroe and Amanda Welch Eikenberry, 1 July 1873.

December 1935 to Bertha by my grandfather, apparently in response to questions about family. The clues in the letter included the parents of Monroe Eikenberry. Then he mentioned Harvey Welsh (his grandfather), who was born near Raleigh,

NC in 1805 and died in Illinois at age 85. He mentioned his grandmother Rachel born 1818 in Virginia, with a maiden name of Woodard or Woodward, and who died at age 90 or older in Iowa. He mentioned they pioneered in Richmond, IN. He also wrote about Rachel's grandfather Amos Woodward, who lived to be 105.

The letter led me to the 1860 census in Wayne County, IN where I found Harvey and Rachel Welch, with daughter Amanda. One brickwall down!

We had determined that Rachel was born in Tennessee, not Virginia, and that her father was John Woodward and her mother Rachel Woodward. With the clue in my grandfather's letter that the younger Rachel's maiden name was Woodward or Woodard, we researched Woodwards in Wayne County, IN and found Rachel named as an underage daughter in the will of John Woodward written on 4 January 1821. The will named wife Rachel, who was still alive in 1850 and living near Harvey and Rachel Welch with daughter Eliza, also named in the will.

There were 399 heads of household with 1,907 family members with some variation of the surname Woodward in the 1790 census. Trying to place John Woodward without a birthplace or date seemed an impossible task. The Amos clue did not work out (we later learned my grandfather meant Amos Williams, Rachel's maternal grandfather.) We had nowhere to go, as we knew only that John went to Indiana from the state of Tennessee, but there were huge numbers of Woodwards in Tennessee.

One day, a sort of epiphany occurred: we realized that one of the executors of John Woodward's will was a Patrick Beard, that John Woodward named a son Patrick, and that descendants of Patrick Beard went to Mercer County, IL, as did Harvey and Rachel Woodward Welch.

We then began to concentrate on Patrick Beard since the two families were obviously very close. Patrick's son John Beard was born in 1796 in Tennessee, while his first child, Alice, was born in North Carolina. We learned that Patrick was a son of John and Martha Beard who immigrated to Rowan County, NC. We also found out that Abraham Woodward also lived in Rowan County, NC, and had a son John (named in his will in Tennessee) who bought land in Jefferson County, TN in 1796, the year that Patrick's oldest son was born in Tennessee. John Woodward was named in Quaker records as a son of Abraham of the right age to be our John Woodward. Another brickwall down.

We attempted to obtain a marriage record for John Woodward from Jefferson County, TN, and were told by the clerk that there wasn't one. By that time we had met several Woodward cousins and one of them was making a trip to Jefferson County and offered to look for the marriage record. He immediately found it as John Woodert married to Rachel Williams on 1 September 1795 in Jefferson County. We learned that Rachel Williams was the daughter of Amos Williams, hence my grandfather's mistake in his letter. Another brickwall down!

Patrick Beard, as it turns out, was likely married to John Woodard's sister Hannah, hence the closeness of the families.

One way of breaking down brickwalls for families with common surnames is to look for connections to families with not-so-common names and research their background. Families seldom moved alone from place to place and often moved together for whole generations. — Nadine D. Holder, AZ, nadineholder72@ssvecnet.com

How I Found My Wife's Grandfather In The 1930 US Census

My wife's grandfather, Benjamin Trotman, immigrated to the US in 1905 (according to the 1920 census, 1915 according to his son). Because he died when my wife was very young and he lived on the east coast and my wife's family lived on the west coast, she knew very little about him. Conversations with my wife's father before he died indicated the family lived either in Philadelphia, PA or Atlantic City, NJ in 1930, but conventional searches on Ancestry.com's 1930 federal census turned up nothing. Every alternative spelling I could conceive (including Tortman, which is how I found Benjamin's brother Isadore in the 1920 census) met with the same negative results. Soundex searches were the same. I had started a manual search, but without an address, in Philadelphia, even in 1930, was just too large to tackle this way.

MapQuest.com.

I decided some more research was in order and checked the 1929 Philadelphia city directory (there was none available for 1930) and the 1931 Atlantic city directory at my local FHC. Benjamin was in both, so I started with his Philadelphia address first.

I went to Mapquest.com and got a map of the area surrounding Ben's address. Then I went to Steve Morse's website for obtaining enumeration districts for US censuses. Unfortunately, this gave me four enumeration districts. However, that significantly narrowed my manual search.

Now came the really hard part, searching each page first for the street, then the address. Ben's street was not the one that the enumerator walked from one end to the other; his was the one that was crossed back and forth many times during the enumeration. About halfway through the second enumeration district, I found Ben and his family, at the address from the 1929 city directory. Looking at the image, the name appeared to have been written Torman, with a T placed later between the R and M. I knew that I had checked for the name Tortman and that had not come up. At least I had finally found Benjamin.

Not one to let success get in my way, I was determined to find out how the name had been indexed. I went back to the search screen and filled in the first name, state, city, age and place of birth and came up with 32 Benjamins, aged 52, born in Russia and living in Philadelphia. A quick scan of the two pages of search results turned up only two Benjamins whose last names started with T. I clicked on the first, Talman, and there he was.

All in all, I spent about six hours over a couple of weeks on all the pieces that I had to put together to find Benjamin. Since I had been looking for over a year, I just wished I had thought of this approach earlier. While difficult, it was well worth the effort and I recommend it as an approach if you are pretty sure you know the city your ancestor or relative lived in 1930, but aren't getting results using conventional, alternative spellings or Soundex searches. — Gerald Mitchell, CA

The Brickwall Of Elma J. Whitelaw

Our family records had Elma J. (Maude) Whitelaw listed as the youngest of 11 children of Edward Whitelaw. These records indicated that she was born on 10 August 1863, in Bloomingdale, Van Buren County, MI, and died on 28 June 1886, in Morton County, KS during childbirth. Some of the records stated she was buried at Gobles, Van Buren County, MI. One copy of a handwritten letter said the writer's mother went to Syracuse for the funeral of Maude who had died in childbirth. Syracuse is in Hamilton County, north of Morton County. I got curious. Who was Elma J./ Maude? What was her married name? Where was she buried? What happened to the baby?

I started with cemetery records of the Gobles Cemetery in Michigan, but there wasn't an Elma buried near the Whitelaw graves.

Some of Edward's children left Michigan and went to Sedgwick County, KS. I wondered if Elma J. was really buried in the town of Morton, Sedgwick County, KS or in Morton County in the far west corner of Kansas. One summer, my husband and I drove across Kansas, and the first cemetery we stopped at was in Richfield, Morton County, KS. We didn't see any gravestones for Elma, but there were other Whitelaw-related cousins who had gone to Morton

County. We also found out the cemetery was established two months after she died. When we got to Kingman and Sedgwick Counties, we found many more cemeteries with ancestors, but no sign of Elma near our families.

I used inter library loan and the Kansas State Historical Society's newspaper microfilm, but there were no obituaries for that time period in Syracuse. I got microfilm of the Richfield newspaper for 1886 and found two deaths in the newspaper. Mrs. F.G. Lester had a small obituary with no cause of death and Mrs. C.R. Hovey, who died of Bright's disease. Old newspapers never printed married women's first names! Through the Internet and queries on county websites, I found another person researching the Lester surname. I wrote to her and received an answer that Mrs. Lester was neither an Elma nor a Whitelaw. The next possibility was Mrs. Hovey, even though that cause of death wasn't related to childbirth.

The Van Buren County, MI, website at USGenWeb posted some marriage data, and a search indicated that Elma J. Maud Whitelaw married Charles R. Hoveg. The initials matched, and the name was close to Hovey from the obituary.

I wrote to the Van Buren District Library and asked if someone there could look for information in the Gobles or Bloomingdale newspapers since they did not have interlibrary

> Mrs. C. R. Hovey who has for years been afflicted with Bright's disease, died last Friday at ten o'clock. Mr. Hovey resided three miles north of Richfield and himself and wife were well known to a number of our people, who always regarded them with the highest esteem and respect and Mrs. Hovey's death is deeply regretted by all friends, who with the LEADER, extend to Mr. Hovey their heartfelt sympathy. The funeral was preached by Rev. Boss at three o'clock Saturday afternoon from the schoolhouse.

Obituary for a Mrs. C.R. Hovey, as it appeared in the Richfield Leader *on 3 July 1886.*

loan microfilms. The librarian wrote back and said that the Gobles and Bloomingdale newspapers did not have many surviving issues before 1900 and nothing with the dates I wanted. However, she found issues of the *Paw Paw True Northerner* with two articles:

July 1, 1886: Mrs. Phil. Bush received a telegram from Kansas, stating that her sister was not expected to live. She immediately left for that state. A subsequent telegram announced that her sister was dead.

July 8, 1886: Our informant was incorrect last week in stating that a telegram had been received in regard to the death of Mrs. Hovey, nee Whitelaw of Kansas, but later advices report her death.

The newspapers helped me find out that Elma J. Whitelaw married Charles R. Hovey, that she died of Bright's disease, there were probably no children, and she is buried in western Kansas, not next to her parents in Michigan. — Cheryl Whitelaw, UT, whitelawcs@suu.edu

Always Check The Surrounding Locales

Because of an incorrect death record it took 16 years to locate the birthplace and parents of my great-grandmother, Maryanna Bauza Majewska.

My journey began in April 1988 when I obtained a copy of my great-grandmother, Maryanna Bauza Majewski's 1917 death record from St. Adalbert's Roman Catholic Church in Glen Lyon, PA. On this record, her place of birth was given as Poland, Poznan, district Dzubin, place of Gencawa. She was 67 (making her birth about 1850). Maryanna's husband was Walenty Majewski. My grandmother had often told me that her grandparents' names were Mathias Bauza and Agnes. The par-

ents of Maryanna on the Pennsylvania death certificate were Mathias and Agnes Boza, a slightly different surname spelling but undoubtedly the correct couple.

In March 1989, the FHL reference librarian suggested Maryanna's birthplace was probably Gasawa, Szubin. I reviewed the only two Gasawa films available at the time, but did not find any Bauza references in the parish.

In 1991, I rechecked Gasawa films, again not finding any references. I then wrote to the Gasawa parish priest. He kindly responded saying that he did not find any Bauza references in his records, or those of the archdiocese, and suggested the name might be Burzy. However, none of the names and dates he provided came even close to matching the information I possessed. At an apparent dead end, I focused on my other genealogical research.

Six years later, in January 1997, David Philip Wilson contacted me regarding his newly published Gora/Znin birth extraction book. He had seen a query of mine in a Polish newsletter. He indicated that there were many Bauza births and marriages in Gora parish, a parish nearby Gasawa.

After purchasing his book, I found a birth of a Michal in 1855 to a Mathias Bauza and Agnes Sobolewska in the village of Podgorzyn, Gora parish. Could these be my second-great-grandparents? A strong possibility existed. Since David Wilson's book covered the dates 1853-81, it did not include the estimated 1850 birth year of my great-grandmother Maryanna Bauza.

In March 1997, I obtained and reviewed locally the Gora birth microfilm and found a Maryanna Bauza born on 19 August 1848 to Mathias Bauza and Agnes Sobolewska. They also had four other children born between 1846 and 1858, including a Rosalie born in 1850. The two Gora films I reviewed had lots of data on four earlier generations. I was thrilled, but needed to check the film of death records to see if this Maryanna survived to adulthood and married.

In June 1997 I did this, reviewing the FHL film covering Gora deaths beginning in 1848. I found a death of a Marianna Bauza — age five. My Maryanna would have been 10-years-old in 1858. A review of Mathias and Agnes Bauza's other children's birth dates showed no child born to them in 1853 in Gora. Could the dead Marianna possibly have been Rosalie, born 1850? Perhaps she was a small eight-year-old that the priest took to be only five?

Family History Library's website.

Another dead end. I let the matter rest and concentrated on other family lines. Meanwhile, I had extracted every record that included the Bauza or Sobolewski name. The notes just sat in my file drawer taking up space. But something told me that this was the right family.

In early 2000, I hired a researcher in Poland to check for the marriage of Maryanna Bauza and Walenty Majewski. In the archive at Gniezno he found the marriage on 17 November 1870 in Barcin parish, Szubin for Maryanna Bauza, age 23, daughter of Mathias Bauza and Agnes (no surname) and Walenty Majewski, age 20, son of Jozef Majewski and Marianna (again no surname). This was definitely the correct couple.

In May 2000, I reviewed films for Barcin parish, but neither Maryanna Bauza nor Walenty Majewski were found in the birth records of the parish. There were very few mentions of the surnames Majewski or Bauza in the parish.

Almost three years later, in January 2003, two new FHL films were released for Gasawa parish. In a review of these films, I found two children born in 1862 and 1864 to Mathias Bauza and Agnes Sobolewska in the village of Lysinin. Obviously, they had moved from Podgorzyn to Lysinin sometime after 1855, Michal's birth year.

Finally in May 2004, I started an area search of Barcin and adjacent parishes. In 1868, in Barcin, I found the marriage record for Rosalie Bauza (daughter of Mathias Bauza and Agnes Sobolewska). If it was not Rosalie that died in 1858, who was it?

Widening my search to nearby Labiszyn parish, I found the birth of Walenty Majewski, born on 7 January 1852 to Jozef Majewski and Marianna Walentowska. I decided to do the same kind of search in the area surrounding Gora parish. In doing earlier research, I noticed that there were several Gora couples that chose to marry in Znin — was Gora lacking a priest at a particular time?

In looking at births in Znin parish for the year 1853, there she was, the mysterious child who died in 1858 — only her name was actually Marcianna, not Marianna. A marginal note says Marcianna was born to Mathias Bauza and Agnes Sobolewska in Podgorzyn, Gora parish, the same village as the other Bauza children in the years 1846-58. Bingo! So the priest at Gora did make an error in the death record in 1858, but not the age, the name!

So after 16 long years, I can finally state with authority that Maryanna

Bauza, born in 1848, and her ancestors are mine. My gut feeling all along was that this was so, but…

Why did my search take so long? The incorrect information in Maryanna Bauza Majewski death record in Pennsylvania started me down the wrong path. I speculate that what happened is that when Walenty and Maryanna were married in 1870 her parents were still living in Gasawa parish. Upon her death, Walenty simply assumed that she, too, had been born there.

If someone is not found where records indicate they should be — always check the surrounding locales. — Sharon Haskin Galitz, AZ, shgalitz@yahoo.com

Coming Out Of The Woodwork!

While working on my father's family, I found I had very little information and few living relatives to turn to. I turned to his obituary and found there were brothers and sisters listed. I used the SSDI to hopefully find the brothers and sisters listed, based on the city named in the obituary. If I found them, I sent a letter to the library in the city of residence. Once I got that obituary, I would check for survivors. I used online sources to try to find those survivors. I had a family tree letter made up that I sent to see if they were actually related and could shed any light on the family.

Within a few weeks, I had unknown cousins coming out of the woodwork with additional information and pictures taking me back several generations. What a jackpot! Two cousins were also working on the family tree and we combined all of our information, culminating in a 300-page book and a reunion held in 2003 where I met more than 85 relations I never knew I had.

I am currently going sideways on my husband's family and waiting to see where that leads me. — Kathy Robarts, FL, grob44@gte.net

Check Those Genealogy Periodicals

Always check genealogy periodicals for others searching your names in the same localities.

Home of Dominick and Mary (Fahy) Benson in Ballysadare, County Sligo.

I am researching the Benson family of Ballysadare County, Sligo, Ireland. I found the address of a New York man also researching the Benson name in Ballysadare during the 19th century. He wrote back telling me that we were not connected but gave me the address of a researcher from Australia. She, too, was not a match but she gave me the name of a Benson family currently living in Ballysadare.

When I wrote them, they informed me that there were no members of my Benson family still there but they were so kind to send me photographs of the farmhouse, the church and the gravestones of my ancestors. — Kevin Cassidy, NE, kmct@earthlink.net

The Second Branch

While working on the family tree of the Villanuevas from northern New Mexico, I quickly realized that there were two main branches. One centered around the village of Villanueva in the Pecos Valley, and the other from Galisteo, about 20 miles south of Santa Fe.

The Villanuevas from Villanueva could easily be traced to one Vicente Villanueva, who came from Parral, Chihuahua, in around 1796. No luck with the other branch, however. They seemed to appear out of nowhere on the 1870 census with a Serefino Villanueva and his family. I thoroughly searched the Villanueva and Galisteo areas in the 1860 census, but could not find a trace.

From an early court document, I knew that Vicente Villanueva had a younger brother, Ramon. Records about him are sparse, but from church records I know that in 1801 in Santa Cruz de la Canada (northern New Mexico) he fathered an illegitimate son, Lazaro Antonio. The mother's name was Rosa Sanches. Could Lazaro have been the ancestor of the Galisteo Villanuevas?

Finally, the long-awaited publication of the Santa Fe, NM, church records provided the all-important clue: the 1850 marriage of Maria Josefa Sanches, daughter of Lazaro Villanueva from 'Real de San Francisco', then a booming mining town south west of Santa Fe. The 1850 census of Real de San Francisco did not yield anything of interest; but now, knowing where to look, in the 1860 census I found Lazaro Villanueva with wife Maria Martha and five children. And only a few houses away, lived Serefino Villanueva with his wife and young son. Could Lazaro be the father of Serefino and the son of Ramon? And why was his young daughter called Sanches at her marriage?

I then revisited the 1850 census — and there they were: Nazaro Sanches, his wife Maria Martha, two of the children listed in 1860, and a young man named Serefino Sanches. Lazaro was using his mother's last name!

Final proof that I had found the right Lazaro (the son of Ramon Villanueva) came when I, based on the 'new' last name, found two more baptism records: one that listed the grandparents of a daughter of Lazaro Sanches as Ramon Billanueba and Rosalia Sanches, and one that gave them as Ramon Sanches and Rosalia Bianueba. As for the mix-up of last names, I am not concerned. Santa Fe, where the baptisms were recorded, was far from the family home, the priest busy, and Lazaro only a poor miner. Maybe even Lazaro himself was not sure of his parents' last names.

On a side note: as essential as census records were for my research, they also re-enforced the old rule to never trust them too much. The ages of Lazaro, Serefino and their wives varied considerably between censuses, and spelling of both first and last names often were rather innovative — cumulating in the 1870 census entries Serferino Vianiara and Laciro Bienuera. — Lis Könnecke, NM, liskonn@yahoo.com

Needle In A Haystack

In early 20th century Memphis, TN, a son was born to my maternal uncle, Leo, and his wife, Bobby. They divorced several years later and the mother left the area taking the child with her. My uncle, who died in 1964, had tried to locate his son, but without success. This is all the information I had to work with in trying to find my first-cousin — no name or other details.

Several trips to Memphis in the 1990s had failed to produce results through the usual sources. A subsequent visit in 1997 took me to the Memphis and Shelby County Archives and it was there that a casual remark provided the key to my success. One of the aides commented that marriage banns were in effect in Memphis during the period in question and, to avoid the delay this caused, many couples simply crossed the nearby state lines to get married in Mississippi or Arkansas.

An Internet telephone directory proved beneficial for Margaret McKinney.

I immediately drove to the nearest courthouse in Mississippi, but failed to find a record of interest. Next, I drove to the first courthouse in Arkansas, which was at Marion, and struck pay dirt. Within 30 minutes I found the marriage record for Leo and Bobby — plus a record of a second marriage for Leo. I also found my parents' marriage record.

Using the dates of Leo's two marriages gave me a probable time frame in which to search for a birth record of my first-cousin. I then went to the Bureau of Vital Statistics in Memphis and requested a search for that period. Within five minutes, the clerk produced the birth record for my long-missing first-cousin. He was born in 1920 and had been named Jack in honor of Leo's brother.

Armed with this information, I returned to my home near Atlanta and

began the daunting task of seeking the needle in the haystack. Somewhat naively, I turned to the Internet telephone directory and requested a nationwide listing using the given and surnames. This produced about 50 hits, of which three had the desired middle initial. I called the two closest to Memphis first, without success. It was the third call, to California, that vaulted me over my brickwall where I discovered my long-missing cousin — who turned out to be one of the most fascinating and wonderful people I have ever met.

Look across state lines for more lenient marriage/divorce requirements and use the Internet telephone directory for a national name search.
— Margaret McKinney, GA

Study That Church Register!

A good way to learn about your family is to study their church register even if you do not expect your ancestor to show up in the records because of a late starting date or gaps in the records.

When I borrowed the Ballysadare Catholic baptismal register for County Sligo, Ireland from my FHC, there was a gap for 1853-58. My aunt assured me that her grandmother was 39 in August of 1893 when my grandfather was born. That would make her birth in June of 1854 and inside the baptismal gap beginning in August of 1853 through to February 1858. I was expecting that my great-grandmother, Bridget Benson, would fall between the cracks and not be listed. I started with the earliest records for the register and recorded every Benson entry I could find.

I was stunned when I got to the baptisms of 3 July 1853 and found Brigida Benson, daughter of Dominick Benson and Maria Fahy of Corhawnagh Townland. This was

Bridget Benson Cassidy and husband Joseph Cassidy.

totally unexpected and very exciting. I also found two unknown siblings in 1859 and 1862 and the youngest brother whose 1864 birth registration had led me to this parish register. Apparently, Bridget was 40 when she became a first-time mother in 1893. — Kevin Cassidy, NE, kmct@earthlink.net

The Mystery Of John's James

My great-grandfather, John Boucher and his wife Anna Maria (Woods) left Ireland in 1819 and settled in March Township, Carleton County, close to present-day Ottawa, ON. The 1821 census for March Township indicates that the couple had one daughter, who we know was Elizabeth, born on 22 April 1821. Four sons followed in the next seven years, with James being born on 24 January 1828, according to the parish records. His death was not recorded, but according to the parish records, another James was born to John on 16 November 1855 and died eight days later. The Boucher gravestone mentions only one James, who died on 25 December 1851, aged 31 years.

We know that John Boucher's father was named James, and that he remained behind in Mountshannon, County Galway/Clare, Ireland. A gravestone there states that a James Bourchier died in 1839, aged 66 years but we have no evidence that this James was the father of our John. According to Irish tradition, the first son is named after his paternal grandfather.

For more than 30 years, these facts confused us. It was obvious that John wanted to name a son James. If, in fact, the first James did die in 1851, as the gravestone stated, then John gave the name James to his next son, born in 1855.

By chance, when I was writing up the family history, I re-read an early Boucher land deed in detail. This 1850 deed documented the transfer of title for 95 acres of land from John Boucher's sister-in-law and nephew, Anne and William Woods, to John's son-in-law Oliver Riddle (the husband of Elizabeth Boucher). Although faint, the names of the witnesses popped out of the screen — John Boucher and James R. Boucher.

In December 1850, the James born in 1828 would have been almost 23, old enough to witness a deed. However, if the gravestone was correct and he had died that month, he would not have appeared in the 1851 census, which was actually recorded in January 1852.

The Boucher cemetery stone was engraved many years after James' death and shows other incorrect information (for example, John Boucher's year of death was recorded incorrectly as 1866 rather than 1869).

This find was significant because five acres of this clergy reserve lot had long been targeted for an Anglican church at the village of South March.

Negotiations for title of the 100-acre lot and transfer of the five acres to the church continued for several years after the death of the settler, John Boucher's brother-in-law, Ringrose Woods. After the five acres had officially been transferred to the church, Ringrose Woods' widow Anne sold the remaining 95 acres to Oliver Riddle. John Boucher and James R. Boucher witnessed the deed and Anne Woods and her family moved into the Riddle house. Perhaps James' middle name was Ringrose, after his uncle, making this land transfer very personal to the family.

This long search demonstrates that we shouldn't forget those little inconsistencies in our research findings and that we may have overlooked some information, no matter how careful we had tried to be. A review of the known data can lead to unexpected and pleasant surprises. — Heather Boucher Ashe, ON

In Search Of Salvation

The year before my grandmother Gladys died, I wrote to her asking her to write down for me everything she knew about our family history. My grandmother was the family historian and I think she passed that onto me. Unfortunately, we had a continent between us and I hardly knew anything about her side of the family. She wrote me a detailed five-page, double-sided letter. It was a wealth of information and I'd recommend that everyone should have such a document. But that is not my story!

Although the information was great, it didn't contain many dates. I had gathered more data over the years with the help of that letter but there were a few things missing. I had all of my grandmother's siblings' vital statistics except for her youngest sister, Irene.

When my grandmother died, my father brought home a box of mementoes including a letter from a cousin written to the family upon my grandmother's death. It was a nice letter about his memories of my grandmother and about how the family joined the Salvation Army. I put the letter in my files and for the most part, forgot about it. Years later, while trying to find any overlooked clues, I realized this cousin was the son of Irene. I noticed that the letter was written on Salvation Army letterhead in Ontario and that cousin Earl was a Lieut.-Colonel.

It was a long shot but I contacted the Ontario branch where he had been located at the time through their website. No reply. I then went to the national Salvation Army website where I found that he had been appointed to an important position in the international headquarters. I thought it should be easy to find him now! However, I only found a couple of articles written by him and his wife on the international site. As a last resort, I left a message on the message board asking if anyone knew how to contact him.

A few days later, I received a message from a lady who said he had retired but lived in Canada and she had his phone number. But the phone number was incorrect. By now it was Christmas time so I gave up the search for a while.

In January, I went through my notes again and decided to try something else. I put his name into Canada411.com. There were a lot of people with the same name. When I looked closer at the phone numbers, I saw that one of them was identical to the one I had been given except the area code was off by one number! It had to be him! His address was also included so I wrote a letter explaining who I was and included a family group sheet and my e-mail address.

A few weeks later, I received an e-

Christina MacLean's grandmother Gladys (left), with her mother and sister.

mail message from cousin Earl. He gave me a lot of information about his mother including some surprising information I never would have gotten had I not found him. — Christina MacLean, NS

Finding The Third Grandfather

My brother, sister and I grew up knowing two loving, supportive grandfathers who influenced our lives in positive ways. However, there was a third grandfather we never knew and about whom we never heard anything good. This was our dad's biological father, Everett Edward Clark.

I probably could have let his story end when he abandoned his family in 1901, leaving a mentally ill wife and five children to face the world alone. As a genealogist, however, I couldn't bear to see a gap in my charts or an

unsolved mystery in the family narrative.

Over time I learned a great deal about Everett's parents and siblings, his wife and the little boy who was adopted by neighbors and became my father. Everett eluded me.

Family members said he "went West." I searched from Michigan to California. I sent what was believed to be his picture to the historical society of a town where he was rumored to have lived. I studied his wife's death record and obituary, both of which indicated that she was still married to him at the time she died. All I hit everywhere was a brickwall.

Then in 2000, a first-cousin once-removed and I both submitted articles on the family for inclusion in a Kalkaska County, MI, history being put together by the local genealogical society. Soon after the book was published, Shirley called me. "We've found Everett!" she exclaimed. "He was right there all the time."

As it turned out, he was actually in the next county north of the one where he had lived. A man from that county had read the articles about Everett Clark and concluded that he was the grandfather that his brother-in-law grew up knowing as Edward. The story, as he and Shirley worked it out, was a simple one but nothing to be proud of.

When the family broke up and his wife was placed in hospital, Everett took the easiest way out. He went off into the woods less than 40 miles from his old home. A strapping 32-year-old with experience in lumbering, he easily found work in a lumber camp. He introduced himself as Edward, added five years to his age, and devised a history for himself that hinted at a past in Texas and a wife from whom he was divorced.

He later married an 18-year-old country girl. They bought a farm and over time had five children of their own. There seems no question this was a bigamous marriage. Searching has not turned up any record of divorce from his first wife, and, as mentioned, her death records show her as married.

Yet this second union appears to have been a satisfactory one. His obituary says: "He has been a faithful husband and father, leaving to mourn his wife…". It also notes: "in 1942 Mr. Clark became a Christian. Since that time his life has been a testimony for the Lord Jesus." Perhaps it was then that he revealed to his wife his parents' names and his own birthplace. At least they appear correctly on his death certificate. If he told her more of his past life, she did not pass it on to their children.

My cousin Shirley found it hard to accept that her dad's grandfather had been a liar and a bigamist who took no responsibility for the children of his first marriage. That he might have come to repent of this did not move her. As for me, why would I care? He did not influence my life.

My father's adoptive parents were my grandparents in the ways that mattered. I am glad, though, to be able to round out my records. I could not have done so, and this brickwall would likely never have been breached, without the forum a contemporary county history provided.
— Catherine R. Clarke, CA

Tapping Into The Extended Family Tree

After becoming addicted to the joys of genealogy with my own family, my wife suggested that I begin working on hers. Living in the same general area where she grew up, I assumed that it would be a breeze. She had aunts, uncles, cousins and other family members living within a few miles of us. However, after talking to her relatives I discovered very little. The family name is McCuiston and supposedly they came from Ireland. My wife thought it might be Cladagh, near Galway. I knew the name of my wife's grandfather but that was it.

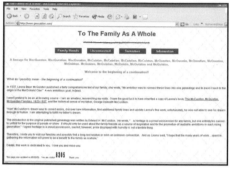

"To the Family As A Whole" website.

One day, while utilizing a search engine for some other things, I casually entered the McCuiston name by itself. The third item on the search response was something about "To the Family as a Whole" and it listed McCuiston with several other spelling variations. Looking through the heads of the families, I found a John with the same spelling and who lived in Ireland. Three of his sons came to the US, landing in New Castle, DE and moving on to Pennsylvania, Virginia or North Carolina. I began to trace each son beginning with the oldest and following through from son to son until that line ended. Then, I would back track and pick up another son. By easing through this maze, I finally encountered a name which looked familiar.

Upon further investigation, it turned out to be my wife's grandfather. It ended there with no further information. This one lucky find actually increased her family tree by seven generations. And somewhat true to family tradition, the three brothers came from County Antrim, Northern Ireland to America before the American Revolutionary War.

With that much information, I

became bold and volunteered as a McCuiston reference person on another local area website. A short time later, I received an e-mail from someone in California who asked me "Who are you? Are you part of the family?" I sent a reply stating that my wife was certainly part of the family and that I was working on her family tree. He sent me an invitation to a private website where I met many more of the family. The name has many different spelling variations: the first part of the name can be McC or McQ, the middle can be uis, hris or ues and he ending can be ton or tion. There are family members with all possible combinations and a few more. This is due to the choice of pronunciation. Some said Mic-Hugh-ston, others Mic-question, others Mic-ooshton, and some sounded like Mic-wishton. However, all spellings led back to these same three brothers.

The owner of the first website I had visited was the family genealogist. There was also a family historian who tracked, documented and published information about the Clan Uisdean, as this group was called. The person who invited me was the family secretary treasurer and he and the family genealogist turned out to be my wife's third-cousins. The family historian is a fifth-cousin. We have since officially joined Clan Uisdean, met with them at an annual gathering and recently I was elected as the Clan Chaplain even though it is my wife who is related.

My research continues but I am not alone anymore. Now I belong to the extended family tree and I am able to utilize their information and other assistance provided. When we have a question, I have dozens of qualified people to help me from their own experiences and information.

So, when you reach a brickwall, try to find another branch of your extended family tree. The results may not be as quickly rewarding as mine

were but it should lead to more opportunities for additional information. — Robert Worden, KY

Did You Hear The One About The Baptism And The Alias?

I was stymied. Finding public and church records of my Irish great-grandfather from the day of his 1852 arrival in the US had been easy. After all, Hugh Haughry was an uncommon, perhaps even unique, name. I was never sidetracked by any coincidental duplication.

I knew from family folklore that Hugh was a coal miner in Pennsylvania and that he died before his last child was born in Illinois in 1880. There were census and baptismal records to prove the family lived in Pennsylvania until the mid 1860s. But then the Haughrys seemed to vanish! I could not find a single record of them under that name.

According to family folklore, Hugh's widow remarried in Illinois. The story went that Hugh and Margaret's children took the surname of their step-father, a Mr. Donahue. In fact, I discovered a number of their baptismal, marriage and cemetery records in Emmetsburg, IA — all under the surname of Donahue. (This confirmed my suspicion that my ancestors had moved from Illinois to Iowa in the early 1880s and ultimately, to Oklahoma by 1889.)

The brickwall was the complete absence of these particular Haughrys in either the 1870 or 1880 census or in any Illinois or Pennsylvania state, county or church files from the period. The last of Hugh and Margaret's children, Ada, was born on 3 March 1880 in Du Quoin, IL. One of my cousins, Ada's granddaughter, insisted that Ada had given her that information personally and that there could be no doubt about its accuracy.

But the sole Catholic parish in Du Quoin had no record of the baptism of Ada Haughry. What's more, the church had no record of any kind pertaining to anyone named Haughry.

The mystery remained unsolved for more than a year. Then suddenly, I had a hunch. I asked Sacred Heart church in Du Quoin to do another search, which yielded a baptismal record of an Ada Donahue in March 1880. The child's mother was Margaret Donahue and her father was Hugh Donahue!

Going back in time, Sacred Heart also had records of the death of Hugh Donahue in 1879 and the baptism of another child born to Hugh and Margaret Donahue in 1873. I could hardly believe my eyes!

I did a quick census search and found that Hugh and Margaret Donahue lived in Grundy County, IL in 1870. The 1880 census listed the widow Margaret Donahue in Perry County (near Du Quoin), IL. In both records, the given names and ages of the children in the household matched those of my great-grandparents children.

The conclusion was obvious: Hugh Haughry took the name Donahue, as an alias and moved his family from Pennsylvania to Illinois sometime in the latter half of the 1860s. All of Hugh's surviving children went by the name of Donahue until they became adults.

Margaret (Haughry) Donahue did, in fact, remarry in 1882. The license was issued to Margaret Donahue of Perry County, IL, and James McDonald of Emmetsburg, IA.

I might never have found the missing pieces of the puzzle had I not been inspired to search for Ada's baptism record under a different surname. — Michael O'Haugherty, GA

Getting Genealogy Goose Bumps

Always check the published family histories located at most historical libraries. Once, while we were passing through Des Moines, my wife and I stopped at the Iowa State Historical Society to check some census returns. After I finished my assignments, I started browsing. With just 15 minutes to go before closing, I hit a goldmine. I saw a book called the *Munson Record 1637-1887 A Genealogical and Biographical Account of Captain Thomas Munson (A Pioneer of Hartford and New Haven) and His Descendants* by Myron A. Munson.

Nelle Munson Miller and daughter Gertrude.

My wife's second-great-grandmother's 1883 wedding invitation said "Mr. and Mrs. O.D. Munson invite you to the wedding of their daughter Nelle". We were able to find Nelle's marriage license at the courthouse and it said she was the daughter of Orson Deriel Munson and Sarah Elizabeth Powell. Our quest had begun.

The Munson family book was indexed and I got goose bumps as I looked in the People Who Married a Munson index and found an S.E. Powell. Could it be our S.E. Powell? Quickly turning the pages as closing time approached, I found that it was indeed the Orson and Sarah Munson family of Omaha, NE and it listed their children including Nelle.

I quickly made notes of Orson's ancestors and got back to Capt. Thomas Munson, an early settler in Connecticut. We made a Xerox of the title page and planned to return when we could make copies.

This was by far the most exciting time in a research library for us. — Kevin Cassidy, NE, kmct@earthlink.net

Helping Others Knock Down Their Brickwalls

There is excitement when we knock down our own brickwalls, but there is also joy and delight when we help a perfect stranger with theirs.

Last spring I received an e-mail from a woman in New York who was struggling to track down her ancestry, and came across a posting of mine on a Niebel Family Forum message board. She told me that her great-grandfather's name was John E. Niebel. He, his wife and daughter were murdered in Mansfield, OH in 1948. She asked me if I could find some information on her family.

I spent about a week "digging" and found more than I had bargained for. I found some articles in a Mansfield newspaper which went into great detail about the murders. John Niebel had been the farm super-intendent at the Ohio State Reformatory in Mansfield, OH. Two former inmates of the prison went on a killing rampage across Ohio. One night they kidnapped John Niebel, his wife and 20-year-old daughter; then

shot and killed them in a nearby field. The killers were apprehended several days later.

From the information she had given me, and with what I had found in the newspaper articles, I was able to put together her ancestry from John Niebel forward. Then, when I went backward looking for his ancestors, I discovered that he was the great-grandson of Joseph Niebel who was the brother of my great-grandfather, Jacob Niebel! So, I not only found the information she had been looking for, but I also found another piece to my own puzzle.

Ohio State Reformatory postcard. The motion picture Shawshank Redemption *was filmed at the prison.*

After I had put all of the information together for her, I went back on the Internet and found quite a few interesting articles about the murders and the history of the prison. All in all, helping her knock down her brickwall was a very rewarding experience. — Georgia Kruse, rockingranny@comcast.net

How To Climb A Brickwall

My mother began searching for information on her father in 1963. By 2002, she was no further ahead at determining his parentage. All we knew about my grandfather was that he and his brother Frank had been placed in

Barnardos Home by their mother when they were very young. When Frank and Bill had been sent to Canada, at ages nine and six, they were split up and sent to different farms in different counties. The farm family which had taken Grandpa Bill worked him very hard, and belittled him by telling him that he had been unwanted and that he was lucky to be living with them. In fact, Grandpa didn't really know much at all until he ran into his brother, some years later. Frank told him a great many things, but even his memory was sketchy.

This is where I came in.

I wrote to Barnardos, but because I was only a granddaughter, I was required to get permission for the information from the oldest child — who luckily happened to be my mother.

Then I was given the greatest gift. Barnardos sent pictures of my grandfather and his brother, the admission note, follow-up notes and ship's boarding information. It was wonderful to see my Grandpa as a boy and see that my brother looks just like him.

Within the admission note was the information that Grandpa's mother, Isabella, wanted the boys placed into the Home under her maiden name, only until she could get a little ahead. The father's name was listed.

Also included was a narrative that the mother and her four children had been living with her sister since the death of her husband the year before. The sister's name and address were given — also the information that she was married and had five children of her own.

The search was on.

For the last 40 years we had been unable to find a marriage certificate for Isabella and Ephraim. But as this had ostensibly occurred in London, that didn't surprise me — what with two World Wars and all.

So I began with the 1901 census. Sure enough, there was Grandpa as a boy in his family with his brother and two sisters. Also in the 1901 census, at the address in the Barnardos note, was a family with three children of the correct name.

Searching for a marriage of the groom and obtaining the certificate, gave me the bride's maiden name — the same as Isabella and her father's name.

Searching the 1891 census, I found a family with the same last name. The problem appeared to be that the family had a daughter Isabella, and an Annie, and an Anna. But according to Barnardos, the sister's name was Hannah.

Through a search of vocal dynamics for the area around which the family lived, it appeared that H was an optional sound. So Hannah could indeed be heard by a census taker as Anna.

Searches for a marriage between Isabella and Ephraim had turned up another union. However, if this was the right Isabella, why had she been married to another fellow?

A continued search indicated that the first husband had died the year before the eldest of Isabella and Ephraim's children were born. He had died, an alcoholic, alone and in a workhouse. So the union of my great-grandma and great-grandpa was easily explained.

The link was further strengthened when, in a journal that my grandfather had started some years before, indicated that he had had a paternal aunt Jesse who had come to Canada to find Grandpa and his brother. She had told them what little she knew about the circumstances of the boys being whisked off to Canada. She had said that the family had had no idea that the boys had left England. She had been searching for some time, and finally Barnardos had surrendered their information. She wanted them to know their actual surname, and that their parents had, in fact, been married. She had been a kindly lady who had wanted the boys to know their heritage, that they had been loved, and that their family wanted to know what happened to them.

It is interesting to me that neither son changed their name to their 'official' surname, but they and their families continued to go by their mother's maiden name, and do so to this day.

Suffice it to say that a search of London census records indicated a family that had a son, Ephraim, and a daughter, Jesse. Although the name was spelled differently, this could be chalked up to being the dialect of the area, and/or the census taker.

Now, we have been able to trace my grandfather's family back several more generations — on both maternal and paternal sides.

And my Mom has a greater sense of the history that is hers. — Wendy Sturgeon Cairns, AB, wpsc@shaw.ca

Seventeenth-Century Genealogy

In his genealogy of the Briggs family, L. Vernon Briggs identified Lydia Gamer as the wife of Scituate settler Humphrey Turner, citing her gravestone erected years after her death. In the 1620-33 segment of his *Great Migration Begins* series, author Robert C. Anderson disparages Briggs and notes concerning Lydia, "[N]owhere is there any evidence for this surname."

But Mr. Anderson does cite a suggestive note in *The American Genealogist* that a Lydia, daughter of Humphrey Turner, was baptized on 17 February 1629 at Little Baddow, Essex, England. A search of the records of adjoining parishes disclosed that Humphrey Turner and Lidda Gamar married at Sandon on 24 October 1618, three miles southwest of Little Baddow.

Was the elder Lydia's family also from one of these small Essex towns along the Blackwater river? Midway between Bocking and Little Baddow, her family was found. Richard Gaymer married, according to the Terling register, Margaret Mason on 23 July 1590, by whom he had Sarah, Elizabeth, a stillborn female, Andrew, and Lydia, baptized on 18 May 1602. Soon after Margaret's death in 1602, he remarried, to Joan Robinson in adjoining Fairsted on 19 February 1603, by whom he had six more children.

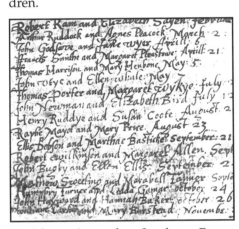

Parish register for Sandon, Essex, England showing marriage entries for 1618, including Humphrey Turner and Lydia Gamer (bottom).

The picture that emerged is that of a Lydia in only her 17th year, marrying Humphrey Turner, in a small parish midway between his home and hers. One can only speculate that her relationship with her stepmother was not a felicitous one, one which led her to embark with her husband and four small children for Plymouth and Scituate, where she gave birth to four more children in America. — David L. Kent, TX, chirologe@hotmail.com

Patience, Persistence And Plenty Of Luck

It was what I didn't know about my grandmother's early antecedents, Thomas and Ann Pattison, that bothered me. I had collected and entered into my Reunion computer program 51 separate items of information about Thomas and a number more about Ann. These came from many books and Internet sources about early Maryland. I had visited libraries in Cincinnati, Baltimore, the Daughters of the American Revolution offices in Washington and the Maryland Archives.

However, I had not uncovered Ann's maiden name nor where they had lived before they moved to Maryland. The important source book, *Revised History of Dorchester County*, says:

Thomas Pattison... came to Maryland... and settled in Dorchester County, December 20, 1671. He proved his right to 400 acres for transporting into the province himself, Ann Pattison (his wife), James, Jacob, Priscilla and Ann Pattison (his children) and two servants.

I was alert for clues. "Two servants" meant they had resources. Did they all sail over from England or Ireland together? And how could I find Ann's maiden name?

Land records reveal that Thomas was a multiple buyer and seller of acreage along Dorchester's major rivers. He was trained as a surveyor. Thomas was also an entrepreneur. He started a grain mill near Secretary, MD and a windmill on James Island. Sometimes he listed himself as a wine cooper, undoubtedly after buying land with a good number of oak trees.

Shortly after his arrival date of 1671, Thomas was appointed County Commissioner. Soon after that, he became the County Surveyor, and then the County Clerk. How could a newcomer be selected for such posts?

While studying another family, I acquired a booklet that reported land records between 1689 and 1732, long after Thomas and Ann's arrival. Tucked between an entry for May 1727 and one for June 1727 was this:

13 August 1669, Francis Armstrong and Frances Armstrong, his wife, to Thomas Paterson of Rappahannock: 400 acres called "Armstrong's Hoggepenne" on James Island.

At first, I didn't realize that this entry opened a completely new trail. This was the first reference to Rappahannock. Was that the name of a Maryland plantation or the river in Virginia?

Daughters of the American Revolution's offices in Washington, DC.

About a year later, visiting Fredericksburg, VA, I had some extra time and stopped at the city's main library. Going down a narrow, circular, iron staircase to the basement, I reached their well-lit, very quiet, local history room. The shelves were full of old books. After browsing, I opened *Old Rappahannock County Deed Abstracts 1656-1664* by Ruth and Sam Sparacio. I checked the index for Pattisons. In this book were 10 citations of a Thomas Pattison who bought and sold land in the Rappahannock area, witnessed signings of official documents, and even, on occasion, acted as an attorney. This pattern matched the activities of my Thomas Pattison in Dorchester County.

However, I saw nothing that could help to prove whether this was our Thomas Pattison. Several weeks later, during another trip to Fredericksburg, I planned for library time.

Suddenly, there it was! In *Old Rappahannock County Deed Abstracts 1663-1668*:

6 May, 1668: Know all men by these presents that I, Elizabeth Haslerton do hereby give the following mentioned cattle and their increase, unto the children of my brother-in-law Thomas Pattison, and my sister Ann, his wife: I give unto their eldest son, James Pattison, two heifers and one yearling. …Secondly, I give… to their youngest son, Jacob Pattison, one black heifer with a calf at her side…. Thirdly, I give unto their daughter, Priscilla Pattison, one yearling heifer of a black color.

There could be no doubt! The names of Thomas' wife and children matched my Thomas. And now we knew his wife's sister was Elizabeth Haslerton! But, was Elizabeth's married name Haslerton or her family name? I bought some booklets covering Old Rappahannock for this era. More good luck!

On 22 May 1655:

I, Abraham Moone do hereby, for consideration from the hands of James Bagnall, …give, grant… two hundred acres of land being upon the freshes of the Rappahannock River… unto Elizabeth Hezeltyn, daughter unto Arther Hezeltyn, deceased.

So, Haslerton (or maybe Hezeltyn) was Elizabeth's — and therefore Ann's — family name. And their father was Arthur Haslerton. But more questions!

Why would James Bagnall buy land for Elizabeth Haslerton? Further reading of the land records showed that James Bagnall married another of Arthur Haslerton's daughters, Priscilla. Twenty years later, Priscilla did "ordain my brother-in-law, Thomas Pattison my lawful attorney to prove the will of my deceased husband, James Bagnall."

Ann was quite young when she arrived in America. She had nine children in 30 years of childbearing, and adopted one more daughter. She must have been one tough lady to raise 10 children, while living out on the edges of civilization with the high-energy, fast-moving, land-trading and entrepreneurial Thomas Pattison.

Patience, persistence and plenty of luck answered the question: "Ann who?" And they revealed that Thomas and Ann had lived in Virginia for almost 20 years before they came to Dorchester County, MD.
— C.E. Peck, MD

Who Is This Baby?

On 30 July 1902, Lola Brown became the second wife of my great-grandfather. His first wife died shortly after the birth of her seventh baby (who died within a month of being born). Lola had one baby, James Brown Whitelaw, who only lived one day. Great-grandfather then died in 1911. By then, all but one of the children of the first marriage were married and gone from the home, but Lola stayed with the youngest daughter, who soon went off to college.

By reading many microfilms, I was able to find out more about Lola. On 23 June 1918, Lola married William Leonidas Sexton, of Wichita, KS. His first wife, Julia, had died in 1916. Lola and William lived together for many years, but had a childless marriage, he died in 1955, and she died in 1961.

I visited the Maple Grove Cemetery in Wichita, KS, and found Lola's gravestone and William's father. I found Julia's gravestone under a bush, and, finally, next to it, I found a gravestone that was knocked over, which was William's. In front of the bush and next to Lola E. Sexton was a small, flat gravestone that said: *Marvin King, Son of Lola S. & C. K. Davis June 20, 1918 - Apr. 10, 1919*

So who was this baby? I had no record of a baby in our family records! Did Lola have another baby who died as an infant?

I checked the cemetery records and they were all Sextons in that section, along with Marvin King Davis. There was no listing for a C. Davis in the cemetery records.

A marriage record book showed that Lola and William were married on 23 June 1918, three days after the baby had been born. The marriage certificate showed that a Reverend Claud K. Davis had performed the marriage. There were no marriages listed for a C. Davis and a Lola.

At the Wichita Public Library, I found The Stork Special: "Rev. and Mrs. Claud K. Davis of Harper announce the birth of a son, Marvin King on June 20…"

The gravestone that started Cheryl Whitelaw's quest.

When I got home, I used several Internet sources to search for Claud. The Sedgwick County marriage index had Claude K. Davis and Lola Fae Sexton married on 14 June 1910. So now I knew the mother's name. The 1900 and 1910 census information confirmed that William and Julia Sexton had a daughter, Lola, born in 1886. Lola had a step-daughter whose name was also Lola, and her husband officiated her step-mother's second marriage. I was still curious why the parents weren't buried near their baby. Where were they?

I did eventually find a handwritten letter that Lola and Claud went to E----s, WV, to a college. I looked on the Internet for colleges in West Virginia and determined it must be Elkins, which had a church college. I don't have definitive answers, only conjecture that after the baby was buried in the logical place with the grandparents, the young couple went off to West Virginia and perhaps lived there for many years, far across the country from their little baby. — Cheryl Whitelaw, UT, whitelawcs@suu.edu

A Brickwall To Cadott

My Rosenthal ancestors immigrated to Washington County in southeastern Wisconsin during the mid 1800s. My great-grandfather, Friedrich, his wife, both sets of parents and Friedrich's adult siblings all immigrated there at various times between 1847 and 1854. I had the names and birth dates of Friedrich's parents and the younger siblings of the family from a response to a query that I wrote to the church in Germany where they had lived. Research of census records for 1850 and 1860 in Washington County revealed names of other Rosenthals all living in Addison Township, probably all related somehow.

The 1850 census listed 10 Rosenthals in succession, in three successive households: Godlip, 34 with Ann, 26 in the first household: Christoph, 61, with Julia, 59, and Godfrey, 31 in the second household. (The older couple was the parents of Friedrich, which the church pastor in Germany had named, and Godfrey was probably a son too old to have been listed with the other children in the church book). In the third household in the census were Fredrich, 24, with Cristen, 24, Augusta, three, Fredrick, four-months old, and August, 21. This was my great-grandfather's household with his wife and two children and also Friedrich's brother, August, whose name and birth date had been supplied by the pastor at the church in Germany.

It was not known how the couple in the first household was related to the others. A search of the 1860 records showed Gotlieb, 44, with Rosanna, 21, and five children, ages nine, eight, six, one and seven months. Still no clue as to how Gotlieb was related, but what happened to his wife, Ann, who would have been age 36 in this census? And who was Rosanna? She was too young to be the mother of all those children, and by 1870, this family was gone from the census with no clues as to where they went.

My grandfather, Frederick Rosenthal, who was the infant in my great-grandfather's household in 1850, homesteaded in Pepin County in northwestern Wisconsin and raised his family there. His younger sister, Sophia married and lived in Chippewa County, also in northwestern Wisconsin. I have found that my maiden name of Rosenthal is fairly common; so when I heard the name Rosenthal in my parish membership at my church in Wisconsin, I assumed that it wasn't likely that they were my relatives.

One year, when I attended a family reunion in the town where I grew up, the subject came up about some Rosenthals living around Cadott, WI. It was not known if they were related or not, and we had no idea how they could possibly be related. They weren't part of my grandfather's sister, Sophia's family because I had done that research and had obtained that family's descendants' information. My cousin, who lived nearby, said that she would send me the pages from the phone book for the Cadott area so that I could contact someone there.

When I received the pages, I wrote to one of the Rosenthals listed

explaining who I was and my Rosenthal relationship. I asked if the Cadott Rosenthals were in any way related to my Rosenthals. I received a wonderful answer from a man named Fritz. Yes, they were related. His grandfather Gottlieb Rosenthal, was a brother of my great-grandfather, Friedrich, and he had moved his family to the Cadott area in the 1860s, traveling by oxcart and oxen a distance of approximately 200 miles. His first wife had died, leaving him with three small children. He then married the younger sister of his first wife.

ROSENTHAL -See also ROSENTHALL	
ROSENTHAL A 4455 Bathurst	633-2673
A 430 Shaw	532-2001
A 555 SheppardAvW	633-1473
Alan 98 Roncesvalles	533-9910
Albert 890 SheppardAvW	630-5756
Arthur 59 NeptuneDr	789-5714
Arthur 59 NeptuneDr	789-5951
B 38 AvenueRd	975-2661
Barry 97 Coady	463-1977
B S 38 AvenueRd	966-2125
D 203 Davisville	488-4522
D 367 PalmerstonBl	929-2754
D J 50 Raeburn	635-0379
E 36 FleanceDr	731-7348
E 27 Lynn	699-5415
E 10 Senlac	227-0776
F 3636 Bathurst	256-2763
G 38 CliftonAv	635-5363
H 550 Glencairn	782-2081

Looking in the phone book helped Sharon Rosenthal Lemley overcome her brickwall.

That solved the question of the census in Washington County. But there was more... Fritz had a brother named Henry living in West Allis, and Henry had a daughter, who was very interested in family history. She lived in the neighboring community of New Berlin. Then I recalled that the name I had heard from my church was Henry. I began a contact with Henry's daughter, and we shared our family data. It was a long way around to find someone so close.

If only I had taken the short-cut and asked Henry if he was related to me, I could have found this branch of the family much sooner than I did. — Sharon Rosenthal Lemley, WI

You Can Run, But You Cannot Hide... Completely

All genealogy research has its difficulties, and I ran into one as I searched for a death record of my second-great-grandfather. I will give him an alias, John Watkins, since the outcome is less than good.

My great-grandmother had left a lot of little notes about her family — and one mentioned that her father, John Watkins, died in 1881, but did not give the location. Since John was living in Chicago in 1880 (he was on the census), I assumed that he most likely died there. I had written for a death record in Chicago, with no luck. I could not find his burial place either. By 1883, his wife Mary had remarried, so I knew that he must have died before that time. Since I couldn't find a death record, I checked for a divorce record — nothing. I knew he was in the Civil War, but his name was common, and I had a difficult time locating the right John Watkins. Luckily his middle name wasn't so common, and this was the link I needed to solve the mystery. One day, at the NARA, I was thumbing through a new volume of the California 1890 Great Register of Voters Index and checking for other Watkins surnames.

There, before my very eyes, was John Watkins with his full name, age, address and birthplace! He was alive — and not buried in Chicago after all, but living (and voting) 2000 miles away in San Francisco. He didn't die or divorce — he ran off!

This led to more census research, which produced another surprise — he had a whole new family! With his new location, I was finally able to narrow down the right name in the Civil War pension records, and received the pension records in the mail. It revealed that he had applied for a pension, but was denied because he had "deserted". Also in the file was a letter from his daughter, (from the second family), asking the Pension Department for the whereabouts of her father since he had deserted their family also! Through city directories, I was able to see where he lived in the late 1890s and early 1900s.

I should say that he is actually still in hiding. He disappeared in 1906, about the time of the San Francisco earthquake, and I have not been able, as of yet, to find a death record or burial place. — Marianne Hale, CA, hhmachshop@aol.com

Family Branches Reconnect

I was doing research on my maternal grandfather's family line when I stumbled upon the naturalization papers of my second-great-uncle, Charles J. Hampel. I had been curious about this uncle ever since reading about him in the autobiography of his younger brother and my great-grandfather, Theodore Hampel Sr.

Charles was the first Hampel in my family to immigrate to the US from Germany in 1884. He then began writing letters home to his brother Theodore, which convinced him to come to the US. Charles even sent his orphaned and sickly brother the money for the voyage, without which he may never have been able to make the passage.

Although I wanted to know more about this uncle, I was discouraged by hitting a brickwall at the very beginning of my search. My maternal great-uncle and aunts spoke in detail about visiting with their mother's family; but they knew nothing about their father's brother, Charles and his family or what may have become of them. I always remembered what my grandfather had said just a few months before his death, when I inquired about his Uncle Charles. He told me that not only did he not know what happened to him but that he knew he had cousins somewhere and wouldn't even be able to recognize them even if he passed them on the street. My mother had never even heard of this relative.

Based upon these interviews, I surmised that Charles had either died young or moved a great distance away. Finally, any descendants of Charles that may still exist, like myself, may not even have Hampel as a last name, making finding them, I thought, virtually hopeless.

Charles J. Hampel and wife Pauline with sons Arthur and Frederick in 1894.

However, the chance discovery of Charles' naturalization documents, convinced me to renew my search in earnest. According to his 1886 petition and subsequent 1890 naturalization filing, Charles resided in Adams, MA. I then checked the 1900 US census and found him still in Adams with a wife, Pauline and three children, Frederick, Arthur and Edna. After calling the Adams Town Clerk's Office, I received some further clarifying information. Charles' wife had died on 24 December 1903 at the young age of 39. Charles had remarried a widow who had children of her own, but then he had died suddenly on 11 November 1915. Charles' second wife then married for a third time and was probably too busy with her current

affairs to visit her step-children's relatives, which may help to explain why contact was lost.

I wondered, could there be any Hampels left in Adams? Upon checking the Adams phone book, I was surprised to find the name of a Hampel listed. Could this be the son or grandson of Charles? I called and an older woman answered. When I mentioned that I was a Hampel descendent and was inquiring about the family of Charles, she became very excited. She told me she was his granddaughter and that Arthur was her father.

We exchanged stories and sent each other copies of old documents and photographs, finding one we each had, picturing both of the Hampel brothers; Charles and Theodore with their respective families at a large family gathering. The two families were obviously very close. In fact, in a small family Bible which had been passed down to Grace by her father, was a poem written in old German script and signed by my great-grandfather, Theodore. After being translated, it appeared to be a blessing to none other than Arthur, his nephew and godson, on the occasion of his baptism.

Besides exchanging genealogical information, I have also visited with my new-found cousin along with my mother, and we have become close. In fact, on my last visit, Grace gave me a wooden machinist chest including tools, which belonged to her grandfather Charles, on some of which he had even engraved his name. I will make sure that this family treasure is passed down along with the interesting story behind it.

I may never learn the exact reason why the two Hampel brothers' families lost contact with each other over the years. However, this doesn't seem to matter, as the two families have finally reconnected due to some luck on my part and the kindness of my second-cousin once-removed, Grace.
— Edward John Dudek, Jr., NY

Glossary Of Terms

FHC (Family History Center): local branches of the LDS Church's FHL. There are approximately 3,400 in operation worldwide (www.familysearch.org).

FHL (Family History Library): The LDS Church's main repository of genealogical information, located in Salt Lake City, UT (www.familysearch.org).

GEDCOM (GEnealogical Data COMmunication): A standardized form of computerized data exchange developed by the Family History Department of the LDS Church. GEDCOM files are a universal code allowing different genealogy programs to communicate with one another.

IGI (International Genealogical Index): A worldwide index of more than 200 million names created by the LDS Church. It is available at www.familysearch.org.

LDS (Latter-day Saints): The abbreviated form of the Church of Jesus Christ of Latter-day Saints, sometimes called the Mormons (www.mormon.org).

NARA (National Archives and Records Administration): A Washington, DC-based organization with facilities throughout the US, such as Research Centers, Records Centers and Presidential Libraries. (http://www.archives.gov).

SSDI (Social Security Death Index): An important research source that lists information about people who held Social Security Numbers (www.RootsWeb.com)

Soundex/Miracode: A code composed of a letter and three numbers, based on the way a surname sounds instead of how it is spelled. The letter represents the first letter of the surname and the numbers represent the remaining sounds of the name.

    1 – B, F, P, V
    2 – C, G, J, K, Q, S, X, Z
    3 – D, T
    4 – L
    5 – M, N
    6 – R

The letters A, E, H, I, O, U, W and Y are ignored. For example the name Lee is Soundexed as L 000. Surnames that sound the same but spelled differently like Smith and Smyth, have the same code (S 530) and are filed together.

Both Soundex and Miracode use the Soundex coding system, Soundex cards are handwritten, while Miracode cards are printed (http://www.archives.gov).

Index

cemetery transcripts 2, 110 *also see* cemetery records

censuses — school 115

censuses 5, 21, 25, 53, 57, 58, 65, 67, 72, 81, 84, 94, 106, 124, 132, 140, 141, 149, 158, 162, 163, 165 *also see* enumeration districts, US — Soundex

certificates — birth *see* birth certificates

certificates — death *see* death certificates

certificates — marriage *see* marriage certificates

Charles R. Hale Collection (index to gravestone inscriptions for more than 2,000 Connecticut cemeteries) 92

christening records *see* baptism records

Christian names *see* names

church records — French-Canadian 91

church records 17, 69, 71, 78, 89, 91, 100, 140, 149, 159 *also see* baptism records, informants, marriage records, parish records, UK — Bishops transcripts

church registers 113, 150

city directories 40, 144, 164

classes/courses/seminars — genealogy 15, 119

collateral-line research 15, 74, 77, 100, 109, 117, 128, 139

correspondence — old 109, 125 *also see* ancestors' possessions

court documents 115

court records 109

D

Daughters of the American Revolution 83

death certificates 21, 34, 129 *also see* burial records

death indexes — online 2

death indexes 113

death notices 8 *also see* obituaries

death records 16 *also see* burial records, cemeteries, cemetery records, funeral homes, gravestones

deeds — land 151

deeds 33, 34

diaries 136 *also see* ancestors' possessions

E

Ellis Island website 96

e-mail 48, 128 *also see* letters/mass mailings, networking queries

England *see* UK

enumeration districts 141, 144 *also see* censuses

estate records *see* wills, probate

executors 143 *also see* wills

F

family Bibles 4 *also see* ancestors' possessions

Family History Centers (FHC) 133

Family History Library (Salt Lake City, UT) (FHL) 32, 50

family names *see* names

family reunions 29, 33 *also see* networking

FamilySearch.org 21, 104 *also see* Family History Centers, Family History Library, Internet, websites

FHC *see* Family History Centers

FHL *see* Family History Library (Salt Lake City, UT)

first names *see* names

FreeBMD.com 43, 57 *also see* Internet, websites

funeral homes 3, 62, 119, 137 *also see* burial records, cemeteries, cemetery records, death records, gravestones

funeral notices *see* obituaries

G

Genealogy.com 20, 32, 141 *also see* Internet, websites

German military records 24 *also see* Germany

Germany 49, 50, 89 *also see* German military records

given names *see* names

gravestones 15, 64, 98 *also see* burial records, cemeteries, cemetery records, death records, funeral homes

H

headstones *see* gravestones

health departments — local 39

Home children 158

I

IGI *see* International Genealogical Index

informants 132 *also see* witnesses
International Genealogical Index (IGI) 56, 138
Internet 10, 46, 47, 50, 55, 62, 81, 97, 121, 128, 162 *also see* e-mail, websites, individual website listings
interviewing friends/family/neighbors 37, 52, 113 *also see* networking
Ireland — Householders Index 137
Ireland 135

J

Jewish 51
journals 19 *also see* ancestors' possessions

L

land transactions 131
last names *see* names
letters/mass mailings 7, 11, 20, 26, 35, 45, 48, 104, 107, 110, 116, 122, 128, 133, 148 *also see* queries
libraries 47, 62 *also see* archives, on-site/local research, museums
listservs *see* message boards (Internet)

M

maiden names *see* names — maiden
mailing lists — Internet *see* message boards (Internet)
MapQuest.com 141, 144 *also see* Internet, map/map research, websites
maps — time-appropriate 121 *also see* maps/map research
maps/map research 137, 141 *also see* maps — time-appropriate
marriage applications 69
marriage certificates 21, 25, 133
marriage indexes 106
marriage records 8, 30, 77, 98, 162 *also see* church records
marriages — previous/subsequent/multiple 17, 57, 69, 77, 111, 127, 131
memorial notices *see* obituaries
message boards (Internet) 5, 25, 35, 37, 47, 56, 60, 93, 101, 116, 152, 157 *also see* Internet, queries, networking
militia rolls 78
museums 85 *also see* archives, libraries, on-site/local research

N

names — aliases 155
names — anglicized 1
names — changes 22, 54, 107 *also see* names — spelling variations
names — maiden 59
names — multiple 34
names — multiple spellings *see* names — spelling variations
names — naming patterns 20, 32, 51, 75, 83, 83, 126
names — spelling variations 1, 73, 96, 128, 135, 154 *also see* names — changes, transcription errors
names — unusual 67, 83, 108
naming patterns *see* names — naming patterns
networking 4, 6, 12, 18, 20, 24, 27, 29, 35, 41, 51, 52, 54, 55, 56, 61, 65, 66, 68, 74, 77, 81, 82, 85, 86, 89, 93, 103, 104, 111, 111, 114, 117, 118, 121, 130, 136, 140, 148, 150, 157, 163, 165 *also see* interviewing friends/family/neighbors, queries, message boards, societies — family history, genealogical, historical, telephone calls
newspapers — local — advertisements 70, 135 *also see* newspapers — local
newspapers — local 122
newspapers 49, 146 *also see* obituaries

O

obituaries 105, 145 *also see* death notices
occupations — ancestors 21, 39, 53, 60, 133, 135, 138, 160
on-site/local research 36, 42, 64, 68, 86, 87, 98, 112, 118, 120, 120, 150 *also see* archives, libraries, museums

P

parish records 160 *also see* church records, UK — Bishops transcripts
phone books/directories/calls *see* telephones books/directories/calls
photographs — old 30, 60, 97, 99, 103, 138 *also see* ancestors' possessions
Poland 146
probate 45, 86 *also see* wills
professional researchers 40, 147

Q

queries (online, journals, newspapers) 8, 12, 23, 32, 66, 73, 78, 82, 115, 142, 145, 146 *also see* advertisements, letters/mass mailings, message boards, networking

R

Random Acts of Genealogical Kindness website 105
records — baptism *see* baptism records
records — birth *see* birth records
records — burial *also see* burial records
records — cemeteries *see* cemetery records
records — chancery court 41, 109
records — christening *see* baptism records
records — church *see* church records
records — court *see* court records
records — death *see* death records
records — estate *see* wills, probate
records — homestead/land 14
records — land 160
records — marriage *see* marriage records
records — military 31, 35
records — parish *see* parish records
records — pension 93
records — records 117, 124 *also see* probate
records — Southern Claims Commission 128
registrations — birth *see* birth registrations
research techniques 11, 26, 39, 58, 65, 71, 72, 75, 80, 92, 101, 107, 114, 131, 141, 144, 150, 155
reunions — family *see* family reunions
RootsWeb.com 91 *also see* Internet, websites

S

Scotland *see* UK
societies — family history, genealogical, historical 1, 16, 44, 103, 106, 118, 133, 136, 153, 156 *also see* networking
SSDI *see* Social Security Death Index
surnames *see* names
Switchboard.com 54 *also see* Internet, websites

T

tax assessments — land 9
tax rolls 124
telephone calls 38, 46, 62, 88 *also see* networking
telephone directories/books — international/domestic/Internet 45, 48, 56, 104, 128, 133, 150, 165
tombstones *see* gravestones
tourist information 112
transcription errors 25, 72, 84, 135, 137, 143 *also see* names — spelling variations

U

UK — Bishops transcripts 133 *also see* church records
UK — Home children 158
unusual names *see* names — unusual
US — Civil War pension applications 5
US — Civil War records 108
US — records — naturalization 126
US — Social Security Death Index 2, 148
US — Soundex 8, 11 *also see* censuses
US — SS-5 (Application for a Social Security Card) 8
US — veterans' census of 1865 — New York 62
USGenWeb.com 91, 107, 130, 137 *see* Internet, websites

V

voters index 164

W

Wales *see* UK
websites — translation 49
websites 8, 25, 27, 44, 48, 55, 60, 100, 110, 154 *also see* Internet, individual website listings
widows' pension papers 6
will indexes 102
wills 3, 33, 78, 102, 143 *also see* probate
witnesses 96, 151 *also see* informants
World Family Trees (Ancestry.com) 20 *also see* Internet, websites
WorldConnect (RootsWeb.com) 116 *also see* Internet, websites

Notes